Stevenson's Scotland

Lighthouse

0   50   100 kilometres

Muckle Flugga
Bluemull Sound — North Unst
Jarlshof
Yell
SHETLAND
ISLANDS   Whalsay
Lerwick

Sumburgh Head

Fair Isle (North)
Fair Isle (South)

ORKNEY
ISLANDS
Skara Brae
Maes Howe   Kirkwall

Pentland Firth   *Scapa Flow*
Thurso   John o'Groats
Castletown
Wick

Golspie

Inverness

SKYE   Aberdeen

RHUM   Braemar   Dunnottar
EIGG
Fort   *Ben Alder*   Blair Atholl   Montrose
William
Glencoe   Pitlochry   Kirriemuir
Loch   Dundee   Arbroath
Leven   *Rannoch*   Perth   *Bell Rock*
Skerryvore   *Moor*   Strathyre   Lower   St Andrews
IONA   MULL   Bridge of   Kirkcaldy   Largo   *Isle of May*
Earraid   Allan   Anstruther
Dubh Artach   Stirling   *Bass Rock*
Limekilns   North Berwick
Greenock   South   Gullane
Glasgow   Queensferry   Inverkeithing
Bothwell   *Pentland*   Edinburgh
Bridge   *Hills*   Colinton

Ayr
Culzean   Dunure Castle
Castle   Maybole
Girvan   Kirkoswald
Balmaclellan   Dumfries
Caerlaverock

STEVENSON'S SCOTLAND

Edited by

TOM HUBBARD & DUNCAN GLEN

mercatpress
www.mercatpress.com

This selection first published in 2003 by Mercat Press
10 Coates Crescent, Edinburgh EH3 7AL
www.mercatpress.com

ISBN: 184183 0569

Set in Ehrhardt and Tiepolo Book at Mercat Press

Printed and bound in Great Britain by
Bell & Bain Ltd., Glasgow

Contents

TO THE MEMORY OF
NEIL R MacCALLUM
1954-2002
New makar
Stevensonian
Native of the Precipitous City

Preface and Acknowledgements

We have arranged our selection from Stevenson's topographical writings on Scotland in the form of a journey, starting in Edinburgh and heading north-east. From Shetland we head south-west through the Highlands as far as Dumfries, then return to the Edinburgh area. There are a number of detours on the way.

We have concentrated on Stevenson's non-fictional prose writings but, on occasion, we have also selected topographically-focused material from the poetry and fiction. The criterion is that the places represented should exist in reality. We have avoided fiction with invented place-names or with descriptions that cannot be firmly associated with an actual location.

Since this aims to be a reader-friendly selection, we have, with one exception, given each work, or extract from a work or a letter, a topographical heading that is not Stevenson's. The exception is *Edinburgh: Picturesque Notes* where we reprint the complete book of 1879. The notes, which also aim to be informal without sacrificing scholarly standards, are headed by our titles but also give Stevenson's titles and details of the sources. The Select Bibliography lists works that we believe will make interesting further reading. Amongst these works are those that have been especially useful in writing the notes but, since we had read widely for earlier works on Stevenson, we acknowledge and thank the authors of the many other works that may have influenced these notes and the introduction. We thank also the staffs of Edinburgh Central Library, Edinburgh University Library, Kirkcaldy Central Library and the National Library of Scotland for assistance. Two previously unpublished pieces were supplied by the Beinecke Rare Book and Manuscript Library, Yale University, in the form of copies of the original manuscripts; we are also grateful to Yale University Press for permission to reprint material previously available only in *The Letters of Robert Louis Stevenson*, edited by Bradford A Booth and Ernest Mehew, 8 vols, New Haven & London, 1994–95. Tom Johnstone and Seán Costello of Mercat Press gave us much encouragement and showed that civilised publishing is alive and well in Stevenson's Edinburgh and Scotland.

DUNCAN GLEN and TOM HUBBARD
Kirkcaldy, Fife, August 2003

INTRODUCTION

Bleak Fertility: Robert Louis Stevenson and Scotland

1

Stevenson's love of his native land is understood mainly by means of his absence from it. He is perhaps the most celebrated 'Scot abroad' and in this respect he leads a literary pantheon occupied by such figures as George Buchanan, Sir Thomas Urquhart, R B Cunninghame Graham, Alastair Reid and Kenneth White. A book remains to be written on this major but neglected area of Scottish literary history.

'There in Samoa is the Scottish laddie... and his head is full of old Scotland and old Edinburgh, and he makes us see them.' These are the words of an anonymous reviewer in the *Elgin Courant* of 5 September 1893, and it's a pleasant irony that this most international of Scottish writers should be so well summed up in a local paper. It's also fitting, for two reasons.

First, although much of the present book reprints Stevenson's accounts of his native city, it well represents small-town and rural Scotland. Dumfries, Bridge of Allan, Kirriemuir, Kirkwall are all here, not to mention some of the most remote corners of the Highlands, islands, and uplands. (We challenge our bolder readers to make their way to Cluny's Cage, on the southern slope of Ben Alder.) Secondly, the *Elgin Courant* journalist is right to emphasise Stevenson's visual power, not least because that raises an issue which is both contentious and complex.

In a letter to Stevenson dated 21 October 1893, Henry James complained that while the novel *Catriona* appealed to the ear, it starved the eye. Many will endorse James's appreciation of the musicality of his friend's prose, but will be baffled by his other claim, and even more by Stevenson's cheerful acceptance of it—one of his aims, he told James, was precisely 'death to the optic nerve'. Are we talking about the same book here? Anyone who knows Edinburgh's Old Town (as James didn't but Stevenson did) will have it vividly before him when he reads David Balfour's narrative of his dangerous sojourn 'in this old, black city, which for all the world was like a rabbit-warren, not only by the number of its indwellers, but the complication of its passages and holes.' (This description, incidentally, reinforces the argument that Jekyll-and-Hyde's city is not London essentially, but Edinburgh). Two chapters later, there is the marvellous ballad-like tableau of David's encounter with the spae-wife near what is now Picardy Place; having read that, even today's visitor can't pass that spot without a shudder. Going further east, we have reprinted the novel's unforgettable evocation of the coast around North Berwick—the islet of Fidra, where 'the sea peeped through like a man's eye'—and we had to represent RLS on the sombre isolation of the Bass Rock, where David is incarcerated.

Reports of the death of the optic nerve, it seems, are greatly exaggerated. It was in Edinburgh, a city of unexpected vistas, that Stevenson acquired a visual power of great subtlety and sophistication: 'You turn a corner, and there is the sun going down into the Highland hills. You look down an alley, and see ships tacking for the Baltic.' From Scotland to the Baltic and the world: in the essay 'Ordered South' Stevenson demonstrated how the slightest change in the angle of vision can reveal a fresh aspect of Mediterranean France. Here is a writer who anticipates the aesthetic of Cubism; it should be noted, too, that he was an early champion of his friend Rodin.

Stevenson's artistry derived from seeing and representing things in what he called their 'significant simplicity'. It may be that Henry James, without knowing it, missed in Stevenson the exhaustive descriptions to be found in earlier nineteenth-century writers—the evocation of the London fog over several pages of the first chapter of Dickens's *Bleak House*, or the patient demographic context-setting of Mme Vauquer's boarding-house in Balzac's *Le père Goriot*. Stevenson, however, opts for the increasing minimalism of his own times. Like those Japanese printmakers whom he and his contemporaries admired so much, he can create an atmosphere with only a few deft touches. For example, the wooded den between Bridge of Allan and Dunblane was a favourite haunt: a cave there is said to be the original of that of Ben Gunn in *Treasure Island*. As early as 1872 he evokes the scene memorably as he walks 'by a colonnade of beeches along the brawling Allan'. Greek? Roman? Rocks, whirlpools? He expands neither on the 'colonnade' nor on the brawling: his half-sentence is all we need. Much later, his French admirer Marcel Schwob—a writer identified with the Symbolist movement—praised Stevenson's techniques of suggestion and what he called (roughly translated) the 'unreal realism' of the Scottish master. By this he meant Stevenson's ability to lure the reader into accepting physical impossibilities as part of the truth of his fiction, but the phrase could apply to any vivid image that hints at more than itself. In his chapter on Edinburgh's Greyfriars Churchyard, he encounters its cats, 'all sleek and fat, and complacently blinking, as if they had fed upon strange meats.' That has all the blood-curdling briskness of a ballad, and is worth far more than any guide-book enunciation of each and every tomb.

2

Stevenson remembered his childhood explorations of Edinburgh for 'a sense of something moving in things of infinite attraction and horror coupled'. *Edinburgh: Picturesque Notes* bears this out, but one might discern another dimension: Stevenson's city exists in a perpetual November. That is the month of his birth, and it's as if it becomes the temporal marker for much of his writing. Janet Adam Smith, in the introduction to her edition of the collected poems, remarks on the adolescent appeal of the early verse. Certainly such pieces are superficial, but those concerned with Edinburgh are not without a wistful resonance that can be rather affecting. Counterpointed as they are by a certain cheeky wit, their nostalgia does not quite dissolve into the lachrymose. Stevenson was particularly drawn back to Duddingston Loch, in a quiet Edinburgh village south-east of Arthur's Seat: there is a sparky little number in ballad-stanzas, recording some early amour that may have been real, imagined, or at least augmented. In the winter, the loch freezes over, and the poet recalls gliding along with his girl; at this point visitors to the National Gallery of Scotland may visualise Sir Henry Raeburn's quirky portrait of a skating minister. In a letter of December 1874, the young Stevenson felt impelled to impress Mrs Sitwell—one of those older women very much to his taste—with a cameo of Duddingston: 'If you had seen the moon rising, a perfect sphere of smoky gold, in the dark air above the trees, and the white loch thick with skaters, and the greater hill, snow-sprinkled overhead. It was a sight for a king.'

That's short-term nostalgia, when he's still close in time and space to the original experience. It's the long-term nostalgia, however, which informs the years after 1887, when he left Scotland for good. We recommend our readers not only to read the passages in the order in which we have printed them, but also to move backwards and forwards, comparing Stevenson's Scotland as experienced in youth with that experienced (from afar) in middle age. In the latter passages, Stevenson gazes at us with the countenance of his portrait by Count Nerli—worn-out, ill, the cheerful front giving way to the realisation that in the few remaining years he will revisit Scotland only (if amply) in his formidable imagination. Writing to Lord Rosebery in 1893, he expresses ambivalence about the Lothians: he misses the area, but confesses that any return would be 'superlatively painful'. He continues: 'Only I wish I could be buried there—among the hills, say, on the head of Allermuir—with a table tombstone like a Cameronian.' In the same year, he told Sidney Colvin that it was 'singular, that I should fulfil the Scots destiny throughout, and live in voluntary exile and have my head filled with the blessed, beastly place all the time!'

Over many years, in the course of his wanderings, he had been reminded of Scotland when the foreign topography somehow didn't seem so foreign: when 'the fine bulk of Tamalpais looking down on San Francisco' made him think of Arthur's Seat, or when the Adirondack mountain wilderness suggested 'a kind of insane mixture of Scotland and a dash of Switzerland and a dash of America', and where he was living in 'a decent house... on a hill-top, with a look down a Scottish river in front, and on one hand a Perthshire hill...' (letter from Saranac Lake, November 21, 1887). At Saranac he works on *The Master of Ballantrae*, whose Scottish chapters he mentions as set 'near Kirkcudbright' (letter of December 24, 1887; the 'Ballantrae' must not be identified with its factual namesake, which is a good forty-odd miles to the north-west on the Ayrshire coast.) One of his last home-thoughts from abroad is of Cramond, once the scene of those cherished but tense walks with his father. Some four pages before *St Ives* breaks off, never to be resumed by him, he gives us this brief sketch of Cramond: 'a little hamlet on a little river, embowered in woods, and looking forth over a great flat of quicksand to where a little islet stood planted in the sea.'

3

There remains that ambivalence about Scotland, and the reader will come across passages that would not feature in a holiday brochure. At seventeen, in a letter to his mother, he complained of 'this bleak fertility' of the East Neuk of Fife; twenty years later, in 'The Coast of Fife' (here reprinted) he was more appreciative. Stevenson is often considered to be Walter Scott's successor as the literary arch-celebrant of romantic Scotland; given that, we might be surprised to discover that he could be less than ecstatic about the topography of *The Lady of the Lake* and points north. '...I suppose the Trossachs would hardly be the Trossachs for most tourists if a man of admirable romantic instinct had not peopled it for them with harmonious figures, and brought them thither with minds rightly prepared for the impression. There is half the battle in this preparation. For instance: I have rarely been able to visit, in the proper spirit, the wild and inhospitable places of our own Highlands. I am happier where it is tame and fertile, and not readily pleased without trees.' This is priggish, even wimpish stuff from a man in his early twenties ('On the Enjoyment of Unpleasant Places', 1874)— more po-faced David Balfour than dashing Alan Breck. Can this be the same Stevenson who indeed became more recklessly Alan Breck-like as he got older, and who in *Kidnapped* relished the grim savagery of coastal outcrops and remote peaks? Ironically, the relish is all the greater for the narration by young fogey David; RLS loved writing for him that journey 'through a labyrinth of dreary glens and hollows and into the heart of that dismal mountain of Ben Alder.' These lines conclude a chapter in the most breathtakingly dramatic manner.

4

In recent years some of the most interesting books of Scottish topography have focused on architecture. In what follows we have Stevenson, on a few occasions, eloquently appraising Scottish buildings. Anyone visiting Kirkwall's St Magnus Cathedral and its neighbouring masterpieces will find in RLS a guide both stimulating and practical. Here is one of the finest prose passages of his youth. His denunciation of the late-Victorian accretions of Kirkwall Pier is all the more cutting for the preceding praise-poem to the town's glories.

He displayed serious and informed interest in projected illustrations to *The Master of Ballantrae,* concerned as he was that the stately home of the Durrisdeers would be authentically depicted. However, the book was a piece of fiction (by an 'unreal realist') and he would not insist on a too-literal requirement that the building be in the style of the South-West. So he suggested that the illustrator might consider as models Craigievar Castle in Aberdeenshire and Pinkie House in Lothian.

That does not mean, though, that he is insensitive to the regional specifics of Scottish architecture, and in 'A Winter's Walk in Carrick and Galloway' he lovingly quotes at length William Abercrombie's detailed account of Maybole, and his own description of the castle tower is richly observant, especially with regard to 'a small oriel window, fluted and corbelled and carved about with stone heads'. That same essay has impressed me for more personal reasons. As a native of Fife, I am familiar with the Bass Rock looming up from the Forth Estuary; as an occasional migrant, I leave Scotland from the west, and my last view of Scotland—as the plane ascends from Prestwick Airport —is of Ailsa Craig guarding the Firth of Clyde. It had never occurred to me to compare these two noble rocks. More than a century ago, it had occurred to Stevenson.

TOM HUBBARD

'The Romance of Destiny': The Varied and Various Stevensons

1

Robert Lewis (later 'Louis') Balfour Stevenson was born on 13 November 1850 at 8 Howard Place, Edinburgh. The house still stands in this street of unpretentious Georgian terraced houses which was built in the 1820s in one of the later phases of the development of Edinburgh's New Town. In 1853 the Stevenson family moved to nearby 1 Inverleith Terrace. That house was more exposed than Howard Place to the cold November wind of Edinburgh that Stevenson disliked and helped to make famous. In 1856 the increasingly prosperous Stevensons moved to the south-facing 17 Heriot Row. This still-prestigious terrace was built in the first decade of the nineteenth century as the first part of the northern or second New Town. It was within this elegant Georgian Edinburgh of ultra-respectable professional families that Stevenson grew up. The house faces across private Queen Street Gardens to Queen Street which runs parallel to George Street and Princes Street. Above Princes Street Gardens the skyline is dominated by the Castle and the 'lands' of the Old Town.

There has been a tendency for those who have written on Stevenson to exaggerate his childhood illnesses and the loneliness of his years as a boy at Heriot Row. It is clear that he enjoyed the company of his cousins in Edinburgh and on holiday at North Berwick. His cousin Charles Stevenson, who was born in 1855 and lived to be 96, wrote of his family resenting that Louis has 'so often been referred to as a more or less permanent invalid. He certainly had all the childhood illnesses that we all got at some time or other and also a chest weakness that was greatly aggravated by the Edinburgh climate. His mother had this too, and both of them did well to escape the winter and head for the South of France. It is generally accepted today that Louis had bronchiectasis which did eventually cause severe haemorrhages but he made good recovery from all the attacks. His death I think was an isolated stroke. He walked many miles on a daily basis and on some walking tours notched up 30 miles without undue fatigue. He had a very strong constitution indeed to withstand all the physical blows life dealt him. All the Stevenson family worked hard at their vocation but none harder than Louis in the 44 years he had in life.'

Charles Stevenson, who lived at 25 Royal Terrace, on Calton Hill, also remembered, 'Only a few hundred yards to the south of Royal

Terrace lay the heart of Louis's playground in his adolescent years and he shared it often with us. Every part of Holyrood and of Arthur's Seat we made our own. A map illustrates the ground we covered from the Haggis Knowe to Dunsappie Loch. Passing Dunsappie Louis always identified a non-existent cave and called it Dick Hatterick's Cave [after the cave in Scott's *Guy Mannering*]. Probably he was also remembering the Grotto known to him in Italy, which he had visited with Bessy (my sister). She had arranged this trip in 1863 at the request of her Uncle Thomas.' During 1862-63, in the company of members of his family, Louis also visited France and Germany. Perhaps the seeds of his compulsion to travel were planted by his mother.

Whilst it may be true that Stevenson never had tuberculosis, he spent many years looking for a cure. He spent the winter of 1880-81 in the 'frosty mountains' of Davos in south-eastern Switzerland. This was a famous centre for the treatment of consumption, with Dr Karl Ruedi, says Stevenson in his Dedication to *Underwoods*, 'the good genius of the English'. Dr Ruedi's prognosis was that two years at Davos might permanently arrest Stevenson's disease, but that was more than he could face in that place where funerals took place every day and new dying consumptives moved in to make the exile very aware of 'the wolverine on my own shoulders'. He did return to Davos for another winter, but after a summer in Scotland he and his wife went south to the Mediterranean to the Châlet La Solitude, at Hyères, another resort for consumptives. Somewhat dramatically, Stevenson wrote to Sidney Colvin, 'I was happy once; that was at Hyères.'

Stevenson probably learned as much that was important to him as a writer from his Calvinistic nurse, Alison Cunningham, as anything he learned from professional teachers, whether at Mr Henderson's school in India Street, or the prestigious Edinburgh Academy in Henderson Row that he attended from 1861 to 1863. Louis was seventeen when, in 1867, he enrolled at Edinburgh University to study engineering in order to be qualified to join the family's engineering business. In the following year he was sent by his father to watch harbour works being undertaken by the family firm at Anstruther and Wick. In 1869 he went with his father on board the *Pharos*, the steamer of the Commissioners of the Board of Northern Lighthouses, on a tour of inspection to Orkney, Shetland and Fair Isle, and we are pleased to print extracts from letters written to his mother from *Pharos* that take the form of a journal. In 1870 Louis spent three weeks on the Isle of Earraid off Mull to watch the Dhu Heartach lighthouse being built and from that experience came not only his essay, 'Memoirs of an Islet' but descriptive passages in *Kidnapped*.

During the following year at university Louis changed course to study law. Although very disappointed by this, Thomas Stevenson must have been proud when in 1875 his son was admitted to the Scottish bar and his name, as Advocate, could be placed on the door of 17 Heriot Row. Before that time, however, Louis had decided on a literary career and for that, as the essays and extracts printed here show, his journeys, by land and sea, to harbours and lighthouses, to learn about engineering were important to both the prolific novelist and the essayist. In his essay 'A College Magazine' (*Memoirs and Portraits*, 1887) Stevenson explained,

> All through my boyhood and youth, I was known and pointed out for the pattern of an idler; and yet I was always busy on my own private end, which was to learn to write. I kept always two books in my pocket, one to read, one to write in. As I walked, my mind was busy fitting what I saw with appropriate words; when I sat by the roadside, I would either read, or a pencil and a penny version-book would be in my hand, to note down the features of the scene or commemorate some halting stanzas. Thus I lived with words. And what I thus wrote was for no ulterior use, it was written consciously for practice. It was not so much that I wished to be an author (though I wished that too) as that I had vowed that I would learn to write. That was a proficiency that tempted me; and I practised to acquire it, as men learn to whittle, in a wager with myself. Description was the principal field of my exercise; for to anyone with senses there is always something worth describing, and town and country are but one continuous subject.

The story of Stevenson's courtship, marriage and life with Fanny van de Grift, whose first husband was Sam Osbourne, is a tempestuous one. The courtship involved Louis in a heroic journey from Glasgow to New York and across the plains to San Francisco to be reunited with Fanny. Stevenson told the story of that courageous expedition in *The Amateur Emigrant* which some consider to be his best non-fiction work. They were married in San Francisco in 1880 and honeymooned in Silverado, an abandoned mining town below Mount Saint Helena in the Napa Valley. From that episode came *The Silverado Squatters*, which was published in 1883 with a frontispiece by Joseph D Strong showing Louis and Fanny in their deserted shack at Silverado. Joe

Strong was an artist with whom Fanny's daughter, Isobel (Belle) Osbourne, eloped but, following a divorce, Belle remained at Vailima as Stevenson's amanuensis. In a light-hearted letter to J M Barrie, April 1893, RLS wrote of Isobel Osbourne Strong, '[She] runs me like a baby in a perambulator, sees I'm dressed properly, bought me silk socks, and made me wear them, takes care of me when I'm well, from writing my books to trimming my nails. Has a growing conviction that she is the author of my works, manages the house and the houseboys, who are very fond of her.'

Having spent the months of June and July 1880 in the Californian mountains, the Stevensons then sailed on 7th August from New York to arrive in Liverpool on the 17th where they were met by RLS's parents on whom Louis, in his thirtieth year, still depended for financial support. As a divorced woman with children and artistic leanings, Fanny was not the wife Thomas Stevenson would have chosen for his son, but surprisingly quickly she charmed him into seeing her as potentially a stabilising influence on Louis.

Following a winter at Davos in the summer of 1881, Stevenson was in the Scottish Highlands; initially, with his wife and mother, at Kinnaird Cottage, near Moulin above Pitlochry 'in the Vale of Atholl'. It was there that he wrote 'Thrawn Janet'. Soon the family moved to Braemar and, as always, his father could not resist offering advice and criticism to his son, but it was at Braemar in 1881 that Stevenson wrote the first chapters of *Treasure Island*. He read chapters to his family as he completed them and, like many another after him, Thomas Stevenson was entranced by his son's ever-popular tale. It was also at Braemar, when his mother showed him Kate Greenaway's *Birthday Book for Children* with text by Sale Barker, that Stevenson wrote the first of his very popular verses for children which were published in 1885 as *A Child's Garden of Verses*.

Seemingly, it was apprehension about an outbreak of cholera at Hyères that prompted the Stevensons to move to Bournemouth in 1885 and in late summer they moved to what RLS's wife thought would be a 'permanent' home. The house was a gift to her from her father-in-law who was still hopeful that his son would settle into a more conventional life. They lived in Bournemouth only till Thomas died in 1887. Situated on the Westbourne cliffs, the yellow-brick villa was known as 'Sea View' until Stevenson renamed it 'Skerryvore', after what he saw as 'the noblest of all the extant deep-sea lights'. It was in Bournemouth that Stevenson wrote *The Strange Case of Dr Jekyll and Mr Hyde* and *Kidnapped* and first met Henry James. Jenni Calder has written that whilst *Dr Jekyll and Mr Hyde* brought him 'popularity' *Kidnapped* brought 'critical respect'. The success of *Dr Jekyll and Mr Hyde* can be seen in the sales figures; 40,000 copies were sold in the first six months from January 1886 and by the end of the century 250,000 copies had been sold in the USA.

2

RLS's relationship with his father Thomas Stevenson (1818-87) was complex and difficult. As a student Louis adopted the bohemian dress of the day which was not then common in Edinburgh; long hair, velvet jacket and black shirt and neckerchief. He also explored the dark side of the Old Town that New-Town Edinburgh liked to pretend did not exist. All this was disagreeable to Louis's father but a bigger break came when the twenty-two-year-old admitted to his father that he was an agnostic, if not an atheist. Although Stevenson's relationship with his father was stormy, Thomas Stevenson's generosity to his wayward son was unusual for an Edinburgh professional man of that time. Without his father's financial support Stevenson could not have been a full-time writer. The best words on Thomas and his only child are by J C Furnas in his *Voyage to Windward: The Life of Robert Louis Stevenson*, 1952: 'Louis and his father paid equal shares in bitterness for every farthing of the thousands of pounds required to crutch the promising invalid into independence.'

Although not such an important lighthouse builder as his father, who built the Bell Rock light, or his brother Alan, who built the magnificent Skerryvore, Thomas Stevenson made a significant contribution to the lighthouses built by his family, with that at Dhu Heartach (or Dubh Artach) which he worked on with his brother David, the most interesting. But, as Louis wrote in 'Thomas Stevenson, Civil Engineer', 1887, 'the great achievement of his life was in optics as applied to lighthouse illumination.' To the mature Louis, his father was 'a man of antique strain with a blend of sternness and softness that was wholly Scottish and at first bewildering; with a profound essential melancholy of disposition and (what sometimes accompanies it) the most humorous geniality in company; shrewd and childish; passionately attached, passionately prejudiced; a man of many extremes, many faults of temper, and no very stable foothold for himself among life's troubles.'

The last time Louis saw Heriot Row was at his father's funeral in 1887 and when he left No 17 for the last time he was also leaving Scotland, never to return physically. Flora Masson gave a lively description of Stevenson leaving Edinburgh for the last time, 'An open cab, with a man and a woman in it, seated side by side, and leaning back— the rest of the cab piled high with rather untidy luggage—came slowly towards us... As it passed... a slender, loose-garbed figure stood up... and waved a wide-brimmed hat. "Goodbye"! he called to us, "Goodbye!"'

Goodbye indeed, but his imagination was never free of memories of Scotland and especially of Edinburgh of which he wrote in 1883, 'it grows on me with every year; there are no stars as lovely as Edinburgh street-lamps. When I forget Auld Reekie, may my right hand forget its cunning!' As the essays, and extracts from his letters and Scottish novels that we have enjoyed selecting for *Stevenson's Scotland* show, that cunning was still there as he wrote the never-to-be-completed *Weir of Hermiston*.

Tom Hubbard and I have been spoiled for choice in making a selection from Stevenson's writing and here I would add some sentences from the essay 'Pastoral', which RLS wrote around spring 1887 and collected in *Memories and Portraits,* 1887, the proofs of which he read during the voyage to New York, and dedicated to his newly-widowed mother 'in the name of past joy and present sorrow'. Hugh MacDiarmid, having named an astonishing diversity of plants on a patch of heather-covered Scottish hillside, asked ironically, 'Scotland Small? This multitudinous Scotland Small?' In 'Pastoral', Stevenson was performing a similar naming of the universal in the particularly Scottish when he wrote of Scottish rivers and burns,

> their sound and colour dwell for ever in the memory. How often and willingly do I not look again in fancy on Tummel, or Manor, or the talking Airdle, or Dee swirling in its Lynn; on the bright burn of Kinnaird, or the golden burn that pours and sulks in the den behind Kingussie. I think shame to leave out one of these enchantresses, but the list would grow too long if I remembered all; only I may not forget Allan Water, nor birch-wetting Rogie, nor yet Almond; nor, for all its pollutions, that Water of Leith of the many and well-named mills—Bell's Mills, and Canon Mills, and Silver Mills; nor Redford Burn of pleasant memories; nor yet, for all its smallness, that nameless trickle that springs in the green bosom of Allermuir, and is fed from Halkerside with a perennial teacupful, and threads the moss under the Shearer's Knowe.

It is the variety and extent of Stevenson's writings on what he clearly saw as a 'multitudinous Scotland' that has made our selection pleasurably difficult.

3

In August 1887, RLS with his wife, her son Lloyd Osbourne, the newly-widowed Mrs Stevenson and 'trusted servant', Valentine Roch, sailed from Tilbury for New York in the tramp freighter SS *Ludgate Hill*, with passenger cabins. Meeting Stevenson in London on the 16th Edmund Gosse was surprised to be greeted by a smartly dressed Louis, 'instead of looking like a Lascar out of employment, as he generally does.' Following a celebrity's enthusiastic welcome in New York for the author of *Jekyll and Hyde*, Stevenson spent almost seven months, from the end of September to the end of April, in upper New York State at Saranac Lake in the Adirondack Mountains. The Lake had become a place 'of cure', with Dr Edward Trude the resident physician, and he diagnosed that Stevenson's consumption was 'in remission'. From the time Stevenson arrived in the USA sixteen months passed without his experiencing a haemorrhage—what he termed his 'old friend Bloodie Jacke'. In a letter of October 1887 to his cousin Robert Stevenson, RLS wrote, 'We have a wooden house on a hill-top, overlooking a river, and a village about a quarter of a mile away, and very wooded hills; the whole scene is very Highland, bar want of heather and the wooden houses.'

In December 1887, after he and his mother were left alone in the low temperatures of Saranac Lake, Stevenson put in much work on *The Master of Ballantrae* which had been 'conceived' on the moors between Pitlochry and Strathairdle and in 'Highland rain, in the blend of the smell of heather and bog-plants, and with a mind full of the Athole correspondence and the Memoirs of the Chevalier de Johnstone.' It is apt that Stevenson, a master of contrast and duality, worked, during the early months of 1889, on *The Master* in the very different climatic conditions of a 'crazy dirty cottage' at the eastern end of Waikiki Beach, four miles out of Honolulu. This is yet another study of duality that we may, in this regard, link not only to *Dr Jekyll and Mr Hyde* but also to Gordon Darnaway of 'The Merry Men', and Tod of the exceptional 'Tale of Tod Lapraik' (in *Catriona*) that is worthy to be placed beside 'Thrawn Janet' which is often seen as Stevenson's finest story in Scots.

On 28th June 1888 the Stevensons sailed from San Francisco Bay in the yacht *Casco*, Captain A H Otis, on the first of the South Seas voyages that led, eventually, to Upolu, Samoa. Arriving just before Christmas 1889 and before leaving for Sydney in February 1890, Louis had bought an estate on the wooded mountainside above Apia on the island of Upolu. It was on that land that the Stevensons began building the distinctive house called Vailima. Stevenson's poem 'The Woodman' was written in 1890 as the jungle was being cleared to make the home at Vailima and he gave himself the task of making a path up the heavily forested gorge of a burn above the house. On 2nd November 1890, from that mountainside in Samoa, Stevenson wrote to Sidney Colvin, 'the whole silent battle, murder, and slow death of the contending forest, weigh upon the imagination.' Envisaging Robert Louis Stevenson, supposedly delicate son of harsh but bourgeois Victorian Edinburgh, fighting a small-scale South Seas jungle, hints at the contradictions of his life and work.

By the end of 1890 the Stevensons were well settled in Vailima and soon Louis became involved in Samoan politics. Stevenson had come to believe that he could not leave the tropical climate of the South Seas, but in February 1893 he did take a 'month's holiday' to Sydney where he found his 'fame much grown on this return to civilisation. *Digito monstrari* [to be pointed at by the finger] is a new experience; people all look at me in the streets; and it was very queer' (letter to Sidney Colvin, April 1893). A photograph taken in Sydney in 1893 shows him looking as bohemianly delicate as ever. Robert Louis Stevenson, who had fought illnesses of his chest and lungs all his life, died suddenly from a brain haemorrhage. The date was 3 December 1894. He was 44. He was buried at the top of Mount Vaea with the now well-known 'Requiem' engraved on his tomb,

> Home is the sailor, home from sea,
> And the hunter home from the hill.

But in his last years Stevenson also lived by words that he wrote for the 'Dedication' of *Catriona* to Charles Baxter, dated Vailima, Upolu, Samoa, 1892,

> You are still—as when first I saw, as when I last addressed you—in the venerable city which I must always think of as my home. And I have come so far; and the sights and thoughts of my youth pursue me; and I see like a vision the youth of my father, and of his father, and the whole stream of lives flowing down there far in the north, with the sound of laughter and tears, to cast me out in the end, as by a sudden freshet, on these ultimate islands. And I admire and bow my head before the romance of destiny.

DUNCAN GLEN

Edinburgh Duality

Early Memories

I was born within the walls of that dear city of Zeus, of which the lightest and (when he chooses) the tenderest singer of my generation sings so well. I was born likewise within the bounds of an earthly city, illustrious for her beauty, her tragic and picturesque associations, and for the credit of some of her brave sons. Writing as I do in a strange quarter of the world, and a late day of my age, I can still behold the profile of her towers and chimneys, and the long trail of her smoke against the sunset; I can still hear those strains of martial music that she goes to bed with, ending each day, like an act of an opera, to the notes of bugles; still recall, with a grateful effort of memory, any one of a thousand beautiful and specious circumstances that pleased me, and that must have pleased anyone, in my half-remembered past. It is the beautiful that I thus actively recall; the august airs of the castle on its rock, nocturnal passages of lights and trees, the sudden song of the blackbird in a suburban lane, rosy and dusky winter sunsets, the uninhabited splendours of the early dawn, the building up of the city on a misty day, house above house, spire above spire, until it was received into a sky of softly glowing clouds, and seemed to pass on and upwards, by fresh grades and rises, city beyond city, a new Jerusalem, bodily scaling heaven...

Memory supplies me, unsolicited, with a mass of other material, where there is nothing to call beauty, nothing to attract—often a great deal to disgust. There are trite street corners, commonplace, well-to-do houses, shabby suburban tan-fields, rainy beggarly slums, taken in at a gulp nigh forty years ago, and surviving to-day, complete sensations, concrete, poignant and essential to the genius of the place. From the melancholy of these remembrances I might suppose them to belong to the wild and bitterly unhappy days of my youth. But it is not so; they date, most of them, from early childhood; they were observed as I walked with my nurse,[1] gaping on the universe, and striving vainly to piece together in words my inarticulate but profound impressions. I seem to have been born with a sentiment of something moving in things, of an infinite attraction and horror coupled.

Edinburgh: Picturesque Notes

Chapter I: Introductory

The ancient and famous metropolis of the North sits overlooking a windy estuary from the slope and summit of three hills. No situation could be more commanding for the head city of a kingdom; none better chosen for noble prospects. From her tall precipice and terraced gardens she looks far and wide on the sea and broad champaigns. To the east you may catch at sunset the spark of the May lighthouse, where the Firth expands into the German Ocean; and away to the west, over all the carse of Stirling, you can see the first snows upon Ben Ledi.

But Edinburgh pays cruelly for her high seat in one of the vilest climates under heaven. She is liable to be beaten upon by all the winds that blow, to be drenched with rain, to be buried in cold sea fogs out of the east, and powdered with the snow as it comes flying southward from the Highland hills. The weather is raw and boisterous in winter, shifty and ungenial in summer, and a downright meteorological purgatory in the spring. The delicate die early, and I, as a survivor, among bleak winds and plumping rain, have been sometimes tempted to envy them their fate. For all who love shelter and the blessings of the sun, who hate dark weather and perpetual tilting against squalls, there could scarcely be found a more unhomely and harassing place of residence. Many such aspire angrily after that Somewhere-else of the imagination, where all troubles are supposed to end. They lean over the great bridge[1] which joins the New Town with the Old—that windiest spot, or high altar, in this northern temple of the winds—and watch the trains smoking out from under them and vanishing into the tunnel on a voyage to brighter skies. Happy the passengers who shake off the dust of Edinburgh, and have heard for the last time the cry of the east wind among her chimney-tops! And yet the place establishes an interest in people's hearts; go where they will, they find no city of the same distinction; go where they will, they take a pride in their old home.

Venice, it has been said, differs from all other cities in the sentiment which she inspires. The rest may have admirers; she only, a famous fair one, counts lovers in her train. And, indeed, even by her kindest friends, Edinburgh is not considered in a similar sense. These like her for many reasons, not any one of which is satisfactory in itself. They like her whimsically, if you will, and somewhat as a virtuoso dotes upon his cabinet. Her attraction is romantic in the narrowest meaning of the term. Beautiful as she is, she is not so much beautiful as

2

interesting. She is pre-eminently Gothic, and all the more so since she has set herself off with some Greek airs, and erected classic temples on her crags. In a word, and above all, she is a curiosity. The Palace of Holyrood[2] has been left aside in the growth of Edinburgh, and stands grey and silent in a workman's quarter and among breweries and gas works. It is a house of many memories. Great people of yore, kings and queens, buffoons and grave ambassadors, played their stately farce for centuries in Holyrood. Wars have been plotted, dancing has lasted deep into the night, murder has been done in its chambers.[3] There Prince Charlie held his phantom levées,[4] and in a very gallant manner represented a fallen dynasty for some hours. Now, all these things of clay are mingled with the dust, the king's crown itself is shown for sixpence to the vulgar; but the stone palace has outlived these changes. For fifty weeks together, it is no more than a show for tourists and a museum of old furniture; but on the fifty-first, behold the palace re-awakened and mimicking its past. The Lord Commissioner, a kind of stage sovereign, sits among stage courtiers; a coach and six and clattering escort come and go before the gate; at night, the windows are lighted up, and its near neighbours, the workmen, may dance in their own houses to the palace music. And in this the palace is typical. There is a spark among the embers; from time to time the old volcano smokes. Edinburgh has but partly abdicated, and still wears, in parody, her metropolitan trappings. Half a capital and half a country town, the whole city leads a double existence; it has long trances of the one and flashes of the other; like the king of the Black Isles, it is half alive and half a monumental marble. There are armed men and cannon in the citadel overhead; you may see the troops marshalled on the high parade; and at night after the early winter even-fall, and in the morning before the laggard winter dawn, the wind carries abroad over Edinburgh the sound of drums and bugles. Grave judges sit bewigged in what was once the scene of imperial deliberations. Close by in the High Street perhaps the trumpets may sound about the stroke of noon; and you see a troop of citizens in tawdry masquerade; tabard above, heather-mixture trowser below, and the men themselves trudging in the mud among unsympathetic bystanders. The grooms of a well-appointed circus tread the streets with a better presence. And yet these are the Heralds and Pursuivants of Scotland, who are about to proclaim a new law of the United Kingdom before two-score boys, and thieves, and hackney-coachmen. Meanwhile every hour the bell of the University rings out over the hum of the streets, and every hour a double tide of students, coming and going, fills the deep archways. And lastly, one night in the spring-time—or say one morning rather, at the peep of

3

day—late folk may hear voices of many men singing a psalm in unison from a church on one side of the old High Street; and a little after, or perhaps a little before, the sound of many men singing a psalm in unison from another church on the opposite side of the way. There will be something in the words about the dew of Hermon, and how goodly it is to see brethren dwelling together in unity. And the late folk will tell themselves that all this singing denotes the conclusion of two yearly ecclesiastical parliaments—the parliaments of Churches which are brothers in many admirable virtues, but not specially like brothers in this particular of a tolerant and peaceful life.

Again, meditative people will find a charm in a certain consonancy between the aspect of the city and its odd and stirring history. Few places, if any, offer a more barbaric display of contrasts to the eye. In the very midst stands one of the most satisfactory crags in nature—a Bass Rock upon dry land, rooted in a garden shaken by passing trains, carrying a crown of battlements and turrets, and describing its warlike shadow over the liveliest and brightest thoroughfare of the New Town. From their smoky beehives, ten stories high, the unwashed look down upon the open squares and gardens of the wealthy; and gay people sunning themselves along Princes Street, with its mile of commercial palaces all beflagged upon some great occasion, see, across a gardened valley set with statues, where the washings of the Old Town flutter in the breeze at its high windows. And then, upon all sides, what a clashing of architecture! In this one valley, where the life of the town goes most busily forward, there may be seen, shown one above and behind another by the accidents of the ground, buildings in almost every style upon the globe. Egyptian and Greek temples, Venetian palaces and Gothic spires, are huddled one over another in a most admired disorder; while, above all, the brute mass of the Castle and the summit of Arthur's Seat look down upon these imitations with a becoming dignity, as the works of Nature may look down upon the monuments of Art. But Nature is a more indiscriminate patroness than we imagine, and in no way frightened of a strong effect. The birds roost as willingly among the Corinthian capitals as in the crannies of the crag; the same atmosphere and daylight clothe the eternal rock and yesterday's imitation portico; and as the soft northern sunshine throws out everything into a glorified distinctness—or easterly mists, coming up with the blue evening, fuse all these incongruous features into one, and the lamps begin to glitter along the street, and faint lights to burn in the high windows across the valley—the feeling grows upon you that this also is a piece of nature in the most intimate sense; that this profusion of eccentricities, this dream in masonry and living rock, is not a drop-scene in a theatre,

4

but a city in the world of everyday reality, connected by railway and telegraph-wire with all the capitals of Europe, and inhabited by citizens of the familiar type, who keep ledgers, and attend church, and have sold their immortal portion to a daily paper. By all the canons of romance, the place demands to be half deserted and leaning towards decay; birds we might admit in profusion, the play of the sun and winds, and a few gipsies encamped in the chief thoroughfare; but these citizens, with their cabs and tramways, their trains and posters, are altogether out of key. Chartered tourists, they make free with historic localities, and rear their young among the most picturesque sites with a grand human indifference. To see them thronging by, in their neat clothes and conscious moral rectitude, and with a little air of possession that verges on the absurd, is not the least striking feature of the place.*

And the story of the town is as eccentric as its appearance. For centuries it was a capital thatched with heather, and more than once, in the evil days of English invasion, it has gone up in flame to heaven, a beacon to ships at sea. It was the jousting-ground of jealous nobles, not only on Greenside,[5] or by the King's Stables, where set tournaments were fought to the sound of trumpets and under the authority of the royal presence, but in every alley where there was room to cross swords, and in the main street, where popular tumult under the Blue Blanket alternated with the brawls of outlandish clansmen and retainers. Down in the palace John Knox[6] reproved his queen in the accents of modern democracy. In the town, in one of those little shops plastered like so many swallows' nests among the buttresses of the old Cathedral, that familiar autocrat, James VI,[7] would gladly share a bottle of wine with George Heriot[8] the goldsmith. Up on the Pentland Hills, that so quietly look down on the Castle with the city lying in waves around it, those mad and dismal fanatics, the Sweet Singers, haggard from long

---

* These sentences have, I hear, given offence in my native town, and a proportionable pleasure to our rivals of Glasgow. I confess the news caused me both pain and merriment. May I remark, as a balm for wounded fellow-townsmen, that there is nothing deadly in my accusations? Small blame to them if they keep ledgers: 'tis an excellent business habit. Churchgoing is not, that ever I heard, a subject of reproach; decency of linen is a mark of prosperous affairs, and conscious moral rectitude one of the tokens of good living. It is not their fault if the city calls for something more specious by way of inhabitants. A man in a frock-coat looks out of place upon an Alp or Pyramid, although he has the virtues of a Peabody and the talents of a Bentham. And let them console themselves—they do as well as anybody else; the population of (let us say) Chicago would cut quite as rueful a figure on the same romantic stage. To the Glasgow people I would say only one word, but that is of gold: *I have not yet written a book about Glasgow.*

exposure on the moors, sat day and night with 'tearful psalms' to see Edinburgh consumed with fire from heaven, like another Sodom or Gomorrah. There, in the Grassmarket, stiff-necked, covenanting heroes[9] offered up the often unnecessary, but not less honourable, sacrifice of their lives, and bade eloquent farewell to sun, moon, and stars, and earthly friendships, or died silent to the roll of drums. Down by yon outlet rode Grahame of Claverhouse[10] and his thirty dragoons, with the town beating to arms behind their horses' tails—a sorry handful thus riding for their lives, but with a man at the head who was to return in a different temper, make a dash that staggered Scotland to the heart, and die happily in the thick of fight. There Aikenhead[11] was hanged for a piece of boyish incredulity; there, a few years afterwards, David Hume ruined Philosophy and Faith, an undisturbed and well-reputed citizen; and thither, in yet a few years more, Burns came from the plough-tail, as to an academy of gilt unbelief and artificial letters.[12] There, when the great exodus was made across the valley, and the New Town began to spread abroad its draughty parallelograms, and rear its long frontage on the opposing hill, there was such a flitting, such a change of domicile and dweller, as was never excelled in the history of cities: the cobbler succeeded the earl; the beggar ensconced himself by the judge's chimney; what had been a palace was used as a pauper refuge; and great mansions were so parcelled out among the least and lowest in society, that the hearthstone of the old proprietor was thought large enough to be partitioned off into a bedroom by the new.

Chapter II: Old Town—The Lands

The Old Town, it is pretended, is the chief characteristic, and, from a picturesque point of view, the liver-wing of Edinburgh. It is one of the most common forms of depreciation to throw cold water on the whole by adroit over-commendation of a part, since everything worth judging, whether it be a man, a work of art, or only a fine city, must be judged upon its merits as a whole. The Old Town depends for much of its effect on the new quarters that lie around it, on the sufficiency of its situation, and on the hills that back it up. If you were to set it somewhere else by itself, it would look remarkably like Stirling in a bolder and loftier edition. The point is to see this embellished Stirling planted in the midst of a large, active, and fantastic modern city; for there the two react in a picturesque sense, and the one is the making of the other.

The Old Town occupies a sloping ridge or tail of diluvial matter, protected, in some subsidence of the waters, by the Castle cliffs which fortify it to the west. On the one side of it and the other the new towns of the south and of the north occupy their lower, broader, and more gentle hill-tops. Thus, the quarter of the Castle overtops the whole city and keeps an open view to sea and land. It dominates for miles on every side; and people on the decks of ships, or ploughing in quiet country places over in Fife, can see the banner on the Castle battlements, and the smoke of the Old Town blowing abroad over the subjacent country. A city that is set upon a hill. It was, I suppose, from this distant aspect that she got her nickname of *Auld Reekie*. Perhaps it was given her by people who had never crossed her doors: day after day, from their various rustic Pisgahs, they had seen the pile of building on the hill-top, and the long plume of smoke over the plain; so it appeared to them; so it had appeared to their fathers tilling the same field; and as that was all they knew of the place, it could be all expressed in these two words.

Indeed, even on a nearer view, the Old Town is properly smoked; and though it is well washed with rain all the year round, it has a grim and sooty aspect among its younger suburbs. It grew, under the law that regulates the growth of walled cities in precarious situations, not in extent, but in height and density. Public buildings were forced, wherever there was room for them, into the midst of thoroughfares; thoroughfares were diminished into lanes; houses sprang up story after story, neighbour mounting upon neighbour's shoulder, as in some Black Hole of Calcutta, until the population slept fourteen or fifteen deep in a vertical direction. The tallest of these *lands*, as they are locally termed, have long since been burnt out; but to this day it is not uncommon to see eight or ten windows at a flight; and the cliff of building which hangs imminent over Waverley Bridge would still put many natural precipices to shame. The cellars are already high above the gazer's head, planted on the steep hill-side; as for the garret, all the furniture may be in the pawn-shop, but it commands a famous prospect to the Highland hills. The poor man may roost up there in the centre of Edinburgh, and yet have a peep of the green country from his window; he shall see the quarters of the well-to-do fathoms underneath, with their broad squares and gardens; he shall have nothing overhead but a few spires, the stone top-gallants of the city; and perhaps the wind may reach him with a rustic pureness, and bring a smack of the sea, or of flowering lilacs in the spring.

It is almost the correct literary sentiment to deplore the revolutionary improvements of Mr. Chambers[13] and his following. It is easy to be a conservator of the discomforts of others; indeed, it is only our good qualities we find it irksome to conserve. Assuredly, in driving streets

7

through the black labyrinth, a few curious old corners have been swept away, and some associations turned out of house and home. But what slices of sunlight, what breaths of clean air, have been let in! And what a picturesque world remains untouched! You go under dark arches, and down dark stairs and alleys. The way is so narrow that you can lay a hand on either wall; so steep that, in greasy winter weather, the pavement is almost as treacherous as ice. Washing dangles above washing from the windows; the houses bulge outwards upon flimsy brackets; you see a bit of sculpture in a dark corner; at the top of all, a gable and a few crowsteps are printed on the sky. Here, you come into a court where the children are at play and the grown people sit upon their doorsteps, and perhaps a church spire shows itself above the roofs. Here, in the narrowest of the entry, you find a great old mansion still erect, with some insignia of its former state—some scutcheon, some holy or courageous motto, on the lintel. The local antiquary points out where famous and well-born people had their lodging; and as you look up, out pops the head of a slatternly woman from the countess's window. The Bedouins camp within Pharaoh's palace walls, and the old warship is given over to the rats. We are already a far way from the days when powdered heads were plentiful in these alleys, with jolly, port-wine faces underneath. Even in the chief thoroughfares Irish washings flutter at the windows, and the pavements are encumbered with loiterers.

These loiterers are a true character of the scene. Some shrewd Scotch workmen may have paused on their way to a job, debating Church affairs and politics with their tools upon their arm. But the most part are of a different order—skulking jail-birds; unkempt, barefoot children; big-mouthed, robust women, in a sort of uniform of striped flannel petticoat and short tartan shawl; among these, a few supervising constables and a dismal sprinkling of mutineers and broken men from higher ranks in society, with some mark of better days upon them, like a brand. In a place no larger than Edinburgh, and where the traffic is mostly centred in five or six chief streets, the same face comes often under the notice of an idle stroller. In fact, from this point of view, Edinburgh is not so much a small city as the largest of small towns. It is scarce possible to avoid observing your neighbours; and I never yet heard of any one who tried. It has been my fortune, in this anonymous accidental way, to watch more than one of these downward travellers for some stages on the road to ruin. One man must have been upwards of sixty before I first observed him, and he made then a decent, personable figure in broadcloth of the best. For three years he kept falling—grease coming and buttons going from the square-skirted coat, the face puffing and pimpling, the shoulders growing bowed, the hair falling scant and grey upon his head; and the last that ever I saw of him, he was standing at the mouth of an entry with several men in moleskin, three parts drunk, and his old black raiment daubed with mud. I fancy that I still can hear him laugh. There was something heart-breaking in this gradual declension at so advanced an age; you would have thought a man of sixty out of the reach of these calamities; you would have thought that he was niched by that time into a safe place in life, whence he could pass quietly and honourably into the grave.

One of the earliest marks of these *dégringolades* is, that the victim begins to disappear from the New Town thoroughfares, and takes to the High Street, like a wounded animal to the woods. And such an one is the type of the quarter. It also has fallen socially. A scutcheon over the door somewhat jars in sentiment where there is a washing at every window. The old man, when I saw him last, wore the coat in which he had played the gentleman three years before; and that was just what gave him so pre-eminent an air of wretchedness.

It is true that the over-population was at least as dense in the epoch of lords and ladies, and that nowadays some customs which made Edinburgh notorious of yore have been fortunately pretermitted. But an aggregation of comfort is not distasteful like an aggregation of the reverse. Nobody cares how many lords and ladies, and divines and lawyers, may have been crowded into these houses in the past—perhaps the more the merrier. The glasses clink around the china punch-bowl, some one touches the virginals, there are peacocks' feathers on the chimney, and the tapers burn clear and pale in the red firelight. That is not an ugly picture in itself, nor will it become ugly upon repetition. All the better if the like were going on in every second room; the *land* would only look the more inviting. Times are changed. In one house, perhaps, two-score families herd together; and, perhaps, not one of them is wholly out of the reach of want. The great hotel is given over to discomfort from the foundation to the chimney-tops; everywhere a pinching, narrow habit, scanty meals, and an air of sluttishness and dirt. In the first room there is a birth, in another a death, in a third a sordid drinking-bout, and the detective and the Bible-reader cross upon the stairs. High words are audible from dwelling to dwelling, and children have a strange experience from the first; only a robust soul, you would think, could grow up in such conditions without hurt. And even if God tempers His dispensations to the young, and all the ill does not arise that our apprehensions may forecast, the sight of such a way of living is disquieting to people who are more happily circumstanced.

9

Social inequality is nowhere more ostentatious than at Edinburgh. I have mentioned already how, to the stroller along Princes Street, the High Street callously exhibits its back garrets. It is true, there is a garden between. And although nothing could be more glaring by way of contrast, sometimes the opposition is more immediate; sometimes the thing lies in a nutshell, and there is not so much as a blade of grass between the rich and poor. To look over the South Bridge and see the Cowgate below full of crying hawkers, is to view one rank of society from another in the twinkling of an eye.

One night I went along the Cowgate after everyone was a-bed but the policeman, and stopped by hazard before a tall *land*. The moon touched upon its chimneys, and shone blankly on the upper windows; there was no light anywhere in the great bulk of building; but as I stood there it seemed to me that I could hear quite a body of quiet sounds from the interior; doubtless there were many clocks ticking, and people snoring on their backs. And thus, as I fancied, the dense life within made itself faintly audible in my ears, family after family contributing its quota to the general hum, and the whole pile beating in tune to its timepieces, like a great disordered heart. Perhaps it was little more than a fancy altogether, but it was strangely impressive at the time, and gave me an imaginative measure of the disproportion between the quantity of living flesh and the trifling walls that separated and contained it.

There was nothing fanciful, at least, but every circumstance of terror and reality, in the fall of the *land* in the High Street. The building had grown rotten to the core; the entry underneath had suddenly closed up so that the scavenger's barrow could not pass; cracks and reverberations sounded through the house at night; the inhabitants of the huge old human beehive discussed their peril when they encountered on the stair; some had even left their dwellings in a panic of fear, and returned to them again in a fit of economy or self-respect; when, in the black hours of a Sunday morning, the whole structure ran together with a hideous uproar and tumbled story upon story to the ground. The physical shock was felt far and near; and the moral shock travelled with the morning milkmaid into all the suburbs. The church-bells never sounded more dismally over Edinburgh than that grey forenoon. Death had made a brave harvest, and, like Samson, by pulling down one roof, destroyed many a home. None who saw it can have forgotten the aspect of the gable; here it was plastered, there papered, according to the rooms; here the kettle still stood on the hob, high overhead; and there a cheap picture of the Queen was pasted over the chimney. So, by this disaster, you had a glimpse into the life of thirty families, all suddenly cut off from the revolving years. The *land* had fallen; and

with the *land* how much! Far in the country, people saw a gap in the
city ranks, and the sun looked through between the chimneys in an
unwonted place. And all over the world, in London, in Canada, in New
Zealand, fancy what a multitude of people could exclaim with truth:
'The house that I was born in fell last night!'

Chapter III: The Parliament Close

Time has wrought its changes most notably around the precincts of St.
Giles's Church. The church itself, if it were not for the spire, would be
unrecognisable; the *Krames*[14] are all gone, not a shop is left to shelter in
its buttresses; and zealous magistrates and a misguided architect have
shorn the design of manhood, and left it poor, naked, and pitifully
pretentious. As St. Giles's must have had in former days a rich and
quaint appearance now forgotten, so the neighbourhood was bustling,
sunless, and romantic. It was here that the town was most overbuilt;
but the overbuilding has been all rooted out, and not only a free fairway left along the High Street with an open space on either side of the
church, but a great porthole, knocked in the main line of the *lands*,
gives an outlook to the north and the New Town.

There is a silly story of a subterranean passage between the Castle
and Holyrood, and a bold Highland piper who volunteered to explore
its windings. He made his entrance by the upper end, playing a strath-
spey; the curious footed it after him down the street, following his
descent by the sound of the chanter from below; until all of a sudden,
about the level of St. Giles's, the music came abruptly to an end, and
the people in the street stood at fault with hands uplifted. Whether he
was choked with gases, or perished in a quag, or was removed bodily
by the Evil One, remains a point of doubt; but the piper has never
again been seen or heard of from that day to this. Perhaps he wandered
down into the land of Thomas the Rhymer, and some day, when it is
least expected, may take a thought to revisit the sunlit upper world.
That will be a strange moment for the cabmen on the stance beside St.
Giles's, when they hear the drone of his pipes reascending from the
bowels of the earth below their horses' feet.

But it is not only pipers who have vanished, many a solid bulk of
masonry has been likewise spirited into the air. Here, for example, is
the shape of a heart let into the causeway. This was the site of the
Tolbooth,[15] the Heart of Midlothian, a place old in story and name-
father to a noble book. The walls are now down in the dust; there is no
more *squalor carceris* for merry debtors, no more cage for the old,
acknowledged prison-breaker; but the sun and the wind play freely

over the foundations of the jail. Nor is this the only memorial that the pavement keeps of former days. The ancient burying-ground of Edinburgh lay behind St. Giles's Church, running downhill to the Cowgate and covering the site of the present Parliament House. It has disappeared as utterly as the prison or the Luckenbooths; and for those ignorant of its history, I know only one token that remains. In the Parliament Close, trodden daily underfoot by advocates, two letters and a date mark the resting-place of the man who made Scotland over again in his own image, the indefatigable, undissuadable John Knox. He sleeps within call of the church that so often echoed to his preaching.

Hard by the reformer, a bandy-legged and garlanded Charles Second, made of lead, bestrides a tun-bellied charger.[16] The King has his backed turned, and, as you look, seems to be trotting clumsily away from such a dangerous neighbour. Often, for hours together, these two will be alone in the Close, for it lies out of the way of all but legal traffic. On one side the south wall of the church, on the other the arcades of the Parliament House, enclose this irregular bight of causeway and describe their shadows on it in the sun. At either end, from round St. Giles's buttresses, you command a look into the High Street with its motley passengers; but the stream goes by, east and west, and leaves the Parliament Close to Charles the Second and the birds. Once in a while, a patient crowd may be seen loitering there all day, some eating fruit, some reading a newspaper; and to judge by their quiet demeanour, you would think they were waiting for a distribution of soup-tickets. The fact is far otherwise; within in the Justiciary Court a man is upon trial for his life, and these are some of the curious for whom the gallery was found too narrow. Towards afternoon, if the prisoner is unpopular, there will be a round of hisses when he is brought forth. Once in a while, too, an advocate in wig and gown, hand upon mouth, full of pregnant nods, sweeps to and fro in the arcade listening to an agent; and at certain regular hours a whole tide of lawyers hurries across the space.

The Parliament Close has been the scene of marking incidents in Scottish history. Thus, when the Bishops were ejected from the Convention in 1688, 'all fourteen of them gathered together with pale faces and stood in a cloud in the Parliament Close'; poor episcopal personages who were done with fair weather for life! Some of the west-country Societarians standing by, who would have 'rejoiced more than in great sums' to be at their hanging, hustled them so rudely that they knocked their heads together. It was not magnanimous behaviour to dethroned enemies; but one, at least, of the Societarians had groaned in the *boots*, and they had all seen their dear friends upon the scaffold. Again, at the

'woeful Union,' it was here that people crowded to escort their favourite from the last of Scottish parliaments: people flushed with nationality,
as Boswell would have said, ready for riotous acts, and fresh from
throwing stones at the author of *Robinson Crusoe* as he looked out of the
window.

One of the pious in the seventeenth century, going to pass his *trials*
(examinations as we now say) for the Scottish Bar, beheld the Parliament Close open and had a vision of the mouth of Hell. This, and
small wonder, was the means of his conversion. Nor was the vision
unsuitable to the locality; for after an hospital, what uglier piece is
there in civilisation than a court of law? Hither come envy, malice, and
all uncharitableness to wrestle it out in public tourney; crimes, broken
fortunes, severed households, the knave and his victim, gravitate to this
low building with the arcade. To how many has not St. Giles's bell told
the first hour after ruin? I think I see them pause to count the strokes,
and wander on again into the moving High Street, stunned and sick at
heart.

A pair of swing doors gives admittance to a hall with a carved roof,[17]
hung with legal portraits, adorned with legal statuary, lighted by windows of painted glass, and warmed by three vast fires. This is the *Salle
des pas perdus* of the Scottish Bar. Here, by a ferocious custom, idle
youths must promenade from ten till two. From end to end, singly or
in pairs or trios, the gowns and wigs go back and forward. Through a
hum of talk and footfalls, the piping tones of a Macer announce a fresh
cause and call upon the names of those concerned. Intelligent men have
been walking here daily for ten or twenty years without a rag of business or a shilling of reward. In process of time, they may perhaps be
made the Sheriff-Substitute and Fountain of Justice at Lerwick or
Tobermory. There is nothing required, you would say, but a little
patience and a taste for exercise and bad air. To breathe dust and
bombazine, to feed the mind on cackling gossip, to hear three parts of
a case and drink a glass of sherry, to long with indescribable longings
for the hour when a man may slip out of his travesty and devote
himself to golf for the rest of the afternoon, and to do this day by day
and year after year, may seem so small a thing to the inexperienced!
But those who have made the experiment are of a different way of
thinking, and count it the most arduous form of idleness.

More swing doors open into pigeon-holes where Judges of the First
Appeal sit singly, and halls of audience where the supreme Lords sit by
three or four. Here, you may see Scott's place within the bar, where he
wrote many a page of Waverley novels to the drone of judicial proceeding. You will hear a good deal of shrewdness, and, as their Lordships

do not altogether disdain pleasantry, a fair proportion of dry fun. The broadest of broad Scotch is now banished from the bench; but the courts still retain a certain national flavour. We have a solemn enjoyable way of lingering on a case. We treat law as a fine art, and relish and digest a good distinction. There is no hurry: point after point must be rightly examined and reduced to principle; judge after judge must utter forth his *obiter dicta* to delighted brethren.

Besides the courts, there are installed under the same roof no less than three libraries: two of no mean order; confused and semi-subterranean, full of stairs and galleries; where you may see the most studious-looking wigs fishing out novels by lanthorn light, in the very place where the old Privy Council tortured Covenanters. As the Parliament House is built upon a slope, although it presents only one story to the north, it measures half-a-dozen at least upon the south; and range after range of vaults extend below the libraries. Few places are more characteristic of this hilly capital. You descend one stone stair after another, and wander, by the flicker of a match, in a labyrinth of stone cellars. Now, you pass below the Outer Hall and hear overhead, brisk but ghostly, the interminable pattering of legal feet. Now, you come upon a strong door with a wicket: on the other side are the cells of the police office and the trap-stair that gives admittance to the dock in the Justiciary Court. Many a foot that has gone up there lightly enough, has been dead-heavy in the descent. Many a man's life has been argued away from him during long hours in the court above. But just now that tragic stage is empty and silent like a church on a week-day, with the bench all sheeted up and nothing moving but the sunbeams on the wall. A little farther and you strike upon a room, not empty like the rest, but crowded with *productions* from bygone criminal cases: a grim lumber: lethal weapons, poisoned organs in a jar, a door with a shot-hole through the panel, behind which a man fell dead. I cannot fancy why they should preserve them unless it were against the Judgment Day. At length, as you continue to descend, you see a peep of yellow gaslight and hear a jostling, whispering noise ahead; next moment you turn a corner, and there, in a whitewashed passage, is a machinery belt industriously turning on its wheels. You would think the engine had grown there of its own accord, like a cellar fungus, and would soon spin itself out and fill the vaults from end to end with its mysterious labours. In truth, it is only some gear of the steam ventilator; and you will find the engineers at hand, and may step out of their door into the sunlight. For all this while, you have not been descending towards the earth's centre, but only to the bottom of the hill and the foundations of the Parliament House; low down, to be sure, but still under the open heaven and in a

field of grass. The daylight shines garishly on the back windows of the
Irish quarter; on broken shutters, wry gables, old palsied houses on the
brink of ruin, a crumbling human pig-sty fit for human pigs. There are
few signs of life, besides a scanty washing or a face at a window: the
dwellers are abroad, but they will return at night and stagger to their
pallets.

Chapter IV: Legends

The character of a place is often most perfectly expressed in its associations. An event strikes root and grows into a legend, when it has
happened amongst congenial surroundings. Ugly actions, above all in
ugly places, have the true romantic quality, and become an undying
property of their scene. To a man like Scott, the different appearances
of nature seemed each to contain its own legend ready made, which it
was his to call forth: in such or such a place, only such or such events
ought with propriety to happen; and in this spirit he made the *Lady of
the Lake* for Ben Venue, the *Heart of Midlothian* for Edinburgh, and
the *Pirate*, so indifferently written but so romantically conceived, for
the desolate islands and roaring tideways of the North.[18] The common
run of mankind have, from generation to generation, an instinct almost
as delicate as that of Scott; but where he created new things, they only
forget what is unsuitable among the old; and by survival of the fittest,
a body of tradition becomes a work of art. So, in the low dens and
high-flying garrets of Edinburgh, people may go back upon dark passages in the town's adventures, and chill their marrow with winter's
tales about the fire: tales that are singularly apposite and characteristic,
not only of the old life, but of the very constitution of built nature in
that part, and singularly well qualified to add horror to horror, when
the wind pipes around the tall *lands*, and hoots adown arched passages,
and the far-spread wilderness of city lamps keeps quavering and flaring
in the gusts.

Here, it is the tale of Begbie the bank-porter, stricken to the heart
at a blow and left in his blood within a step or two of the crowded High
Street. There, people hush their voices over Burke and Hare;[19] over
drugs and violated graves, and the resurrection-men smothering their
victims with their knees. Here, again, the fame of Deacon Brodie[20] is
kept piously fresh. A great man in his day was the Deacon; well seen in
good society, crafty with his hands as a cabinet-maker, and one who
could sing a song with taste. Many a citizen was proud to welcome the
Deacon to supper, and dismissed him with regret at a timeous hour,
who would have been vastly disconcerted had he known how soon, and

15

in what guise, his visitor returned. Many stories are told of this redoubtable Edinburgh burglar, but the one I have in my mind most vividly gives the key of all the rest. A friend of Brodie's, nested some way towards heaven in one of these great *lands*, had told him of a projected visit to the country, and afterwards, detained by some affairs, put it off and stayed the night in town. The good man had lain some time awake; it was far on in the small hours by the Tron bell; when suddenly there came a creak, a jar, a faint light. Softly he clambered out of bed and up to a false window which looked upon another room, and there, by the glimmer of a thieves' lantern, was his good friend the Deacon in a mask. It is characteristic of the town and the town's manners that this little episode should have been quietly tided over, and quite a good time elapsed before a great robbery, an escape, a Bow Street runner, a cock-fight, an apprehension in a cupboard in Amsterdam, and a last step into the air off his own greatly-improved gallows drop, brought the career of Deacon William Brodie to an end. But still, by the mind's eye, he may be seen, a man harassed below a mountain of duplicity, slinking from a magistrate's supper-room to a thieves' ken, and pickeering among the closes by the flicker of a dark lamp.

Or where the Deacon is out of favour, perhaps some memory lingers of the great plagues, and of fatal houses still unsafe to enter within the memory of man. For in time of pestilence the discipline had been sharp and sudden, and what we now call 'stamping out contagion' was carried on with deadly rigour. The officials, in their gowns of grey, with a white St. Andrew's cross on back and breast, and a white cloth carried before them on a staff, perambulated the city, adding the terror of man's justice to the fear of God's visitation. The dead they buried on the Borough Muir; the living who had concealed the sickness were drowned, if they were women, in the Quarry Holes, and if they were men, were hanged and gibbeted at their own doors; and wherever the evil had passed, furniture was destroyed and houses closed. And the most bogeyish part of the story is about such houses. Two generations back they still stood dark and empty; people avoided them as they passed by; the boldest schoolboy only shouted through the keyhole and made off; for within, it was supposed, the plague lay ambushed like a basilisk, ready to flow forth and spread blain and pustule through the city. What a terrible next-door neighbour for superstitious citizens! A rat scampering within would send a shudder through the stoutest heart. Here, if you like, was a sanitary parable, addressed by our uncleanly forefathers to their own neglect.

And then we have Major Weir;[21] for although even his house is now demolished, old Edinburgh cannot clear herself of his unholy memory.

16

He and his sister lived together in an odour of sour piety. She was a marvellous spinster; he had a rare gift of supplication, and was known among devout admirers by the name of Angelical Thomas. 'He was a tall, black man, and ordinarily looked down to the ground; a grim countenance, and a big nose. His garb was still a cloak, and somewhat dark, and he never went without his staff.' How it came about that Angelical Thomas was burned in company with his staff, and his sister in gentler manner hanged, and whether these two were simply religious maniacs of the more furious order, or had real as well as imaginary sins upon their old-world shoulders, are points happily beyond the reach of our intention. At least, it is suitable enough that out of this superstitious city some such example should have been put forth: the outcome and fine flower of dark and vehement religion. And at least the facts struck the public fancy and brought forth a remarkable family of myths. It would appear that the Major's staff went upon his errands, and even ran before him with a lantern on dark nights. Gigantic females, 'stentoriously laughing and gaping with tehees of laughter' at unseasonable hours of night and morning, haunted the purlieus of his abode. His house fell under such a load of infamy that no one dared to sleep in it, until municipal improvement levelled the structure with the ground. And my father has often been told in the nursery how the devil's coach, drawn by six coal-black horses with fiery eyes, would drive at night into the West Bow, and belated people might see the dead Major through the glasses.

Another legend is that of the two maiden sisters. A legend I am afraid it may be, in the most discreditable meaning of the term; or perhaps something worse—a mere yesterday's fiction. But it is a story of some vitality, and is worthy of a place in the Edinburgh kalendar. This pair inhabited a single room; from the facts, it must have been double-bedded; and it may have been of some dimensions: but when all is said, it was a single room. Here our two spinsters fell out—on some point of controversial divinity belike: but fell out so bitterly that there was never a word spoken between them, black or white, from that day forward. You would have thought they would separate: but no; whether from lack of means, or the Scottish fear of scandal, they continued to keep house together where they were. A chalk line drawn upon the floor separated their two domains; it bisected the doorway and the fireplace, so that each could go out and in, and do her cooking, without violating the territory of the other. So, for years, they coexisted in a hateful silence; their meals, their ablutions, their friendly visitors, exposed to an unfriendly scrutiny; and at night, in the dark watches, each could hear the breathing of her enemy. Never did four walls look down upon an uglier spectacle than these sisters rivalling in unsisterliness. Here is a canvas for Hawthorne to have turned into a cabinet picture— he had a Puritanic vein, which would have fitted him to treat this Puritanic horror; he could have shown them to us in their sicknesses and at their hideous twin devotions, thumbing a pair of great Bibles, or praying aloud for each other's penitence with marrowy emphasis; now each, with kilted petticoat, at her own corner of the fire on some tempestuous evening; now sitting each at her window, looking out upon the summer landscape sloping far below them towards the firth, and the field-paths where they had wandered hand in hand; or, as age and infirmity grew upon them and prolonged their toilettes, and their hands began to tremble and their heads to nod involuntarily, growing only the more steeled in enmity with years; until one fine day, at a word, a look, a visit, or the approach of death, their hearts would melt and the chalk boundary be overstepped for ever.

Alas! to those who know the ecclesiastical history of the race—the most perverse and melancholy in man's annals—this will seem only a figure of much that is typical of Scotland and her high-seated capital above the Forth—a figure so grimly realistic that it may pass with strangers for a caricature. We are wonderful patient haters for con- science' sake up here in the North. I spoke, in the first of these papers, of the Parliaments of the Established and Free Churches, and how they can hear each other singing psalms across the street. There is but a street between them in space, but a shadow between them in principle; and yet there they sit, enchanted, and in damnatory accents pray for each other's growth in grace. It would be well if there were no more than two; but the sects in Scotland form a large family of sisters, and the chalk lines are thickly drawn, and run through the midst of many private homes. Edinburgh is a city of churches, as though it were a place of pilgrimage. You will see four within a stone-cast at the head of the West Bow. Some are crowded to the doors; some are empty like monuments; and yet you will ever find new ones in the building. Hence that surprising clamour of church bells that suddenly breaks out upon the Sabbath morning from Trinity and the sea-skirts to Morningside on the borders of the hills. I have heard the chimes of Oxford playing their symphony in a golden autumn morning, and beautiful it was to hear. But in Edinburgh all manner of loud bells join, or rather disjoin, in one swelling, brutal babblement of noise. Now one overtakes an- other, and now lags behind it; now five or six all strike on the pained tympanum at the same punctual instant of time, and make together a dismal chord of discord; and now for a second all seem to have con- spired to hold their peace. Indeed, there are not many uproars in this world more dismal than that of the Sabbath bells in Edinburgh: a harsh ecclesiastical tocsin; the outcry of incongruous orthodoxies, calling on every separate conventicler to put up a protest, each in his own synagogue, against 'right-hand extremes and left-hand defections.' And surely there are few worse extremes than this extremity of zeal; and few more deplorable defections than this disloyalty to Christian love. Shakespeare wrote a comedy of 'Much Ado about Nothing.' The Scottish nation made a fantastic tragedy on the same subject. And it is for the success of this remarkable piece that these bells are sounded every Sabbath morning on the hills above the Forth. How many of them might rest silent in the steeple, how many of these ugly churches might be demolished and turned once more into useful building material, if people who think almost exactly the same thoughts about religion would condescend to worship God under the same roof! But there are the chalk lines. And which is to pocket pride, and speak the foremost word?

Chapter V: Greyfriars

It was Queen Mary who threw open the gardens of the Grey Friars: a new and semi-rural cemetery in those days, although it has grown an antiquity in its turn and been superseded by half a dozen others. The Friars must have had a pleasant time on summer evenings; for their gardens were situated to a wish, with the tall castle and the tallest of the castle crags in front. Even now, it is one of our famous Edinburgh points of view; and strangers are led thither to see, by yet another instance, how strangely the city lies upon her hills. The enclosure is of an irregular shape; the double church of Old and New Greyfriars stands on the level at the top; a few thorns are dotted here and there, and the ground falls by terrace and steep slope towards the north. The open shows many slabs and table tombstones; and all round the margin, the place is girt by an array of aristocratic mausoleums appallingly adorned.

Setting aside the tombs of Roubilliac, which belong to the heroic order of graveyard art, we Scots stand, to my fancy, highest among nations in the matter of grimly illustrating death. We seem to love for their own sake the emblems of time and the great change; and even around country churches you will find a wonderful exhibition of skulls, and crossbones, and noseless angels, and trumpets pealing for the Judgment Day. Every mason was a pedestrian Holbein: he had a deep consciousness of death, and loved to put its terrors pithily before the churchyard loiterer; he was brimful of rough hints upon mortality, and any dead farmer was seized upon to be a text. The classical examples of this art are in Greyfriars. In their time, these were doubtless costly monuments, and reckoned of a very elegant proportion by contemporaries; and now, when the elegance is not so apparent, the significance remains. You may perhaps look with a smile on the profusion of Latin mottoes—some crawling endwise up the shaft of a pillar, some issuing on a scroll from angels' trumpets—on the emblematic horrors, the figures rising headless from the grave, and all the traditional ingenuities in which it pleased our fathers to set forth their sorrow for the dead and their sense of earthly mutability. But it is not a hearty sort of mirth. Each ornament may have been executed by the merriest apprentice, whistling as he plied the mallet; but the original meaning of each, and the combined effect of so many of them in this quiet enclosure, is serious to the point of melancholy.

Round a great part of the circuit, houses of a low class present their backs to the churchyard. Only a few inches separate the living from the dead. Here, a window is partly blocked up by the pediment of a tomb; there, where the street falls far below the level of the graves, a chimney has been trained up the back of a monument, and a red pot looks vulgarly over from behind. A damp smell of the graveyard finds its way into houses where workmen sit at meat. Domestic life on a small scale goes forward visibly at the windows. The very solitude and stillness of the enclosure, which lies apart from the town's traffic, serves to accentuate the contrast. As you walk upon the graves, you see children scattering crumbs to feed the sparrows; you hear people singing or washing dishes, or the sound of tears and castigation; the linen on a clothes-pole flaps against funereal sculpture; or perhaps the cat slips over the lintel and descends on a memorial urn. And as there is nothing else astir, these incongruous sights and noises take hold on the attention and exaggerate the sadness of the place.

Greyfriars is continually overrun by cats. I have seen one afternoon, as many as thirteen of them seated on the grass beside old Milne,[22] the Master Builder, all sleek and fat, and complacently blinking, as if they had fed upon strange meats. Old Milne was chaunting with the saints, as we may hope, and cared little for the company about his grave; but I confess the spectacle had an ugly side for me; and I was glad to step forward and raise my eyes to where the Castle and the roofs of the Old Town, and the spire of the Assembly Hall, stood deployed against the sky with the colourless precision of engraving. An open outlook is to be desired from a churchyard, and a sight of the sky and some of the world's beauty relieves a mind from morbid thoughts.

I shall never forget one visit. It was a grey, dropping day; the grass was strung with raindrops; and the people in the houses kept hanging out their shirts and petticoats and angrily taking them in again, as the weather turned from wet to fair and back again. A gravedigger, and a friend of his, a gardener from the country, accompanied me into one after another of the cells and little courtyards in which it gratified the wealthy of old days to enclose their old bones from neighbourhood. In one, under a sort of shrine, we found a forlorn human effigy, very realistically executed down to the detail of his ribbed stockings, and holding in his hand a ticket with the date of his demise. He looked most pitiful and ridiculous, shut up by himself in his aristocratic precinct, like a bad old boy or an inferior forgotten deity under a new dispensation; the burdocks grew familiarly about his feet, the rain dripped all round him; and the world maintained the most entire indifference as to who he was or whither he had gone. In another, a vaulted tomb, handsome externally but horrible inside with damp and cobwebs, there were three mounds of black earth and an uncovered thigh bone. This was the place of interment, it appeared, of a family with whom the gardener had been long in service. He was among old acquaintances. 'This'll be Miss Marg'et's,' said he, giving the bone a friendly kick. 'The auld—!' I have always an uncomfortable feeling in a graveyard, at sight of so many tombs to perpetuate memories best forgotten; but I never had the impression so strongly as that day. People had been at some expense in both these cases: to provoke a melancholy feeling of derision in the one, and an insulting epithet in the other. The proper inscription for the most part of mankind, I began to think, is the cynical jeer, *cras tibi*. That, if anything, will stop the mouth of a carper; since it both admits the worst and carries the war triumphantly into the enemy's camp.

Greyfriars is a place of many associations. There was one window in a house at the lower end, now demolished, which was pointed out to me by the gravedigger as a spot of legendary interest. Burke, the resurrection man, infamous for so many murders at five shillings a head, used to sit thereat, with pipe and nightcap, to watch burials going forward on the green. In a tomb higher up, which must then have been but newly finished, John Knox, according to the same informant, had taken refuge in a turmoil of the Reformation. Behind the church is the haunted mausoleum of Sir George Mackenzie:[23] Bloody Mackenzie, Lord Advocate in the Covenanting troubles and author of some pleasing sentiments on toleration. Here, in the last century, an old Heriot's Hospital boy once harboured from the pursuit of the police. The Hospital is next door to Greyfriars—a courtly building among lawns, where, on Founder's Day, you may see a multitude of children playing Kiss-in-the-Ring and Round the Mulberry-bush. Thus, when the fugitive had managed to conceal himself in the tomb, his old schoolmates had a hundred opportunities to bring him food; and there he lay in safety till a ship was found to smuggle him abroad. But his must have been indeed a heart of brass, to lie all day and night alone with the dead persecutor; and other lads were far from emulating him in courage. When a man's soul is certainly in hell, his body will scarce lie quiet in a tomb however costly; some time or other the door must open, and the reprobate come forth in the abhorred garments of the grave. It was thought a high piece of prowess to knock at the Lord Advocate's mausoleum and challenge him to appear. 'Bluidy Mackenzie, come oot if ye daur!' sang the foolhardy urchins. But Sir George had other affairs on hand; and the author of an essay on toleration continues to sleep peacefully among the many whom he so intolerantly helped to slay.

For this *infelix campus*, as it is dubbed in one of its own inscriptions—an inscription over which Dr. Johnson passed a critical eye—is in many ways sacred to the memory of the men whom Mackenzie persecuted. It was here, on the flat tombstones, that the Covenant was signed by an enthusiastic people. In the long arm of the churchyard that extends to Lauriston, the prisoners from Bothwell Bridge[24]—fed on bread and water and guarded, life for life, by vigilant marksmen—lay five months looking for the scaffold or the plantations. And while the good work was going forward in the Grassmarket,[25] idlers in Greyfriars might have heard the throb of the military drums that drowned the voices of the martyrs. Nor is this all: for down in the corner farthest from Sir George, there stands a monument dedicated, in uncouth Covenanting verse, to all who lost their lives in that contention. There is no moorsman shot in a snow shower beside Irongray or Co'monell; there is not one of the two hundred who were drowned off the Orkneys; nor so much as a poor, over-driven, Covenanting slave in the American plantations; but can lay claim to a share in that memorial, and, if such things interest just men among the shades, can boast he has a monument on earth as well as Julius Caesar or the Pharaohs. Where they may all lie, I know not. Far-scattered bones, indeed! But if the reader cares to learn how some of them—or some part of some of them—found their way at length to such honourable sepulture, let him listen to the words of one who was their comrade in life and their apologist when they were dead. Some of the insane controversial matter I omit, as well as some digressions, but leave the rest in Patrick Walker's[26] language and orthography:

'The never to be forgotten Mr. *James Renwick* told me, that he was Witness to their Public Murder at the *Gallowlee*, between *Leith* and *Edinburgh*, when he saw the Hangman hash and hagg off all their Five

Heads, with *Patrick Foreman's* Right Hand: Their Bodies were all buried at the Gallows Foot; their Heads, with *Patrick's* Hand, were brought
and put upon five Pikes on the *Pleasaunce-Port*... Mr. *Renwick* told me
also that it was the first public Action that his Hand was at, to conveen
Friends, and lift their murthered Bodies, and carried them to the West
Churchyard of *Edinburgh*,'—not Greyfriars, this time,—'and buried
them there. Then they came about the City... and took down these
Five Heads and that Hand; and Day being come, they went quickly up
the *Pleasaunce*; and when they came to *Lauristoun* Yards, upon the
South-side of the City, they durst not venture, being so light, to go and
bury their Heads with their Bodies, which they designed; it being
present Death, if any of them had been found. *Alexander Tweedie*, a
Friend, being with them, who at that Time was Gardner in these
Yards, concluded to bury them in his Yard, being in a Box (wrapped in
Linen), where they lay 45 Years except 3 Days, being executed upon
the 10th of *October* 1681, and found the 7th Day of *October* 1726. That
Piece of Ground lay for some Years unlaboured; and trenching it, the
Gardner found them, which affrighted him; the Box was consumed.
Mr. *Schaw*, the Owner of these Yards, caused lift them, and lay them
upon a Table in his Summer-house: Mr. *Schaw's* mother was so kind,
as to cut out a Linen-cloth, and cover them. They lay Twelve Days
there, where all had Access to see them. *Alexander Tweedie*, the foresaid
Gardner, said, when dying, There was a Treasure hid in his Yard, but
neither Gold nor Silver. *Daniel Tweedie*, his Son, came along with me
to that Yard, and told me that his Father planted a white Rose-bush
above them, and farther down the Yard a red Rose-bush, which were
more fruitful than any other Bush in the Yard... Many came'—to see
the heads—'out of Curiosity; yet I rejoiced to see so many concerned
grave Men and Women favouring the Dust of our Martyrs. There were
Six of us concluded to bury them upon the Nineteenth Day of *October*
1726, and every One of us to acquaint Friends of the Day and Hour,
being *Wednesday*, the Day of the Week on which most of them were
executed, and at 4 of the Clock at Night, being the Hour that most of
them went to their resting Graves. We caused make a compleat Coffin
for them in Black, with four Yards of fine Linen, the way that our
Martyrs Corps were managed... Accordingly we kept the aforesaid
Day and Hour, and doubled the Linen, and laid the Half of it below
them, their nether Jaws being parted from their Heads; but being
young Men, their Teeth remained. All were Witness to the Holes in
each of their Heads, which the Hangman broke with his Hammer; and
according to the Bigness of their Sculls, we laid the Jaws to them, and
drew the other Half of the Linen above them, and stufft the Coffin

with Shavings. Some prest hard to go thorow the chief Parts of the City as was done at the Revolution; but this we refused, considering that it looked airy and frothy, to make such Show of them, and inconsistent with the solid serious Observing of such an affecting, surprizing unheard-of Dispensation: But took the ordinary Way of other Burials from that Place, to wit, we went east the Back of the Wall, and in at *Bristo-Port*, and down the Way to the Head of the *Cowgate*, and turned up to the Church-yard, where they were interred closs to the Martyrs Tomb, with the greatest Multitude of People Old and Young, Men and Women, Ministers and others, that ever I saw together.'

And so there they were at last, in 'their resting graves.' So long as men do their duty, even if it be greatly in a misapprehension, they will be leading pattern lives; and whether or not they come to lie beside a martyrs' monument, we may be sure they will find a safe haven somewhere in the providence of God. It is not well to think of death, unless we temper the thought with that of heroes who despised it. Upon what ground, is of small account; if it be only the bishop who was burned for his faith in the antipodes, his memory lightens the heart and makes us walk undisturbed among graves. And so the martyrs' monument is a wholesome, heartsome spot in the field of the dead; and as we look upon it, a brave influence comes to us from the land of those who have won their discharge and, in another phrase of Patrick Walker's, got 'cleanly off the stage.'

Chapter VI: New Town—Town and Country

It is as much a matter of course to decry the New Town as to exalt the Old; and the most celebrated authorities have picked out this quarter as the very emblem of what is condemnable in architecture. Much may be said, much indeed has been said, upon the text; but to the unsophisticated, who call anything pleasing if it only pleases them, the New Town of Edinburgh seems, in itself, not only gay and airy, but highly picturesque. An old skipper, invincibly ignorant of all theories of the sublime and beautiful, once propounded as his most radiant notion for Paradise: 'The new town of Edinburgh, with the wind a matter of a point free.' He has now gone to that sphere where all good tars are promised pleasant weather in the song, and perhaps his thoughts fly somewhat higher. But there are bright and temperate days—with soft air coming from the inland hills, military music sounding bravely from the hollow of the gardens, the flags all waving on the palaces of Princes Street—when I have seen the town through a sort of glory, and shaken hands in sentiment with the old sailor. And indeed, for a man who has been much tumbled round Orcadian skerries, what scene could be more agreeable to witness? On such a day, the valley wears a surprising air of festival. It seems (I do not know how else to put my meaning) as if it were a trifle too good to be true. It is what Paris ought to be. It has the scenic quality that would best set off a life of unthinking, open-air diversion. It was meant by nature for the realisation of the society of comic operas. And you can imagine, if the climate were but towardly, how all the world and his wife would flock into these gardens in the cool of the evening, to hear cheerful music, to sip pleasant drinks, to see the moon rise from behind Arthur's Seat and shine upon the spires and monuments and the green tree-tops in the valley. Alas! and the next morning the rain is splashing on the windows, and the passengers flee along Princes Street before the galloping squalls.

It cannot be denied that the original design was faulty and short-sighted, and did not fully profit by the capabilities of the situation. The architect was essentially a town bird, and he laid out the modern city with a view to street scenery, and to street scenery alone. The country did not enter into his plan; he had never lifted his eyes to the hills. If he had so chosen, every street upon the northern slope might have been a noble terrace and commanded an extensive and beautiful view. But the space has been too closely built; many of the houses front the wrong way, intent, like the Man with the Muck-Rake, on what is not worth observation, and standing discourteously back-foremost in the ranks; and, in a word, it is too often only from attic-windows, or here and there at a crossing, that you can get a look beyond the city upon its diversified surroundings. But perhaps it is all the more surprising, to come suddenly on a corner, and see a perspective of a mile or more of falling street, and beyond that woods and villas, and a blue arm of the sea, and the hills upon the farther side.

Fergusson, our Edinburgh poet, Burns's model, once saw a butterfly at the Town Cross; and the sight inspired him with a worthless little ode.[27] This painted countryman, the dandy of the rose garden, looked far abroad in such a humming neighbourhood; and you can fancy what moral considerations a youthful poet would supply. But the incident, in a fanciful sort of way, is characteristic of the place. Into no other city does the sight of the country enter so far; if you do not meet a butterfly, you shall certainly catch a glimpse of far-away trees upon your walk; and the place is full of theatre tricks in the way of scenery. You peep under an arch, you descend stairs that look as if they would land you in a cellar, you turn to the back-window of a grimy tenement in a lane:—and behold! you are face-to-face with distant and bright prospects. You turn a corner, and there is the sun going down into the Highland hills. You look down an alley, and see ships tacking for the Baltic.

For the country people to see Edinburgh on her hill-tops, is one thing; it is another for the citizen, from the thick of his affairs, to overlook the country. It should be a genial and ameliorating influence in life; it should prompt good thoughts and remind him of Nature's unconcern: that he can watch from day to day, as he trots officeward, how the Spring green brightens in the wood or the field grows black under a moving ploughshare. I have been tempted, in this connexion, to deplore the slender faculties of the human race, with its penny-whistle of a voice, its dull ears, and its narrow range of sight. If you could see as people are to see in heaven, if you had eyes such as you can fancy for a superior race, if you could take clear note of the objects of vision, not only a few yards, but a few miles from where you stand:— think how agreeably your sight would be entertained, how pleasantly your thoughts would be diversified, as you walked the Edinburgh streets! For you might pause, in some business perplexity, in the midst of the city traffic, and perhaps catch the eye of a shepherd as he sat down to breathe upon a heathery shoulder of the Pentlands; or perhaps some urchin, clambering in a country elm, would put aside the leaves and show you his flushed and rustic visage; or a fisher racing seawards, with the tiller under his elbow, and the sail sounding in the wind, would fling you a salutation from between Anst'er and the May.[28]

To be old is not the same thing as to be picturesque; nor because the Old Town bears a strange physiognomy, does it at all follow that the New Town shall look commonplace. Indeed, apart from antique houses, it is curious how much description would apply commonly to either. The same sudden accidents of ground, a similar dominating site above the plain, and the same superposition of one rank of society over another, are to be observed in both. Thus, the broad and comely approach to Princes Street from the east, lined with hotels and public offices, makes a leap over the gorge of the Low Calton; if you cast a glance over the parapet, you look direct into that sunless and disreputable confluent of Leith Street; and the same tall houses open upon both thoroughfares. This is only the New Town passing overhead above its own cellars; walking, so to speak, over its own children, as is the way of cities and the human race. But at the Dean Bridge, you may behold a spectacle of a more novel order. The river runs at the bottom of a deep valley, among rocks and between gardens; the crest of either bank is occupied by some of the most commodious streets and crescents in the modern city; and a handsome bridge unites the two summits. Over this, every afternoon, private carriages go spinning by, and ladies with card-cases pass to and fro about the duties of society. And yet down below, you may still see, with its mills and foaming weir, the little rural village of Dean. Modern improvement has gone overhead on its high-level viaduct; and the extended city has cleanly overleapt, and left unaltered, what was once the summer retreat of its comfortable citizens. Every town embraces hamlets in its growth; Edinburgh herself has embraced a good few; but it is strange to see one still surviving— and to see it some hundreds of feet below your path. Is it Torre del Greco that is built above buried Herculaneum? Herculaneum was dead at least; but the sun still shines upon the roofs of Dean; the smoke still rises thriftily from its chimneys; the dusty miller comes to his door, looks at the gurgling water, hearkens to the turning wheel and the birds about the shed, and perhaps whistles an air of his own to enrich the symphony—for all the world as if Edinburgh were still the old Edinburgh on the Castle Hill, and Dean were still the quietest of hamlets buried a mile or so in the green country.

It is not so long ago since magisterial David Hume lent the authority of his example to the exodus from the Old Town, and took up his new abode in a street which is still (so oddly may a jest become perpetuated) known as Saint David Street. Nor is the town so large but a holiday schoolboy may harry a bird's nest within half a mile of his own door. There are places that still smell of the plough in memory's nostrils. Here, one had heard a blackbird on a hawthorn; there, another was taken on summer evenings to eat strawberries and cream; and you have seen a waving wheatfield on the site of your present residence. The memories of an Edinburgh boy are but partly memories of the town. I look back with delight on many an escalade of garden walls; many a ramble among lilacs full of piping birds; many an exploration in obscure quarters that were neither town nor country; and I think that both for my companions and myself, there was a special interest, a point of romance, and a sentiment as of foreign travel, when we hit in our excursions on the butt-end of some former hamlet, and found a few rustic cottages embedded among streets and squares. The tunnel to the Scotland Street Station, the sight of the trains shooting out of its dark maw with the two guards upon the brake, the thought of its length and the many ponderous edifices and open thoroughfares above, were certainly things of paramount impressiveness to a young mind. It was a subterranean passage, although of a larger bore than we were accustomed to in Ainsworth's novels; and these two words, 'subterreanean passage,' were in themselves an irresistible attraction, and seemed to bring us nearer in spirit to the heroes we loved and the black rascals we secretly aspired to imitate. To scale the Castle Rock from West Princes

Street Gardens, and lay a triumphal hand against the rampart itself, was to taste a high order of romantic pleasure. And there are other sights and exploits which crowd back upon my mind under a very strong illumination of remembered pleasure. But the effect of not one of them all will compare with the discoverer's joy, and the sense of old Time and his slow changes on the face of this earth, with which I explored such corners as Canonmills or Water Lane, or the nugget of cottages at Broughton Market. They were more rural than the open country, and gave a greater impression of antiquity than the oldest *land* upon the High Street. They too, like Fergusson's butterfly, had a quaint air of having wandered far from their own place; they looked abashed and homely, with their gables and their creeping plants, their outside stairs and running mill-streams; there were corners that smelt like the end of the country garden where I spent my Aprils; and the people stood to gossip at their doors, as they might have done in Colinton or Cramond.[29]

In a great measure we may, and shall, eradicate this haunting flavour of the country. The last elm is dead in Elm Row; and the villas and the workmen's quarters spread apace on all the borders of the city. We can cut down the trees; we can bury the grass under dead paving-stones; we can drive brisk streets through all our sleepy quarters; and we may forget the stories and the playgrounds of our boyhood. But we have some possessions that not even the infuriate zeal of builders can utterly abolish and destroy. Nothing can abolish the hills, unless it be a cataclysm of nature which shall subvert Edinburgh Castle itself and lay all her florid structures in the dust. And as long as we have the hills and the Firth, we have a famous heritage to leave our children. Our windows, at no expense to us, are most artfully stained to represent a landscape. And when the Spring comes round, and the hawthorns begin to flower, and the meadows to smell of young grass, even in the thickest of our streets, the country hilltops find out a young man's eyes, and set his heart beating for travel and pure air.

Chapter VII: The Villa Quarters

Mr. Ruskin's[30] denunciation of the New Town of Edinburgh includes, as I have heard it repeated, nearly all the stone and lime we have to show. Many however find a grand air and something settled and imposing in the better parts; and upon many, as I have said, the confusion of styles induces an agreeable stimulation of the mind. But upon the subject of our recent villa architecture, I am frankly ready to mingle my tears with Mr. Ruskin's, and it is a subject which makes one envious of his large declamatory and controversial eloquence.

Day by day, one new villa, one new object of offence, is added to another; all around Newington and Morningside, the dismallest structures keep springing up like mushrooms; the pleasant hills are loaded with them, each impudently squatted in its garden, each roofed and carrying chimneys like a house. And yet a glance of an eye discovers their true character. They are not houses; for they were not designed with a view to human habitation, and the internal arrangements are, as they tell me, fantastically unsuited to the needs of man. They are not buildings; for you can scarcely say a thing is built where every measurement is in clamant disproportion with its neighbour. They belong to no style of art, only to a form of business much to be regretted.

Why should it be cheaper to erect a structure where the size of the windows bears no rational relation to the size of the front? Is there any profit in a misplaced chimney-stalk? Does a hard-working, greedy builder gain more on a monstrosity than on a decent cottage of equal plainness? Frankly, we should say, No. Bricks may be omitted, and green timber employed, in the construction of even a very elegant design; and there is no reason why a chimney should be made to vent, because it is so situated as to look comely from without. On the other hand, there is a noble way of being ugly: a high-aspiring fiasco like the fall of Lucifer. There are daring and gaudy buildings that manage to be offensive, without being contemptible; and we know that 'fools rush in where angels fear to tread.' But to aim at making a commonplace villa, and to make it insufferably ugly in each particular; to attempt the homeliest achievement, and to attain the bottom of derided failure; not to have any theory but profit and yet, at an equal expense, to outstrip all competitors in the art of conceiving and rendering permanent deformity; and to do all this in what is, by nature, one of the most agreeable neighbourhoods in Britain:—what are we to say, but that this also is a distinction, hard to earn although not greatly worshipful?

Indifferent buildings give pain to the sensitive; but these things offend the plainest taste. It is a danger which threatens the amenity of the town; and as this eruption keeps spreading on our borders, we have ever the farther to walk among unpleasant sights, before we gain the country air. If the population of Edinburgh were a living, autonomous body, it would arise like one man and make night hideous with arson; the builders and their accomplices would be driven to work, like the Jews of yore, with the trowel in one hand and the defensive cutlass in the other; and as soon as one of these masonic wonders had been consummated, right-minded iconoclasts should fall thereon and make an end of it at once.

29

Possibly these words may meet the eye of a builder or two. It is no use asking them to employ an architect; for that would be to touch them in a delicate quarter, and its use would largely depend on what architect they were minded to call in. But let them get any architect in the world to point out any reasonably well-proportioned villa, not his own design; and let them reproduce that model to satiety.

Chapter VIII: The Calton Hill

The east of new Edinburgh is guarded by a craggy hill, of no great elevation, which the town embraces. The old London road runs on one side of it; while the New Approach, leaving it on the other hand, completes the circuit. You mount by stairs in a cutting of the rock to find yourself in a field of monuments.[31] Dugald Stewart[32] has the honours of situation and architecture; Burns is memorialised lower down upon a spur; Lord Nelson, as befits a sailor, gives his name to the topgallant of the Calton Hill. This latter erection has been differently and yet, in both cases, aptly compared to a telescope and a butter-churn; comparisons apart, it ranks among the vilest of men's handiworks. But the chief feature is an unfinished range of columns, 'the Modern Ruin' as it has been called, an imposing object from far and near, and giving Edinburgh, even from the sea, that false air of a Modern Athens which has earned for her so many slighting speeches. It was meant to be a National Monument; and its present state is a very suitable monument to certain national characteristics. The old Observatory—a quaint brown building on the edge of the steep—and the new Observatory—a classical edifice with a dome—occupy the central portion of the summit. All these are scattered on a green turf, browsed over by some sheep.

The scene suggests reflections on fame and on man's injustice to the dead. You see Dugald Stewart rather more handsomely commemorated than Burns. Immediately below, in the Canongate churchyard, lies Robert Fergusson, Burns's master in his art, who died insane while yet a stripling; and if Dugald Stewart has been somewhat too boisterously acclaimed, the Edinburgh poet, on the other hand, is most unrighteously forgotten. The votaries of Burns, a crew too common in all ranks in Scotland and more remarkable for number than discretion, eagerly suppress all mention of the lad who handed to him the poetic impulse and, up to the time when he grew famous, continued to influence him in his manner and the choice of subjects. Burns himself not only acknowledged his debt in a fragment of autobiography, but erected a tomb over the grave in Canongate churchyard. This was worthy of an artist, but it was done in vain; and although I think I have read nearly all the biographies of Burns, I cannot remember one in which the modesty of nature was not violated, or where Fergusson was not sacrificed to the credit of his follower's originality. There is a kind of gaping admiration that would fain roll Shakespeare and Bacon into one, to have a bigger thing to gape at; and a class of men who cannot edit one author without disparaging all others. They are indeed mistaken if they think to please the great originals; and whoever puts Fergusson right with fame, cannot do better than dedicate his labours to the memory of Burns, who will be the best delighted of the dead.

Of all places for a view, this Calton Hill is perhaps the best; since you can see the Castle, which you lose from the Castle, and Arthur's Seat, which you cannot see from Arthur's Seat. It is the place to stroll on one of those days of sunshine and east wind which are so common in our more than temperate summer. The breeze comes off the sea, with a little of the freshness, and that touch of chill, peculiar to the quarter, which is delightful to certain very ruddy organisations and greatly the reverse to the majority of mankind. It brings with it a faint, floating haze, a cunning decolouriser, although not thick enough to obscure outlines near at hand. But the haze lies more thickly to windward at the far end of Musselburgh Bay; and over the Links of Aberlady and Berwick Law and the hump of the Bass Rock it assumes the aspect of a bank of thin sea fog.

Immediately underneath upon the south, you command the yards of the High School, and the towers and courts of the new Jail—a large place, castellated to the extent of folly, standing by itself on the edge of a steep cliff, and often joyfully hailed by tourists as the Castle. In the one, you may perhaps see female prisoners taking exercise like a string of nuns; in the other, schoolboys running at play and their shadows keeping step with them. From the bottom of the valley, a gigantic chimney rises almost to the level of the eye, a taller and a shapelier edifice than Nelson's Monument. Look a little farther, and there is Holyrood Palace, with its Gothic frontal and ruined abbey, and the red sentry pacing smartly to and fro before the door like a mechanical figure in a panorama. By way of an outpost, you can single out the little peak-roofed lodge, over which Rizzio's murderers made their escape and where Queen Mary herself, according to gossip, bathed in white wine to entertain her loveliness. Behind and overhead, lie the Queen's Park, from Muschat's Cairn to Dumbiedykes, St. Margaret's Loch, and the long wall of Salisbury Crags: and thence, by knoll and rocky bulwark and precipitous slope, the eye rises to the top of Arthur's Seat, a hill for magnitude, a mountain in virtue of its bold design. This upon your left. Upon the right, the roofs and spires of the Old Town climb

31

one above another to where the citadel prints its broad bulk and jagged crown of bastions on the western sky.—Perhaps it is now one in the afternoon; and at the same instant of time, a ball rises to the summit of Nelson's flagstaff close at hand, and, far away, a puff of smoke followed by a report bursts from the half-moon battery at the Castle. This is the time-gun by which people set their watches, as far as the sea coast or in hill farms upon the Pentlands.—To complete the view, the eye enfilades Princes Street, black with traffic, and has a broad look over the valley between the Old Town and the New: here, full of railway trains and stepped over by the high North Bridge upon its many columns, and there, green with trees and gardens.

On the north, the Calton Hill is neither so abrupt in itself nor has it so exceptional an outlook; and yet even here it commands a striking prospect. A gully separates it from the New Town. This is Greenside, where witches were burned and tournaments held in former days. Down that almost precipitous bank, Bothwell launched his horse, and so first, as they say, attracted the bright eyes of Mary. It is now tesselated with sheets and blankets out to dry, and the sound of people beating carpets is rarely absent. Beyond all this, the suburbs run out to Leith; Leith camps on the seaside with her forest of masts; Leith roads are full of ships at anchor; the sun picks out the white pharos upon Inchkeith Island; the Firth extends on either hand from the Ferry to the May; the towns of Fifeshire sit, each in its bank of blowing smoke, along the opposite coast; and the hills enclose the view, except to the farthest east, where the haze of the horizon rests upon the open sea. There lies the road to Norway: a dear road for Sir Patrick Spens and his Scots Lords; and yonder smoke on the hither side of Largo Law is Aberdour, from whence they sailed to seek a queen for Scotland.[33]

> 'O lang, lang, may the ladies sit,
>   Wi' their fans into their hand,
> Or e'er they see Sir Patrick Spens
>   Come sailing to the land!'

The sight of the sea, even from a city, will bring thoughts of storm and sea disaster. The sailors' wives of Leith and the fisherwomen of Cockenzie, not sitting languorously with fans, but crowding to the tail of the harbour with a shawl about their ears, may still look vainly for brave Scotsmen who will return no more, or boats that have gone on their last fishing. Since Sir Patrick sailed from Aberdour, what a multitude have gone down in the North Sea! Yonder is Auldhame, where the London smack went ashore and wreckers cut the rings from ladies' fingers; and a few miles round Fife Ness is the fatal Inchcape, now a star of guidance; and the lee shore to the east of the Inchcape, is that Forfarshire coast where Mucklebackit[34] sorrowed for his son.

These are the main features of the scene roughly sketched. How they are all tilted by the inclination of the ground, how each stands out in delicate relief against the rest, what manifold detail, and play of sun and shadow, animate and accentuate the picture, is a matter for a person on the spot, and turning swiftly on his heels, to grasp and bind together in one comprehensive look. It is the character of such a pros-pect, to be full of change and of things moving. The multiplicity embarrasses the eye; and the mind, among so much, suffers itself to grow absorbed with single points. You remark a tree in a hedgerow, or follow a cart along a country road. You turn to the city, and see children, dwarfed by distance into pigmies, at play about suburban doorsteps; you have a glimpse upon a thoroughfare where people are densely moving; you note ridge after ridge of chimney-stacks running downhill one behind another, and church spires rising bravely from the sea of roofs. At one of the innumerable windows, you watch a figure moving; on one of the multitude of roofs, you watch clambering chimney-sweeps. The wind takes a run and scatters the smoke; bells are heard, far and near, faint and loud, to tell the hour; or perhaps a bird goes dipping evenly over the housetops, like a gull across the waves. And here you are in the meantime, on this pastoral hillside, among nibbling sheep and looked upon by monumental buildings.

Return thither on some clear, dark, moonless night, with a ring of frost in the air, and only a star or two set sparsely in the vault of heaven; and you will find a sight as stimulating as the hoariest summit of the Alps. The solitude seems perfect; the patient astronomer, flat on his back under the Observatory dome and spying heaven's secrets, is your only neighbour; and yet from all round you there come up the dull hum of the city, the tramp of countless people marching out of time, the rattle of carriages and the continuous keen jingle of the tram-way bells. An hour or so before, the gas was turned on; lamplighters scoured the city; in every house, from kitchen to attic, the windows kindled and gleamed forth into the dusk. And so now, although the town lies blue and darkling on her hills, innumerable spots of the bright element shine far and near along the pavements and upon the high facades. Moving lights of the railway pass and repass below the stationary lights upon the bridge. Lights burn in the Jail. Lights burn high up in the tall *lands* and on the Castle turrets, they burn low down in Greenside or along the Park. They run out one beyond the other into the dark country. They walk in a procession down to Leith, and shine singly far along Leith Pier. Thus, the plan of the city and her suburbs is mapped out upon the ground of blackness, as when a child pricks a drawing full of pinholes and exposes it before a candle; not the darkest night of winter can conceal her high station and fanciful design; every evening in the year she proceeds to illuminate herself in honour of her own beauty; and as if to complete the scheme—or rather as if some prodigal Pharaoh were beginning to extend to the adjacent sea and country—half-way over to Fife, there is an outpost of light upon Inchkeith, and far to seaward, yet another on the May.

And while you are looking, across upon the Castle Hill, the drums and bugles begin to recall the scattered garrison; the air thrills with the sound; the bugles sing aloud; and the last rising flourish mounts and melts into the darkness like a star: a martial swan-song, fitly rounding in the labours of the day.

Chapter IX: Winter and New Year

The Scots dialect is singularly rich in terms of reproach against the winter wind. *Snell, blae, nirly,* and *scowthering,* are four of these significant vocables; they are all words that carry a shiver with them; and for my part, as I see them aligned before me on the page, I am persuaded that a big wind comes tearing over the Firth from Burntisland and the northern hills; I think I can hear it howl in the chimney, and as I set my face northwards, feel its smarting kisses on my cheek. Even in the names of places there is often a desolate, inhospitable sound; and I remember two from the near neighbourhood of Edinburgh, Cauldhame and Blawweary, that would promise but starving comfort to their inhabitants. The inclemency of heaven, which has thus endowed the language of Scotland with words, has also largely modified the spirit of its poetry. Both poverty and a northern climate teach men the love of the hearth and the sentiment of the family; and the latter, in its own right, inclines a poet to the praise of strong waters. In Scotland, all our singers have a stave or two for blazing fires and stout potations:—to get indoors out of the wind and to swallow something hot to the stomach, are benefits so easily appreciated where they dwelt!

And this is not only so in country districts where the shepherd must wade in the snow all day after his flock, but in Edinburgh itself, and nowhere more apparently stated than in the works of our Edinburgh poet, Fergusson. He was a delicate youth, I take it, and willingly slunk from the robustious winter to an inn fireside. Love was absent from his life, or only present, if you prefer, in such a form that even the least serious of Burns's amourettes was ennobling by comparison; and so there is nothing to temper the sentiment of indoor revelry which pervades the poor boy's verses. Although it is characteristic of his native town, and the manners of its youth to the present day, this spirit has perhaps done something to restrict his popularity He recalls a supper-party pleasantry with something akin to tenderness; and sounds the praises of the act of drinking as if it were virtuous, or at least witty, in itself. The kindly jar, the warm atmosphere of tavern parlours, and the revelry of lawyers' clerks, do not offer by themselves the materials of a rich existence. It was not choice, so much as an external fate, that kept Fergusson in this round of sordid pleasures. A Scot of poetic temperament, and without religious exaltation, drops as if by nature into the public-house. The picture may not be pleasing; but what else is a man to do in this dog's weather?

To none but those who have themselves suffered the thing in the body, can the gloom and depression of our Edinburgh winter be brought home. For some constitutions there is something almost physically disgusting in the bleak ugliness of easterly weather; the wind wearies, the sickly sky depresses them; and they turn back from their walk to avoid the aspect of the unrefulgent sun going down among perturbed and pallid mists. The days are so short that a man does much of his business, and certainly all his pleasure, by the haggard glare of gas lamps. The roads are as heavy as a fallow. People go by, so drenched and draggle-tailed that I have often wondered how they found the heart to undress. And meantime the wind whistles through the town as if it were an open meadow; and if you lie awake all night, you hear it shrieking and raving overhead with a noise of shipwrecks and of falling houses. In a word, life is so unsightly that there are times when the heart turns sick in a man's inside; and the look of a tavern, or the thought of the warm, fire-lit study, is like the touch of land to one who has been long struggling with the seas.

As the weather hardens towards frost, the world begins to improve for Edinburgh people. We enjoy superb, sub-arctic sunsets, with the profile of the city stamped in indigo upon a sky of luminous green. The wind may still be cold, but there is a briskness in the air that stirs good blood. People do not all look equally sour and downcast. They fall into two divisions: one, the knight of the blue face and hollow paunch, whom Winter has gotten by the vitals; the other well lined with New-year's fare, conscious of the touch of cold on his periphery, but stepping through it by the glow of his internal fires. Such an one I remember, triply cased in grease, whom no extremity of temperature could vanquish. 'Well,' would be his jovial salutation, 'here's a sneezer!' And the look of these warm fellows is tonic, and upholds their drooping fellow-townsmen. There is yet another class who do not depend on corporal advantages, but support the winter in virtue of a brave and merry heart. One shivering evening, cold enough for frost but with too high a wind, and a little past sundown, when the lamps were beginning to enlarge their circles in the growing dusk, a brace of barefoot lassies were seen coming eastward in the teeth of the wind. If the one was as much as nine, the other was certainly not more than seven. They were miserably clad; and the pavement was so cold, you would have thought no one could lay a naked foot on it unflinching. Yet they came along waltzing, if you please, while the elder sang a tune to give them music. The person who saw this, and whose heart was full of bitterness at the moment, pocketed a reproof which has been of use to him ever since, and which he now hands on, with his good wishes, to the reader.

At length, Edinburgh, with her satellite hills and all the sloping country, are sheeted up in white. If it has happened in the dark hours, nurses pluck their children out of bed and run with them to some commanding window, whence they may see the change that has been worked upon earth's face. 'A' the hills are covered wi' snaw,' they sing, 'and Winter's noo come fairly!' And the children, marvelling at the silence and the white landscape, find a spell appropriate to the season in the words. The reverberation of the snow increases the pale daylight, and brings all objects nearer the eye. The Pentlands are smooth and glittering, with here and there the black ribbon of a dry-stone dyke, and here and there, if there be wind, a cloud of blowing snow upon a shoulder. The Firth seems a leaden creek, that a man might almost jump across, between well-powdered Lothian and well-powdered Fife. And the effect is not, as in other cities, a thing of half a day; the streets are soon trodden black, but the country keeps its virgin white; and you have only to lift your eyes and look over miles of country snow. An indescribable cheerfulness breathes about the city; and the well-fed heart sits lightly and beats gaily in the bosom. It is New-year's weather.

New-year's Day, the great national festival, is a time of family expansions and of deep carousal. Sometimes, by a sore stroke of fate for this Calvinistic people, the year's anniversary falls upon a Sunday, when the public-houses are inexorably closed, when singing and even whistling is banished from our homes and highways, and the oldest toper feels called upon to go to church. Thus pulled about, as if between two loyalties, the Scots have to decide many nice cases of conscience, and ride the marches narrowly between the weekly and the annual observance. A party of convivial musicians, next door to a friend of mine, hung suspended in this manner on the brink of their diversions. From ten o'clock on Sunday night, my friend heard them tuning their instruments: and as the hour of liberty drew near, each must have had his music open, his bow in readiness across the fiddle, his foot already raised to mark the time, and his nerves braced for execution; for hardly had the twelfth stroke sounded from the earliest steeple, before they had launched forth into a secular bravura.

Currant-loaf is now popular eating in all households. For weeks before the great morning, confectioners display stacks of Scots bun—a dense, black substance, inimical to life—and full moons of shortbread adorned with mottoes of peel or sugar-plum, in honour of the season and the family affections. 'Frae Auld Reekie,' 'A guid New Year to ye a',' 'For the Auld Folk at Hame,' are among the most favoured of these devices. Can you not see the carrier, after half a day's journey on pinching hill-roads, draw up before a cottage in Teviotdale, or perhaps in Manor Glen among the rowans, and the old people receiving the parcel with moist eyes and a prayer for Jock or Jean in the city? For at this season, on the threshold of another year of calamity and stubborn conflict, men feel a need to draw closer the links that unite them; they reckon the number of their friends, like allies before a war; and the prayers grow longer in the morning as the absent are recommended by name into God's keeping.

On the day itself, the shops are all shut as on a Sunday; only taverns, toyshops, and other holiday magazines, keep open doors. Every one looks for his handsel. The postman and the lamplighters have left, at every house in their districts, a copy of vernacular verses, asking and thanking in a breath; and it is characteristic of Scotland that these verses may have sometimes a touch of reality in detail or sentiment and a measure of strength in the handling. All over the town, you may see comforter'd schoolboys hasting to squander their half-crowns. There are an infinity of visits to be paid; all the world is in the street, except the daintier classes; the sacramental greeting is heard upon all sides; Auld Lang Syne is much in people's mouths; and whisky and short-bread are staple articles of consumption. From an early hour a stranger will be impressed by the number of drunken men; and by afternoon drunkenness has spread to the women. With some classes of society, it is as much a matter of duty to drink hard on New-year's Day as to go to church on Sunday. Some have been saving their wages for perhaps a month to do the season honour. Many carry a whisky-bottle in their pocket, which they will press with embarrassing effusion on a perfect stranger. It is not expedient to risk one's body in a cab, or not, at least, until after a prolonged study of the driver. The streets, which are thronged from end to end, become a place for delicate pilotage. Singly or arm-in-arm, some speechless, others noisy and quarrelsome, the votaries of the New Year go meandering in and out and cannoning one against another; and now and again, one falls and lies as he has fallen. Before night, so many have gone to bed or the police office, that the streets seem almost clearer. And as *guisards* and *first-footers* are now not much seen except in country places, when once the New Year has been rung in and proclaimed at the Tron railings, the festivities begin to find their way indoors and something like quiet returns upon the town. But think, in these piled *lands*, of all the senseless snorers, all the broken heads and empty pockets!

Of old, Edinburgh University was the scene of heroic snowballing; and one riot obtained the epic honours of military intervention. But the great generation, I am afraid, is at an end; and even during my own college days, the spirit appreciably declined. Skating and sliding, on the other hand, are honoured more and more; and curling, being a creature of the national genius, is little likely to be disregarded. The patriotism that leads a man to eat Scots bun will scarce desert him at the curling-pond. Edinburgh, with its long, steep pavements, is the proper home of sliders; many a happy urchin can slide the whole way to school; and the profession of errand-boy is transformed into a holiday amusement. As for skating, there is scarce any city so handsomely provided. Duddingston Loch lies under the abrupt southern side of Arthur's Seat; in summer a shield of blue, with swans sailing from the reeds; in winter, a field of ringing ice. The village church sits above it on a green promontory; and the village smoke rises from among goodly trees. At the church gates, is the historical *jougs*, a place of penance for the neck of detected sinners, and the historical *louping-on stane*, from which Dutch-built lairds and farmers climbed into the saddle. Here Prince Charlie slept before the battle of Prestonpans; and here Deacon Brodie, or one of his gang, stole a plough coulter before the burglary in Chessel's Court. On the opposite side of the loch, the ground rises to Craigmillar Castle, a place friendly to Stuart Mariolaters. It is worth a climb, even in summer, to look down upon the loch from Arthur's Seat; but it is tenfold more so on a day of skating. The surface is thick with people moving easily and swiftly and leaning over at a thousand graceful inclinations; the crowd opens and closes, and keeps moving through itself like water; and the ice rings to half a mile away, with the flying steel. As night draws on, the single figures melt into the dusk, until only an obscure stir, and coming and going of black clusters, is visible upon the loch. A little longer, and the first torch is kindled and begins to flit rapidly across the ice in a ring of yellow reflection, and this is followed by another and another, until the whole field is full of skimming lights.

Chapter X: To the Pentland Hills

On three sides of Edinburgh, the country slopes downward from the city, here to the sea, there to the fat farms of Haddington, there to the mineral fields of Linlithgow. On the south alone, it keeps rising until it not only out-tops the Castle but looks down on Arthur's Seat. The character of the neighbourhood is pretty strongly marked by a scarcity of hedges; by many stone walls of varying height; by a fair amount of timber, some of it well grown, but apt to be of a bushy, northern profile and poor in foliage; by here and there a little river, Esk or Leith or Almond, busily journeying in the bottom of its glen; and from almost every point, by a peep of the sea or the hills. There is no lack of variety, and yet most of the elements are common to all parts; and the southern district is alone distinguished by considerable summits and a wide view.

From Boroughmuirhead, where the Scottish army encamped before Flodden,[35] the road descends a long hill, at the bottom of which and just as it is preparing to mount upon the other side, it passes a toll-bar and issues at once into the open country. Even as I write these words, they are being antiquated in the progress of events, and the chisels are tinkling on a new row of houses. The builders have at length adventured beyond the toll which held them in respect so long, and proceed to career in these fresh pastures like a herd of colts turned loose. As Lord Beaconsfield proposed to hang an architect by way of stimulation, a man, looking on these doomed meads, imagines a similar example to deter the builders; for it seems as if it must come to an open fight at last to preserve a corner of green country unbedevilled. And here, appropriately enough, there stood in old days a crow-haunted gibbet, with two bodies hanged in chains. I used to be shown, when a child, a flat stone in the roadway to which the gibbet had been fixed. People of a willing fancy were persuaded, and sought to persuade others, that this stone was never dry. And no wonder, they would add, for the two men had only stolen fourpence between them.

For about two miles the road climbs upwards, a long hot walk in summer time. You reach the summit at a place where four ways meet, beside the toll of Fairmilehead. The spot is breezy and agreeable both in name and aspect. The hills are close by across a valley: Kirk Yetton, with its long, upright scars visible as far as Fife, and Allermuir the tallest on this side: with wood and tilled field running high upon their borders, and haunches all moulded into innumerable glens and shelvings and variegated with heather and fern. The air comes briskly and sweetly off the hills, pure from the elevation and rustically scented by the upland plants; and even at the toll, you may hear the curlew calling on its mate. At certain seasons, when the gulls desert their surfy forelands, the birds of sea and mountain hunt and scream together in the same field by Fairmilehead. The winged, wild things intermix their wheelings, the sea-birds skim the tree-tops and fish among the furrows of the plough. These little craft of air are at home in all the world, so long as they cruise in their own element; and, like sailors, ask but food and water from the shores they coast.

Below, over a stream, the road passes Bow Bridge, now a dairy-farm, but once a distillery of whisky. It chanced, some time in the past century, that the distiller was on terms of good-fellowship with the visiting officer of excise. The latter was of an easy, friendly disposition, and a master of convivial arts. Now and again, he had to walk out of Edinburgh to measure the distiller's stock; and although it was agreeable to find his business lead him in a friend's direction, it was unfortunate that the friend should be a loser by his visits. Accordingly, when he got about the level of Fairmilehead, the gauger would take his flute, without which he never travelled, from his pocket, fit it together, and set manfully to playing, as if for his own delectation and inspired by the beauty of the scene. His favourite air, it seems, was 'Over the hills and far away.' At the first note, the distiller pricked his ears. A flute at Fairmilehead? and playing 'Over the hills and far away?' This must be his friendly enemy, the gauger. Instantly horses were harnessed, and sundry barrels of whisky were got upon a cart, driven at a gallop round Hill End, and buried in the mossy glen behind Kirk Yetton. In the same breath, you may be sure, a fat fowl was put to the fire, and the whitest napery prepared for the back parlour. A little after, the gauger, having had his fill of music for the moment, came strolling down with the most innocent air imaginable, and found the good people at Bow Bridge taken entirely unawares by his arrival, but none the less glad to see him. The distiller's liquor and the gauger's flute would combine to speed the moments of digestion; and when both were somewhat mellow, they would wind up the evening with 'Over the hills and far away' to an accompaniment of knowing glances. And at least, there is a smuggling story, with original and half-idyllic features.

A little further, the road to the right passes an upright stone in a field. The country people call it General Kay's monument. According to them, an officer of that name had perished there in battle at some indistinct period before the beginning of history. The date is reassuring; for I think cautious writers are silent on the General's exploits. But the stone is connected with one of those remarkable tenures of land which linger on into the modern world from Feudalism. Whenever the reigning sovereign passes by, a certain landed proprietor is held bound to climb on to the top, trumpet in hand, and sound a flourish according to the measure of his knowledge in that art. Happily for a respectable family, crowned heads have no great business in the Pentland Hills. But the story lends a character of comicality to the stone; and the passer-by will sometimes chuckle to himself.

The district is dear to the superstitious. Hard by, at the back-gate of Comiston, a belated carter beheld a lady in white, 'with the most beautiful, clear shoes upon her feet,' who looked upon him in a very ghastly manner and then vanished; and just in front is the Hunters' Tryst, once a roadside inn, and not so long ago haunted by the devil in person. Satan led the inhabitants a pitiful existence. He shook the four corners of the building with lamentable outcries, beat at the doors and windows, overthrew crockery in the dead hours of the morning, and danced unholy dances on the roof. Every kind of spiritual disinfectant was put in requisition; chosen ministers were summoned out of Edinburgh and prayed by the hour; pious neighbours sat up all night making a noise of psalmody; but Satan minded them no more than the wind about the hill-tops; and it was only after years of persecution, that he left the Hunters' Tryst in peace to occupy himself with the remainder of mankind. What with General Kay, and the white lady, and this singular visitation, the neighbourhood offers great facilities to the makers of sun-myths; and without exactly casting in one's lot with that disenchanting school of writers, one cannot help hearing a good deal of the winter wind in the last story. 'That nicht,' says Burns, in one of his happiest moments,—

> 'That nicht a child might understand
> The deil had business on his hand.'[36]

And if people sit up all night in lone places on the hills, with Bibles and tremulous psalms, they will be apt to hear some of the most fiendish noises in the world; the wind will beat on doors and dance upon roofs for them, and make the hills howl around their cottage with a clamour like the judgment-day.

The road goes down through another valley, and then finally begins to scale the main slope of the Pentlands. A bouquet of old trees stands round a white farmhouse; and from a neighbouring dell, you can see smoke rising and leaves ruffling in the breeze. Straight above, the hills climb a thousand feet into the air. The neighbourhood, about the time of lambs, is clamorous with the bleating of flocks; and you will be awakened, in the grey of early summer mornings, by the barking of a dog or the voice of a shepherd shouting to the echoes. This, with the hamlet lying behind unseen, is Swanston.[37]

The place in the dell is immediately connected with the city. Long ago, this sheltered field was purchased by the Edinburgh magistrates for the sake of the springs that rise or gather there. After they had built their water-house and laid their pipes, it occurred to them that the place was suitable for junketing. Once entertained, with jovial magistrates and public funds, the idea led speedily to accomplishment; and Edinburgh could soon boast of a municipal Pleasure House. The dell was turned into a garden; and on the knoll that shelters it from the plain and the sea winds, they built a cottage looking to the hills. They brought crockets and gargoyles from old St. Giles's which they were then restoring, and disposed them on the gables and over the door and about the garden; and the quarry which had supplied them with building material, they draped with clematis and carpeted with beds of roses. So much for the pleasure of the eye; for creature comfort, they made a capacious cellar in the hillside and fitted it with bins of the hewn stone. In process of time, the trees grew higher and gave shade to the cottage, and the evergreens sprang up and turned the dell into a thicket. There, purple magistrates relaxed themselves from the pursuit of municipal ambition; cocked hats paraded soberly about the garden and in and out among the hollies; authoritative canes drew ciphering upon the path; and at night, from high upon the hills, a shepherd saw lighted windows through the foliage and heard the voice of city dignitaries raised in song.

The farm is older. It was first a grange of Whitekirk Abbey, tilled and inhabited by rosy friars. Thence, after the Reformation, it passed into the hands of a true-blue Protestant family. During the Covenanting troubles, when a night conventicle was held upon the Pentlands, the farm doors stood hospitably open till the morning; the dresser was laden with cheese and bannocks, milk and brandy; and the worshippers kept slipping down from the hill between two exercises, as couples visit the supper-room between two dances of a modern ball. In the Forty-Five, some foraging Highlanders from Prince Charlie's army fell upon Swanston in the dawn. The great-grandfather of the late farmer was then a little child; him they awakened by plucking the blankets from his bed, and he remembered, when he was an old man, their truculent looks and uncouth speech. The churn stood full of cream in the dairy, and with this they made their brose in high delight. 'It was braw brose,' said one of them. At last they made off, laden like camels with their booty; and Swanston Farm has lain out of the way of history from that time forward. I do not know what may be yet in store for it. On dark days, when the mist runs low upon the hill, the house has a gloomy air as if suitable for private tragedy. But in hot July, you can fancy nothing more perfect than the garden, laid out in alleys and arbours and bright, old-fashioned flower-plots, and ending in a miniature ravine, all trellis-work and moss and tinkling waterfall, and housed from the sun under fathoms of broad foliage.

The hamlet behind is one of the least considerable of hamlets, and consists of a few cottages on a green beside a burn. Some of them (a strange thing in Scotland) are models of internal neatness; the beds adorned with patchwork, the shelves arrayed with willow-pattern plates, the floors and tables bright with scrubbing or pipe-clay, and the very kettle polished like silver. It is the sign of a contented old age in country places, where there is little matter for gossip and no street sights. Housework becomes an art; and at evening, when the cottage interior shines and twinkles in the glow of the fire, the housewife folds her hands and contemplates her finished picture; the snow and the wind may do their worst, she has made herself a pleasant corner in the world. The city might be a thousand miles away, and yet it was from close by that Mr. Bough[38] painted the distant view of Edinburgh which has been engraved for this collection; and you have only to look at the cut,* to see how near it is at hand. But hills and hill people are not easily sophisticated; and if you walk out here on a summer Sunday, it is as like as not the shepherd may set his dogs upon you. But keep an unmoved countenance; they look formidable at the charge, but their hearts are in the right place, and they will only bark and sprawl about you on the grass, unmindful of their master's excitations.

Kirk Yetton forms the north-eastern angle of the range; thence, the Pentlands trend off to south and west. From the summit you look over a great expanse of champaign sloping to the sea, and behold a large variety of distant hills. There are the hills of Fife, the hills of Peebles, the Lammermoors and the Ochils, more or less mountainous in out-line, more or less blue with distance. Of the Pentlands themselves, you see a field of wild heathery peaks with a pond gleaming in the midst; and to that side the view is as desolate as if you were looking into Galloway or Applecross. To turn to the other is like a piece of travel. Far out in the lowlands Edinburgh shows herself, making a great smoke on clear days and spreading her suburbs about her for miles; the Castle rises darkly in the midst, and close by, Arthur's Seat makes a bold figure in the landscape. All around, cultivated fields, and woods, and smoking villages, and white country roads, diversify the uneven surface of the land. Trains crawl slowly abroad upon the railway lines; little ships are tacking in the Firth; the shadow of a mountainous cloud, as

* One of the illustrations of the First Edition.

large as a parish, travels before the wind; the wind itself ruffles the wood and standing corn, and sends pulses of varying colour across the landscape. So you sit, like Jupiter upon Olympus, and look down from afar upon men's life. The city is as silent as a city of the dead: from all its humming thoroughfares, not a voice, not a footfall, reaches you upon the hill. The sea-surf, the cries of ploughmen, the streams and the mill-wheels, the birds and the wind, keep up an animated concert through the plain; from farm to farm, dogs and crowing cocks contend together in defiance; and yet from this Olympian station, except for the whispering rumour of a train, the world has fallen into a dead silence, and the business of town and country grown voiceless in your ears. A crying hill-bird, the bleat of a sheep, a wind singing in the dry grass, seem not so much to interrupt, as to accompany, the stillness; but to the spiritual ear, the whole scene makes a music at once human and rural, and discourses pleasant reflections on the destiny of man. The spiry habitable city, ships, the divided fields, and browsing herds, and the straight highways, tell visibly of man's active and comfortable ways; and you may be never so laggard and never so unimpressionable, but there is something in the view that spirits up your blood and puts you in the vein for cheerful labour.

Immediately below is Fairmilehead, a spot of roof and a smoking chimney, where two roads, no thicker than packthread, intersect beside a hanging wood. If you are fanciful, you will be reminded of the gauger in the story. And the thought of this old exciseman, who once lipped and fingered on his pipe and uttered clear notes from it in the mountain air, and the words of the song he affected, carry your mind 'Over the hills and far away' to distant countries; and you have a vision of Edinburgh not, as you see her, in the midst of a little neighbourhood, but as a boss upon the round world with all Europe and the deep sea for her surroundings. For every place is a centre to the earth, whence highways radiate or ships set sail for foreign ports; the limit of a parish is not more imaginary than the frontier of an empire; and as a man sitting at home in his cabinet and swiftly writing books, so a city sends abroad an influence and a portrait of herself. There is no Edinburgh emigrant, far or near, from China to Peru, but he or she carries some lively pictures of the mind, some sunset behind the Castle cliffs, some snow scene, some maze of city lamps, indelible in the memory and delightful to study in the intervals of toil. For any such, if this book fall in their way, here are a few more home pictures. It would be pleasant, if they should recognise a house where they had dwelt, or a walk that they had taken.

Edinburgh—The Water of Leith

Unpublished fragment

It is not possible to exaggerate the hold that is taken on the mind of men by a familiar river. It is a piece of nature set apart from its surroundings, the author and the genius of its own valley, wearing the physiognomy of life, and equally delightful to the eye and ear. It is quick with fishes; it flashes to the eye with the sun, darkens and swells in volume with the rain storm; the country freshens as it approaches it; pleasant trees congregate along its course; birds, the cattle, the flies, wading children, and the angler love to frequent its margin, the road follows or crosses it on bridges, which are in themselves delightful and a part of the stage properties of romance; and here and there it leads us to the mill-dam, the mill, with its wheel, and the dusty miller.

Every child has his own adopted river, that he was born or has played beside, and whose ancient voice returns to the ear of memory; but the stream my childhood boasted of was neither great nor very beautiful nor at all known to public acclamation; and its name is not well fitted to adorn the accents of the Muse. It was called the Water of Leith;[1] ran from some not very memorable hills down a not very noticeable glen; skirted the outposts, vacant lots and half-rural slums of a great city, and at last, running between the repose of a graveyard and the clatter of an engine factory, lapsed, through dark gates and groves of masts and a long alley of weedy piers, into an islanded salt estuary. There it may seek to conjoin itself with the waters of another and more famous river, already indistinguishably whelmed in ocean, the Black [?] Avon of Forth, the wild Highlandman's hurdle, and lingering in images within view of the towers of Stirling, and left the place of the heather and the curlew for the society of the gull and herring. It shames my little stream to name it in the same breath with that influential stream of which it is a belated confluent, like mustard after beef. It cannot even bear a comparison with the nearest of its rivals, Esk or Almond, both softlier named and both the architects of more romantic channels. Such as it was, however, it was the river whose streams made glad my childhood and for that reason ever memorable to me.

Edinburgh—Colinton

'The Manse'

I have named, among many rivers that make music in my memory, that dirty Water of Leith. Often and often I desire to look upon it again; and the choice of a point of view is easy to me. It should be at a certain water-door, embowered in shrubbery. The river is there dammed back for the service of the flour-mill just below, so that it lies deep and darkling, and the sand slopes into brown obscurity with a glint of gold; and it has but newly been recruited by the borrowings of the snuff-mill just above, and these, tumbling merrily in, shake the pool to its black heart, fill it with drowsy eddies, and set the curded froth of many other mills solemnly steering to and fro upon the surface. Or so it was when I was young; for change, and the masons, and the pruning-knife, have been busy; and if I could hope to repeat a cherished experience, it must be on many and impossible conditions. I must choose, as well as the point of view, a certain moment in my growth, so that the scale may be exaggerated, and the trees on the steep opposite side may seem to climb to heaven, and the sand by the water-door, where I am standing, seem as low as Styx. And I must choose the season also, so that the valley may be brimmed like a cup with sunshine and the songs of birds;—and the year of grace, so that when I turn to leave the riverside I may find the old manse[1] and its inhabitants unchanged.

It was a place in that time like no other: the garden cut into provinces by a great hedge of beech, and overlooked by the church and the terrace of the churchyard, where the tombstones were thick, and after nightfall 'spunkies' might be seen to dance at least by children; flower-plots lying warm in sunshine; laurels and the great yew making elsewhere a pleasing horror of shade; the smell of water rising from all round, with an added tang of paper-mills; the sound of water everywhere, and the sound of mills—the wheel and the dam singing their alternate strain; the birds on every bush and from every corner of the overhanging woods pealing out their notes until the air throbbed with them; and in the midst of this, the manse. I see it, by the standard of my childish stature, as a great and roomy house. In truth, it was not so large as I supposed, nor yet so convenient, and, standing where it did, it is difficult to suppose that it was healthful. Yet a large family of stalwart sons and tall daughters was housed and reared, and came to man and womanhood in that nest of little chambers; so that the face of the earth was peppered with the children of the manse, and letters with outlandish stamps became familiar to the local postman, and the walls of the little chambers brightened with the wonders of the East. The dullest could see this was a house that had a pair of hands in divers foreign places: a well-beloved house—its image fondly dwelt on by many travellers.

Here lived an ancestor of mine, who was a herd of men. I read him, judging with older criticism the report of childish observation, as a man of singular simplicity of nature; unemotional, and hating the display of what he felt; standing contented on the old ways; a lover of his life and innocent habits to the end. We children admired him: partly for his beautiful face and silver hair, for none more than children are concerned for beauty and, above all, for beauty in the old; partly for the solemn light in which we beheld him once a week, the observed of all observers, in the pulpit. But his strictness and distance, the effect, I now fancy, of old age, slow blood, and settled habit, oppressed us with a kind of terror. When not abroad, he sat much alone, writing sermons or letters to his scattered family in a dark and cold room with a library of bloodless books—or so they seemed in those days, although I have some of them now on my own shelves and like well enough to read them; and these lonely hours wrapped him in the greater gloom for our imaginations. But the study had a redeeming grace in many Indian pictures, gaudily coloured and dear to young eyes. I cannot depict (for I have no such passions now) the greed with which I beheld them; and when I was once sent in to say a psalm to my grandfather, I went, quaking indeed with fear, but at the same time glowing with hope that, if I said it well, he might reward me with an Indian picture.

> 'Thy foot He'll not let slide, nor will
> He slumber that thee keeps,'[2]

it ran: a strange conglomerate of the unpronounceable, a sad model to set in childhood before one who was himself to be a versifier, and a task in recitation that really merited reward. And I must suppose the old man thought so too, and was either touched or amused by the performance; for he took me in his arms with most unwonted tenderness, and kissed me, and gave me a little kindly sermon for my psalm; so that, for that day, we were clerk and parson. I was struck by this reception into so tender a surprise that I forgot my disappointment. And indeed the hope was one of those that childhood forges for a pastime, and with no design upon reality. Nothing was more unlikely than that my grandfather should strip himself of one of those pictures, love-gifts and reminders of his absent sons; nothing more unlikely than that he should bestow it upon me. He had no idea of spoiling children, leaving all that to my aunt; he had fared hard himself, and blubbered under the rod in the last century; and his ways were still Spartan for the young. The last word I heard upon his lips was in this Spartan key. He had over-walked in the teeth of an east wind, and was now near the end of his many days. He sat by the dining-room fire, with his white hair, pale face and bloodshot eyes, a somewhat awful figure; and my aunt had given him a dose of our good old Scots medicine, Dr. Gregory's powder. Now that remedy, as the work of a near kinsman of Rob Roy himself, may have a savour of romance for the imagination; but it comes uncouthly to the palate. The old gentleman had taken it with a wry face; and that being accomplished, sat with perfect simplicity, like a child's, munching a 'barley-sugar kiss.' But when my aunt, having the canister open in her hands, proposed to let me share in the sweets, he interfered at once. I had had no Gregory; then I should have no barley-sugar kiss: so he decided with a touch of irritation. And just then the phaeton coming opportunely to the kitchen door—for such was our unlordly fashion—I was taken for the last time from the presence of my grandfather.

Now I often wonder what I have inherited from this old minister. I must suppose, indeed, that he was fond of preaching sermons, and so am I, though I never heard it maintained that either of us loved to hear them. He sought health in his youth in the Isle of Wight, and I have sought it in both hemispheres; but whereas he found and kept it, I am still on the quest. He was a great lover of Shakespeare, whom he read aloud, I have been told, with taste; well, I love my Shakespeare also, and am persuaded I can read him well, though I own I never have been told so. He made embroidery, designing his own patterns; and in that kind of work I never made anything but a kettle-holder in Berlin wool, and an odd garter of knitting, which was as black as the chimney before I had done with it. He loved port, and nuts, and porter; and so do I, but they agreed better with my grandfather, which seems to me a breach of contract. He had chalk-stones in his fingers; and these, in good time, I may possibly inherit, but I would much rather have inher-ited his noble presence. Try as I please, I cannot join myself on with the reverend doctor; and all the while, no doubt, and even as I write the phrase, he moves in my blood, and whispers words to me, and sits efficient in the very knot and centre of my being. In his garden, as I played there, I learned the love of mills—or had I an ancestor a miller?—and a kindness for the neighbourhood of graves, as homely things not without their poetry—or had I an ancestor a sexton? But what of the garden where he played himself?—for that, too, was a scene of my education. Some part of me played there in the eighteenth century, and ran races under the green avenue at Pilrig; some part of me trudged up

Leith Walk, which was still a country place, and sat on the High School benches, and was thrashed, perhaps, by Dr. Adam.[3] The house where I spent my youth was not yet thought upon; but we made holiday parties among the cornfields on its site, and ate strawberries and cream near by at a gardener's. All this I had forgotten; only my grandfather remembered and once reminded me. I have forgotten, too, how we grew up, and took orders, and went to our first Ayrshire parish, and fell in love with and married a daughter of Burns's Dr. Smith—'Smith opens out his cauld harangues.'[4] I have forgotten, but I was there all the same, and heard stories of Burns at first hand.

And there is a thing stranger than all that; for this *homunculus* or part-man of mine that walked about the eighteenth century with Dr. Balfour in his youth, was in the way of meeting other *homunculos* or part-men, in the persons of my other ancestors. These were of a lower order, and doubtless we looked down upon them duly. But as I went to college with Dr. Balfour, I may have seen the lamp and oil man[5] taking down the shutters from his shop beside the Tron—we may have had a rabbit-hutch or a bookshelf made for us by a certain carpenter in I know not what wynd of the old, smoky city; or, upon some holiday excursion, we may have looked into the windows of a cottage in a flower-garden and seen a certain weaver plying his shuttle. And these were all kinsmen of mine upon the other side; and from the eyes of the lamp and oil man one-half of my unborn father, and one-quarter of myself, looked out upon us as we went by to college. Nothing of all this would cross the mind of the young student, as he posted up the Bridges with trim, stockinged legs, in that city of cocked hats and good Scots still unadulterated. It would not cross his mind that he should have a daughter; and the lamp and oil man, just then beginning, by a not unnatural metastasis, to bloom into a lighthouse-engineer, should have a grandson; and that these two, in the fulness of time, should wed; and some portion of that student himself should survive yet a year or two longer in the person of their child.

But our ancestral adventures are beyond even the arithmetic of fancy; and it is the chief recommendation of long pedigrees, that we can follow backward the careers of our *homunculos* and be reminded of our antenatal lives. Our conscious years are but a moment in the history of the elements that build us. Are you a bank-clerk, and do you live at Peckham? It was not always so. And though today I am only a man of letters, either tradition errs or I was present when there landed at St. Andrews a French barber-surgeon, to tend the health and the beard of the great Cardinal Beaton; I have shaken a spear in the Debateable Land and shouted the slogan of the Elliots; I was present when a skipper, plying from Dundee, smuggled Jacobites to France after the '15; I was in a West India merchant's office, perhaps next door to Bailie Nicol Jarvie's, and managed the business of a plantation in St. Kitt's; I was with my engineer-grandfather (the son-in-law of the lamp and oil man) when he sailed north about Scotland on the famous cruise that gave us the *Pirate* and the *Lord of the Isles*; I was with him, too, on the Bell Rock, in the fog, when the *Smeaton* had drifted from her moorings, and the Aberdeen men, pick in hand, had seized upon the only boats, and he must stoop and lap sea-water before his tongue could utter audible words; and once more with him when the Bell Rock beacon took a 'thrawe,' and his workmen fled into the tower, then nearly finished, and he sat unmoved reading in his Bible—or affecting to read—till one after another slunk back with confusion of countenance to their engineer. Yes, parts of me have seen life, and met adventures, and sometimes met them well. And away in the still cloudier past, the threads that make me up can be traced by fancy into the bosoms of thousands and millions of ascendants: Picts who rallied round Macbeth and the old (and highly preferable) system of descent by females, fleers from before the legions of Agricola, marchers in Pannonian morasses, star-gazers on Chaldaean plateaus; and, furthest of all, what face is this that fancy can see peering through the disparted branches? What sleeper in green tree-tops, what muncher of nuts, concludes my pedigree? Probably Arboreal in his habits...

And I know not which is the more strange, that I should carry about with me some fibres of my minister-grandfather; or that in him, as he sat in his cool study, grave, reverend, contented gentleman, there was an aboriginal frisking of the blood that was not his; tree-top memories, like undeveloped negatives, lay dormant in his mind; tree-top instincts awoke and were trod down; and Probably Arboreal (scarce to be distinguished from a monkey) gambolled and chattered in the brain of the old divine.

Midlothian

Excursion First
Craigmillar Castle

On Saturday the 23d Feby/61 I left Edinb to visit Craigmillar Castle.

Driving along the Dalkeith road we passed Peffer Mill, a quaint old gable ended house in the Scottish Baronial style, standing among trees. Shortly after this we arrived at Craigmillar. We entered the outer court from which we had a full view of the front. Craigmillar is not like most Scottish edifices a cluster of towers and turrets. It is surrounded by a wall with round towers filled with loop holes for archery. In front of this there is a space enclosed by walls which are now completely ruinous. Entering the inner courtyard in front of us stood the Keefe tower, the most ancient part of the building which is completely mantled with ivy. Proceeding up the stair which is very wide & easy to ascend & in perfect preservation, we arrived at the

Great Hall
a largish apartment lighted by deep windows pierced through walls ten feet thick. Opposite the door stands the fireplace which is very large & formed in the style which is usual in these buildings. On the east side of the fireplace a few steps descend to a window. Closely adjoining this chamber is

Queen Mary's boudoir
this room has been restored by the present proprietor Mrs Little Gilmour. Above the fireplace is a heraldic coat of arms & manuscript (this has been restored). In one of the corners lay a curious old gun the lock of which was perfectly scarlet with rust. Ascending another flight of steps we came to a commodious room supposed to be a bedroom, no comment need be made upon this. From the top of the tower we obtained a fine view of the surrounding country. The next place worthy of notice which we visited was

Queen Mary's Prison
an uncommonly small chamber where she was confined for two days after the battle of Carberry[2] & just before she was removed to Loch Leven. The bed which she occupied in this room is said to have been a hammock swung from the roof. In the tower part of the Castle we saw

51

Mar's Prison

A dark vault lighted by a small loop hole in which John Earl of Mar, brother of James III, was confined in 1479, charged with conspiring against his brother & in which by some historians he is said to have been murdered. There are no other chambers of any consequence in the east side of the building except the servants' hall, a large room but which is now rendered totally dark by the windows being built up. Crossing the inner court toward the west we see the

Wine Cellar

This is a large room one part of which is walled from the rest, the walls not going all the height of the roof. At one corner there are the remains of a passage formerly communicating with Queen Mary's private room by which she might fetch a bottle of claret when she felt inclined. Passing from this we enter what I suppose must have been a small side court on which opens

The Confessional

This is a small narrow room, scarcely larger than a passage. In the wall are several recesses with stone benches along the sides. Here the prisoners were confessed & then led down a few steps to the

Execution Cell

A dark apartment partly under ground. In a recess of this room is a smooth stone said to have been worn by the executioner sharpening his axe upon it. Still farther to the west are the remains of a more modern part of the building built by Sir John Gilmour the first of this family who possessed the property. He built it a year or so before the Castle was finally destroyed by fire during Cromwell's wars. The most peculiar feature of the architecture of this castle is the open corbelling. For a further account of this interesting ruin you may look at *The Baronial & Ecclesiastical Antiquities of Scotland* Vol: 1st.

Excursion Second
Corstorphine Church

On Saturday the 2nd March I set out for Corstorphine Church.

This queer little building is situated in the village of the same name about 3 miles to the west of Edinb. It is in the form of a cross with an additional transept at one of the sides. In the chancel which is not fitted up are two tombs both of which bear the arms of the Forresters in front of them. A stone covered with writing is on one side of the door. One part of the inscription, supposed to have been a date, has been completely effaced.

The fitted up part of the building is partly divided by a thick wall pierced by an arch. The order of architecture in which this Church is built (if it is built in any) is the Norman, but at the end of one of the transepts is a window of pointed Gothic (I'm not quite sure of the kind). Below this window is another of the Forresters' tombs.

The tower is a stumpy little erection neither resembling the Grecian nor the Gothic style.

North Berwick

Extract from 'The Lantern-Bearers'

These boys congregated every autumn about a certain easterly fisher-village, where they tasted in a high degree the glory of existence.[1] The place was created seemingly on purpose for the diversion of young gentlemen. A street or two of houses, mostly red and many of them tiled; a number of fine trees clustered about the manse and the kirkyard, and turning the chief street into a shady alley; many little gardens more than usually bright with flowers; nets a-drying, and fisher-wives scolding in the backward parts; a smell of fish, a genial smell of seaweed; whiffs of blowing sand at the street-corners; shops with golf-balls and bottled lollipops; another shop with penny pickwicks (that remarkable cigar) and the *London Journal*, dear to me for its startling pictures, and a few novels, dear for their suggestive names: such, as well as memory serves me, were the ingredients of the town. These, you are to conceive posted on a spit between two sandy bays, and sparsely flanked with villas—enough for the boys to lodge in with their subsidiary parents, not enough (not yet enough) to cocknify the scene: a haven in the rocks in front: in front of that, a file of gray islets: to the left, endless links and sand wreaths, a wilderness of hiding-holes, alive with popping rabbits and soaring gulls; to the right, a range of seaward crags, one rugged brow beyond another; the ruins of a mighty and ancient fortress on the brink of one; coves between—now charmed into sunshine quiet, now whistling with wind and clamorous with bursting surges; the dens and sheltered hollows redolent of thyme and southernwood, the air at the cliff's edge brisk and clean and pungent of the sea—in front of all, the Bass Rock, tilted seaward like a doubtful bather, the surf ringing it with white, the solan-geese[2] hanging round its summit like a great and glittering smoke. This choice piece of seaboard was sacred, besides, to the wrecker; and the Bass, in the eye of fancy, still flew the colours of

King James; and in the ear of fancy the arches of Tantallon still rang with horse-shoe iron, and echoed to the commands of Bell-the-Cat.[3]

There was nothing to mar your days, if you were a boy summering in that part, but the embarrassment of pleasure. You might golf if you wanted; but I seem to have been better employed. You might secrete yourself in the Lady's Walk, a certain sunless dingle of elders, all mossed over by the damp as green as grass, and dotted here and there by the stream-side with roofless walls, the cold homes of anchorites. To fit themselves for life, and with a special eye to acquire the art of smoking, it was even common for the boys to harbour there; and you might have seen a single penny pickwick, honestly shared in lengths with a blunt knife, bestrew the glen with these apprentices. Again, you might join our fishing parties, where we sat perched as thick as solan-geese, a covey of little anglers, boy and girl, angling over each other's heads, to the much entanglement of lines and loss of podleys and consequent shrill recrimination—shrill as the geese themselves. Indeed, had that been all, you might have done this often; but though fishing be a fine pastime, the podley is scarce to be regarded as a dainty for the table; and it was a point of honour that a boy should eat all that he had taken. Or again, you might climb the Law,[4] where the whale's jawbone stood landmark in the buzzing wind, and behold the face of many counties, and the smoke and spires of many towns, and the sails of distant ships. You might bathe, now in the flaws of fine weather, that we pathetically call our summer, now in a gale of wind, with the sand scourging your bare hide, your clothes thrashing abroad from underneath their guardian stone, the froth of the great breakers casting you headlong ere it had drowned your knees. Or you might explore the tidal rocks, above all in the ebb of springs, when the very roots of the hills were for the nonce discovered; following my leader from one group to another, groping in slippery tangle for the wreck of ships, wading in pools after the abominable creatures of the sea, and ever with an eye cast backward on the march of the tide and the menaced line of your retreat. And then you might go Crusoeing, a word that covers all extempore eating in the open air: digging perhaps a house under the margin of the links, kindling a fire of the sea-ware, and cooking apples there—if they were truly apples, for I sometimes suppose the merchant must have played us off with some inferior and quite local fruit, capable of resolving, in the neighbourhood of fire, into mere sand and smoke and iodine; or perhaps pushing to Tantallon, you might lunch on sandwiches and visions in the grassy court, while the wind hummed in the crumbling turrets; or clambering along the coast, eat geans [wild cherries] (the worst, I must suppose, in Christendom) from an adventurous gean tree that had taken root under a cliff, where it was shaken with an ague of east wind, and silvered after gales with salt, and grew so foreign among its bleak surroundings that to eat of its produce was an adventure in itself.

There are mingled some dismal memories with so many that were joyous. Of the fisher-wife, for instance, who had cut her throat at Canty Bay; and of how I ran with the other children to the top of the Quadrant, and beheld a posse of silent people escorting a cart, and on the cart, bound in a chair, her throat bandaged, and the bandage all bloody—horror!—the fisher-wife herself, who continued thenceforth to hag-ride my thoughts, and even to-day (as I recall the scene) darkens daylight. She was lodged in the little old jail in the chief street; but whether or no she died there, with a wise terror of the worst, I never inquired. She had been tippling; it was but a dingy tragedy; and it seems strange and hard that, after all these years, the poor crazy sinner should be still pilloried on her cart in the scrap-book of my memory. Nor shall I readily forget a certain house in the Quadrant where a visitor died, and a dark old woman continued to dwell alone with the dead body; nor how this old woman conceived a hatred to myself and one of my cousins, and in the dread hour of the dusk, as we were clambering on the garden-walls, opened a window in that house of mortality and cursed us in a shrill voice and with a marrowy choice of language. It was a pair of very colourless urchins that fled down the lane from this remarkable experience! But I recall with a more doubtful sentiment, compounded out of fear and exultation, the coil of equinoctial tempests; trumpeting squalls, scouring flaws of rain; the boats with their reefed lug-sails scudding for the harbour mouth, where danger lay, for it was hard to make when the wind had any east in it; the wives clustered with blowing shawls at the pierhead, where (if fate was against them) they might see boat and husband and sons—their whole wealth and their whole family—engulfed under their eyes; and (what I saw but once) a troop of neighbours forcing such an unfortunate homeward, and she squalling and battling in their midst, a figure scarcely human, a tragic Maenad.

These are things that I recall with interest; but what my memory dwells upon the most, I have been all this while withholding. It was a sport peculiar to the place, and indeed to a week or so of our two months' holiday there. Maybe it still flourishes in its native spot; for boys and their pastimes are swayed by periodic forces inscrutable to man; so that tops and marbles reappear in their due season, regular like the sun and moon; and the harmless art of knucklebones has seen the fall of the Roman empire and the rise of the United States. It may still flourish in its native spot, but nowhere else, I am persuaded; for I tried myself to introduce it on Tweedside, and was defeated lamentably; its charm being quite local, like a country wine that cannot be exported.

The idle manner of it was this:—

Toward the end of September, when school-time was drawing near and the nights were already black, we would begin to sally from our respective villas, each equipped with a tin bull's-eye lantern. The thing was so well known that it had worn a rut in the commerce of Great Britain; and the grocers, about the due time, began to garnish their windows with our particular brand of luminary. We wore them buckled to the waist upon a cricket belt, and over them, such was the rigour of the game, a buttoned top-coat. They smelled noisomely of blistered tin; they never burned aright, though they would always burn our fingers; their use was naught; the pleasure of them merely fanciful; and yet a boy with a bull's-eye under his top-coat asked for nothing more. The fishermen used lanterns about their boats, and it was from them, I suppose, that we had got the hint; but theirs were not bull's-eyes, nor did we ever play at being fishermen. The police carried them at their belts, and we had plainly copied them in that; yet we did not pretend to be policemen. Burglars, indeed, we may have had some haunting thoughts of; and we had certainly an eye to past ages when lanterns were more common, and to certain story-books in which we had found them to figure very largely. But take it for all in all, the pleasure of the thing was substantive; and to be a boy with a bull's-eye under his top-coat was good enough for us.

When two of these asses met, there would be an anxious 'Have you got your lantern?' and a gratified 'Yes!' That was the shibboleth, and very needful too; for, as it was the rule to keep our glory contained, none could recognise a lantern-bearer, unless (like the polecat) by the smell. Four or five would sometimes climb into the belly of a ten-man lugger, with nothing but the thwarts above them—for the cabin was usually locked; or choose out some hollow of the links where the wind might whistle overhead. There the coats would be unbuttoned and the bull's-eyes discovered; and in the chequering glimmer, under the huge windy hall of the night, and cheered by a rich steam of toasting tin-ware, these fortunate young gentlemen would crouch together in the cold sand of the links or on the scaly bilges of the fishing-boat, and delight themselves with inappropriate talk. Woe is me that I may not give some specimens—some of their foresights of life, or deep inquiries into the rudiments of man and nature, these were so fiery and so innocent, they were so richly silly, so romantically young. But the talk, at any rate, was but a condiment; and these gatherings themselves only accidents in the career of the lantern-bearer. The essence of this bliss was to walk by yourself in the black night; the slide shut, the top-coat buttoned; not a ray escaping, whether to conduct your footsteps or to make your glory public: a mere pillar of darkness in the dark; and all the while, deep down in the privacy of your fool's heart, to know you had a bull's-eye at your belt, and to exult and sing over the knowledge.

Gillane Sands—Tantallon

From Chapter 13 of *Catriona:* Gillane Sands

As we had first made inland, so our road came in the end to lie very near due north; the old Kirk of Aberlady for a landmark on the left; on the right, the top of the Berwick Law; and it was thus we struck the shore again, not far from Dirleton. From North Berwick west to Gillane Ness there runs a string of four small islets, Craigleith, the Lamb, Fidra, and Eyebrough,[1] notable by their diversity of size and shape. Fidra is the most particular, being a strange grey islet of two humps, made the more conspicuous by a piece of ruin; and I mind that (as we drew closer to it) by some door or window of these ruins the sea peeped through like a man's eye. Under the lee of Fidra there is a good anchorage in westerly winds, and there, from a far way off, we could see the *Thistle* riding.

The shore in face of these islets is altogether waste. Here is no dwelling of man, and scarce any passage, or at most of vagabond children running at their play. Gillane is a small place on the far side of the Ness, the folk of Dirleton go to their business in the inland fields, and those of North Berwick straight to the sea-fishing from their haven; so that few parts of the coast are lonelier. But I mind, as we crawled upon our bellies into that multiplicity of heights and hollows, keeping a bright eye upon all sides, and our hearts hammering at our ribs, there was such a shining of the sun and the sea, such a stir of the wind in the bent grass, and such a bustle of down-popping rabbits and up-flying gulls, that the desert seemed to me like a place alive. No doubt it was in all ways well chosen for a secret embarcation, if the secret had been kept; and even now that it was out, and the place watched, we were able to creep unperceived to the front of the sandhills, where they look down immediately on the beach and sea.

* * *

57

We were at one time close at the foot of Berwick Law on the south side; at another, as we passed over some open hills, I spied the lights of a clachan and the old tower of a church among some trees not far off, but too far to cry for help, if I had dreamed of it. At last we came again within sound of the sea. There was moonlight, though not much; and by this I could see the three huge towers and broken battlements of Tantallon, that old chief place of the Red Douglases. The horse was picketed in the bottom of the ditch to graze, and I was led within, and forth into the court, and thence into the tumble-down stone hall. Here my conductors built a brisk fire in the midst of the pavement, for there was a chill in the night. My hands were loosed, I was set by the wall in the inner end, and (the Lowlander having produced provisions) I was given oatmeal bread and a pitcher of French brandy. This done, I was left once more alone with my three Highlandmen. They sat close by the fire drinking and talking; the wind blew in by the breaches, cast about the smoke and flames, and sang in the tops of the towers; I could hear the sea under the cliffs, and, my mind being reassured as to my life, and my body and spirits wearied with the day's employment, I turned upon one side and slumbered.

I had no means of guessing at what hour I was wakened, only the moon was down and the fire low. My feet were now loosed, and I was carried through the ruins and down the cliffside by a precipitous path to where I found a fisher's boat in a haven of the rocks. This I was had on board of, and we began to put forth from the shore in a fine starlight.

The Bass Rock

From Chapter 14 of *Catriona:* The Bass

There began to fall a greyness on the face of the sea; little dabs of pink and red, like coals of slow fire, came in the east; and at the same time the geese awakened, and began crying about the top of the Bass.[1] It is just the one crag of rock, as everybody knows, but great enough to carve a city from. The sea was extremely little, but there went a hollow plowter round the base of it. With the growing of the dawn I could see it clearer and clearer; the straight crags painted with sea-birds' droppings like a morning frost, the sloping top of it green with grass, the clan of white geese that cried about the sides, and the black, broken buildings of the prison sitting close on the sea's edge.

At the sight the truth came in upon me in a clap.

'It's there you're taking me!' I cried.

'Just to the Bass, mannie,' said he; 'Whaur the auld saints' were afore ye, and I misdoubt if ye have come so fairly by your preeson.'

'But none dwells there now,' I cried; 'the place is long a ruin.'

'It'll be the mair pleisand a change for the solan geese, then,' quoth Andie dryly.

The day coming slowly brighter I observed on the bilge, among the big stones with which fisherfolk ballast their boats, several kegs and baskets, and a provision of fuel. All these were discharged upon the crag. Andie, myself, and my three Highlanders (I call them mine, although it was the other way about), landed along with them. The sun was not yet up when the boat moved away again, the noise of the oars on the thole-pins echoing from the cliffs, and left us in our singular reclusion.

* * *

All the time of my stay on the rock we lived well. We had small ale and brandy, and oatmeal, of which we made our porridge night and morning. At times a boat came from the Castleton and brought us a quarter of mutton, for the sheep upon the rock we must not touch, these being specially fed to market. The geese were unfortunately out of season, and we let them be. We fished ourselves, and yet more often made the geese to fish for us: observing one when he had made a capture and scaring him from his prey ere he had swallowed it.

The strange nature of this place, and the curiosities with which it abounded, held me busy and amused. Escape being impossible, I was allowed my entire liberty, and continually explored the surface of the isle wherever it might support the foot of man. The old garden of the prison was still to be observed, with flowers and pot-herbs running wild, and some ripe cherries on a bush. A little lower stood a chapel or a hermit's cell; who built or dwelt in it, none may know, and the thought of its age made a ground of many meditations. The prison, too, where I now bivouacked with Highland cattle-thieves, was a place full of history, both human and divine. I thought it strange so many saints and martyrs should have gone by there so recently, and left not so much as a leaf out of their Bibles, or a name carved upon the wall, while the rough soldier lads that mounted guard upon the battlements had filled the neighbourhood with their mementoes—broken tobacco-pipes for the most part, and that in a surprising plenty, but also metal buttons from their coats. There were times when I thought I could have

59

heard the pious sound of psalms out of the martyrs' dungeons, and seen the soldiers tramp the ramparts with their glinting pipes, and the dawn rising behind them out of the North Sea.

Edinburgh/Granton—Cramond

Letter to Mrs Frances Sitwell from 17 Heriot Row, Edinburgh, 12 September 1873

After lunch, my father and I went down to the coast and walked a little way along the shore between Granton and Cramond. This has always been with me a very favourite walk. The firth closes gradually together before you, the coast runs in a series of the most beautifully moulded bays, hill after hill, wooded and softly outlined, trends away in front till the two shores join together. When the tide is out, there are great, gleaming flats of wet sand, over which the gulls go flying and crying; and every cape runs down into them with its little spit of wall and trees. We lay together a long time on the beach; the sea just babbled among the stones; and at one time we heard the hollow, sturdy beat of the paddles of an unseen steamer, somewhere round the cape. I am glad to say that the peace of day and scenery was not marred by unpleasantness between us two; indeed I do think things are going a little better with us...[1]

Edinburgh/Granton—South Queensferry

Letter to Mrs Frances Sitwell from Heriot Row, Edinburgh, 24 September 1873

All this beautiful, quiet, sunlit day, I have been out in the country; down by the sea on my own favourite coast between Granton and Queensferry.[1] There was a delicate delicious haze over the firth and sands on one side, and on the other the shadow of the woods was all riven with great golden wefts of sunshine. A little, faint talk of waves upon the beach; the wild strange crying of sea gulls over the sea; and the hoarse wood-pigeons and shrill, sweet robins full of their autumn lovemaking among the trees, made up a delectable concerto of peaceful noises.

South Queensferry and Hawes Inn

From Chapter 6 of *Kidnapped:* I Go to the Queen's Ferry

Just then we came to the top of the hill, and looked down on the Ferry and the Hope. The Firth of Forth (as is very well known) narrows at this point to the width of a good-sized river, which makes a convenient ferry going north, and turns the upper reach into a land-locked haven for all manner of ships. Right in the midst of the narrows lies an islet with some ruins; on the south shore they have built a pier for the service of the Ferry; and at the end of the pier, on the other side of the road, and backed against a pretty garden of holly-trees and hawthorns, I could see the building which they call the Hawes Inn.[1]

The town of Queensferry lies farther west, and the neighbourhood of the inn looked pretty lonely at that time of day, for the boat had just gone north with passengers. A skiff, however, lay beside the pier, with some seamen sleeping on the thwarts; this, as Ransome told me, was the brig's boat waiting for the captain; and about half a mile off, and all alone in the anchorage, he showed me the *Covenant* herself. There was a sea-going bustle on board; yards were swinging into place; and as the wind blew from that quarter, I could hear the song of the sailors as they pulled upon the ropes. After all I had listened to upon the way, I looked at that ship with an extreme abhorrence; and from the bottom of my heart I pitied all poor souls that were condemned to sail in her.

Limekilns, Fife

From Chapter 26 of *Kidnapped:* End of the Flight: We Pass the Forth

All night, then, we walked through the north side of the Carse under the high line of the Ochil mountains; and by Alloa and Clackmannan and Culross, all of which we avoided; and about ten in the morning, mighty hungry and tired, came to the little clachan of Limekilns.[1] This is a place that sits near in by the waterside, and looks across the Hope

61

to the town of the Queensferry. Smoke went up from both of these, and from other villages and farms upon all hands. The fields were being reaped; two ships lay anchored, and boats were coming and going on the Hope. It was altogether a right pleasant sight to me; and I could not take my fill of gazing at these comfortable, green, cultivated hills and the busy people both of the field and sea.

From Inverkeithing to Anstruther

'The Coast of Fife'

Many writers have vigorously described the pains of the first day or the first night at school; to a boy of any enterprise, I believe, they are more often agreeably exciting. Misery—or at least misery unrelieved—is confined to another period, to the days of suspense and the 'dreadful looking-for' of departure; when the old life is running to an end, and the new life, with its new interests, not yet begun; and to the pain of an imminent parting, there is added the unrest of a state of conscious pre-existence. The area-railings, the beloved shop-window, the smell of semi-suburban tanpits, the song of the church bells upon a Sunday, the thin, high voices of compatriot children in a playing-field—what a sudden, what an overpowering pathos breathes to him from each familiar circumstance! The assaults of sorrow come not from within, as it seems to him, but from without. I was proud and glad to go to school; had I been let alone, I could have borne up like any hero; but there was around me, in all my native town, a conspiracy of lamentation: 'Poor little boy, he is going away—unkind little boy, he is going to leave us'; so the unspoken burthen followed me as I went, with yearning and reproach. And at length, one melancholy afternoon in the early autumn, and at a place where it seems to me, looking back, it must be always autumn and generally Sunday, there came suddenly upon the face of all I saw—the long empty road, the lines of the tall houses, the church upon the hill, the woody hillside garden—a look of such a piercing sadness that my heart died; and seating myself on a door-step, I shed tears of miserable sympathy. A benevolent cat cumbered me the while with consolations—we two were alone in all that was visible of the London Road: two poor waifs who had each tasted sorrow—and she fawned upon the weeper, and gambolled for his entertainment, watching the effect, it seemed, with motherly eyes.

For the sake of the cat, God bless her! I confessed at home the story of my weakness; and so it comes about that I owed a certain journey, and the reader owes the present paper, to a cat in the London Road. It was judged, if I had thus brimmed over on the public highway, some change of scene was (in the medical sense) indicated; my father at the time was visiting the harbour lights of Scotland; and it was decided he should take me along with him around a portion of the shores of Fife; my first professional tour, my first journey in the complete character of man, without the help of petticoats.

The Kingdom of Fife (that royal province) may be observed by the curious on the map, occupying a tongue of land between the firths of Forth and Tay. It may be continually seen from many parts of Edinburgh (among the rest, from the windows of my father's house) dying away into the distance and the easterly *haar* with one smoky seaside town beyond another, or in winter printing on the grey heaven some glittering hill-tops. It has no beauty to recommend it, being a low, sea-salted, wind-vexed promontory; trees very rare, except (as common on the east coast) along the dens of rivers; the fields well cultivated, I understand, but not lovely to the eye. It is of the coast I speak: the interior may be the garden of Eden. History broods over that part of the world like the easterly *haar*. Even on the map, its long row of Gaelic place-names bear testimony to an old and settled race. Of these little towns, posted along the shore as close as sedges, each with its bit of harbour, its old weather-beaten church or public building, its flavour of decayed prosperity and decaying fish, not one but has its legend, quaint or tragic: Dunfermline, in whose royal towers the king may be still observed (in the ballad) drinking the blood-red wine;[1] somnolent Inverkeithing, once the quarantine of Leith; Aberdour, hard by the monastic islet of Inchcolm, hard by Donibristle where the 'bonny face was spoiled';[2] Burntisland, where, when Paul Jones[3] was off the coast, the Reverend Mr. Shirra had a table carried between tide-marks, and publicly prayed against the rover at the pitch of his voice and his broad lowland dialect; Kinghorn, where Alexander[4] 'brak's neckbane' and left Scotland to the English wars; Kirkcaldy, where the witches once prevailed extremely and sank tall ships and honest mariners in the North Sea; Dysart, famous—well famous at least to me for the Dutch ships that lay in its harbour, painted like toys and with pots of flowers and cages of song-birds in the cabin windows, and for one particular Dutch skipper who would sit all day in slippers on the break of the poop, smoking a long German pipe; Wemyss (pronounce Weems) with its bat-haunted caves,[5] where the Chevalier Johnstone,[6] on his flight from Culloden, passed a night of superstitious terrors; Leven, a bald, quite modern place, sacred to summer visitors, whence there has gone but

63

yesterday the tall figure and the white locks of the last Englishman in Delhi, my uncle Dr. Balfour,[7] who was still walking his hospital rounds, while the troopers from Meerut clattered and cried 'Deen, Deen' along the streets of the imperial city, and Willoughby mustered his handful of heroes at the magazine, and the nameless brave one in the telegraph office was perhaps already fingering his last despatch; and just a little beyond Leven, Largo Law and the smoke of Largo town mounting about its feet, the town of Alexander Selkirk,[8] better known under the name of Robinson Crusoe. So on, the list might be pursued (only for private reasons, which the reader will shortly have an opportunity to guess) by St. Monans, and Pittenweem, and the two Anstruthers, and Cellardyke, and Crail, where Primate Sharpe[9] was once a humble and innocent country minister: on to the heel of the land, to Fife Ness, overlooked by a sea-wood of matted elders, and the quaint old mansion of Balcomie, itself overlooking but the breach or the quiescence of the deep—the Carr Rock beacon rising close in front, and as night draws in, the star of the Inchcape reef springing up on the one hand, and the star of the May Island on the other, and farther off yet a third and a greater on the craggy foreland of St. Abb's. And but a little way round the corner of the land, imminent itself above the sea, stands the gem of the province and the light of mediaeval Scotland, St. Andrews, where the great Cardinal Beaton held garrison against the world, and the second of the name and title perished (as you may read in Knox's jeering narrative)[10] under the knives of true-blue Protestants, and to this day (after so many centuries) the current voice of the professor is not hushed.

Here it was that my first tour of inspection began, early on a bleak easterly morning. There was a crashing run of sea upon the shore, I recollect, and my father and the man of the harbour light must sometimes raise their voices to be audible. Perhaps it is from this circumstance, that I always imagine St. Andrews to be an ineffectual seat of learning, and the sound of the east wind and the bursting surf to linger in its drowsy classrooms and confound the utterance of the professor, until teacher and taught are alike drowned in oblivion, and only the sea-gull beats on the windows and the draught of the sea-air rustles in the pages of the open lecture. But upon all this, and the romance of St. Andrews in general, the reader must consult the works of Mr. Andrew Lang;[11] who has written of it but the other day in his dainty prose and with his incommunicable humour, and long ago in one of his best poems, with grace, and local truth, and a note of unaffected pathos. Mr. Lang knows all about the romance, I say, and the educational advantages, but I doubt if he had turned his attention to the harbour lights; and it may be news even to him, that in the year 1863 their case was pitiable. Hanging about with the east wind humming in my teeth, and my hands (I make no doubt) in my pockets, I looked for the first time upon that tragi-comedy of the visiting engineer which I have seen so often re-enacted on a more important stage. Eighty years ago, I find my grandfather[12] writing: 'It is the most painful thing that can occur to me to have a correspondence of this kind with any of the keepers, and when I come to the Light House, instead of having the satisfaction to meet them with approbation and welcome their Family, it is distressing when one is obliged to put on a most angry countenance and demean-our.' This painful obligation has been hereditary in my race. I have myself, on a perfectly amateur and unauthorised inspection of Turnberry Point, bent my brows upon the keeper on the question of storm-panes; and felt a keen pang of self-reproach, when we went downstairs again and I found he was making a coffin for his infant child; and then regained my equanimity with the thought that I had done the man a service, and when the proper inspector came, he would be readier with his panes. The human race is perhaps credited with more duplicity than it deserves. The visitation of a lighthouse at least is a business of the most transparent nature. As soon as the boat grates on the shore, and the keepers step forward in their uniformed coats, the very slouch of the fellows' shoulders tells their story, and the engineer may begin at once to assume his 'angry countenance.' Certainly the brass of the hand-rail will be clouded; and if the brass be not immaculate, certainly all will be to match—the reflectors scratched, the spare lamp unready, the storm-panes in the storehouse. If a light is not rather more than middling good, it will be radically bad. Mediocrity (except in literature) appears to be unattainable by man. But of course the unfortunate of St. Andrews was only an amateur, he was not in the Service, he had no uniform coat, he was (I believe) a plumber by his trade and stood (in the mediaeval phrase) quite out of the danger of my father; but he had a painful interview for all that, and perspired extremely.

From St. Andrews, we drove over Magus Muir. My father had announced we were 'to post,' and the phrase called up in my hopeful mind visions of top-boots and the pictures in Rowlandson's *Dance of Death*;[13] but it was only a jingling cab that came to the inn door, such as I had driven in a thousand times at the low price of one shilling on the streets of Edinburgh. Beyond this disappointment, I remember nothing of that drive. It is a road I have often travelled, and of not one of these journeys do I remember any single trait. The fact has not been suffered to encroach on the truth of the imagination. I still see Magus Muir two hundred years ago; a desert place, quite unenclosed; in the midst, the primate's carriage fleeing at the gallop; the assassins loose-reined in pursuit, Burley Balfour,[14] pistol in hand, among the first. No scene of history has ever written itself so deeply on my mind; not because Balfour, that questionable zealot, was an ancestral cousin of my own; not because of the pleadings of the victim and his daughter; not even because of the live bum-bee that flew out of Sharpe's 'bacco-box, thus clearly indicating his complicity with Satan; nor merely because, as it was after all a crime of a fine religious flavour, it figured in Sunday books and afforded a grateful relief from *Ministering Children* or the *Memoirs of Mrs. Katherine Winslowe*. The figure that always fixed my attention is that of Hackston of Rathillet, sitting in the saddle with his cloak about his mouth, and through all that long, bungling, vociferous hurly-burly, revolving privately a case of conscience.[15] He would take no hand in the deed, because he had a private spite against the victim, and 'that action' must be sullied with no suggestion of a worldly motive; on the other hand, 'that action,' in itself was highly justified, he had cast in his lot with 'the actors,' and he must stay there, inactive but publicly sharing the responsibility. 'You are a gentleman—you will protect me!' cried the wounded old man, crawling towards him. 'I will never lay a hand on you,' said Hackston, and put his cloak about his mouth. It is an old temptation with me, to pluck away that cloak and see the face—to open that bosom and to read the heart. With incomplete romances about Hackston, the drawers of my youth were lumbered. I read him up in every printed book that I could lay my hands on. I even dug among the Wodrow[16] manuscripts, sitting shamefaced in the very room where my hero had been tortured two centuries before, and keenly conscious of my youth in the midst of other and (as I fondly thought) more gifted students. All was vain: that he had passed a riotous nonage, that he was a zealot, that he twice displayed (compared with his grotesque companions) some tincture of soldierly resolution and even of military common sense, and that he figured memorably in the scene on Magus Muir, so much and no more could I make out. But whenever I cast my eyes backward, it is to see him like a landmark on the plains of history, sitting with his cloak about his mouth, inscrutable. How small a thing creates an immortality! I do not think he can have been a man entirely commonplace; but had he not thrown his cloak about his mouth, or had the witnesses forgot to chronicle the action, he would not thus have haunted the imagination of my boyhood, and today he would scarce delay me for a paragraph. An incident, at once romantic and dramatic, which at once awakes the judgment and makes a picture for the eye, how little do we realise its perdurable power! Perhaps no one does so but the author, just as none but he appreciates the influence of jingling words; so that he looks on upon life, with something of a covert smile, seeing people led by what they fancy to be thoughts and what are really the accustomed artifices of his own trade, or roused by what they take to be principles and are really picturesque effects. In a pleasant book about a school-class club, Colonel Fergusson has recently told a little anecdote. A 'Philosophical Society' was formed by some Academy boys—among them, Colonel Fergusson[17] himself, Fleeming Jenkin,[18] and Andrew Wilson, the Christian Buddhist and author of *The Abode of Snow*.[19] Before these learned pundits, one member laid the following ingenious problem: 'What would be the result of putting a pound of potassium in a pot of porter?' 'I should think there would be a number of interesting bi-products,' said a smatterer at my elbow; but for me the tale itself was a bi-product, and stands as a type of much that is most human. For this inquirer who conceived himself to burn with a zeal entirely chemical, was really immersed in a design of a quite different nature; unconsciously to his own recently breeched intelligence, he was engaged in literature. Putting, pound, potassium, pot, porter; initial p, mediant t—that was his idea, poor little boy! So with politics and that which excites men in the present, so with history and that which rouses them in the past: there lie at the root of what appears most serious unsuspected elements. The triple town of Anstruther Wester, Anstruther Easter, and Cellardyke, all three Royal Burghs—or two Royal Burghs and a less distinguished suburb, I forget which—lies continuously along the seaside, and boasts of either two or three separate parish churches, and either two or three separate harbours. These ambiguities are painful; but the fact is (although it argue me uncultured), I am but poorly posted upon Cellardyke. My business lay in the two Anstruthers. A tricklet of a stream divides them, spanned by a bridge; and over the bridge at the time of my knowledge, the celebrated Shell House stood outpost on the west. This had been the residence of an agreeable eccentric; during his fond tenancy, he had illustrated the outer walls, as high (if I remember rightly) as the roof, with elaborate patterns and pictures, and snatches of verse in the vein of *exegi monumentum*; shells and pebbles, artfully contrasted and conjoined, had been his medium; and I like to think of him standing back upon the bridge, when all was finished, drinking in the general effect and (like Gibbon) already lamenting his employment.

The same bridge saw another sight in the seventeenth century. Mr. Thomson, the 'curat' of Anstruther Easter,[20] was a man highly obnoxious to the devout: in the first place, because he was a 'curat'; in the second place, because he was a person of irregular and scandalous life; and in the third place, because he was generally suspected of dealings with the Enemy of Man. These three disqualifications, in the popular literature of the time, go hand in hand; but the end of Mr. Thomson was a thing quite by itself, and in the proper phrase, a manifest judgment. He had been at a friend's house in Anstruther Wester, where (and elsewhere, I suspect) he had partaken of the bottle; indeed, to put the thing in our cold modern way, the reverend gentleman was on the brink of *delirium tremens*. It was a dark night, it seems; a little lassie came carrying a lantern to fetch the curate home; and away they went down the street of Anstruther Wester, the lantern swinging a bit in the child's hand, the barred lustre tossing up and down along the front of slumbering houses, and Mr. Thomson not altogether steady on his legs nor (to all appearance) easy in mind. The pair had reached the middle of the bridge when (as I conceive the scene) the poor tippler started in some baseless fear and looked behind him; the child, already shaken by the minister's strange behaviour, started also; in so doing, she would jerk the lantern; and for the space of a moment the lights and the shadows would be all confounded. Then it was that to the unhinged toper and the twittering child, a huge bulk of blackness seemed to sweep down, to pass them close by as they stood upon the bridge, and to vanish on the farther side in the general darkness of the night. 'Plainly the devil come for Mr. Thomson!' thought the child. What Mr. Thomson thought himself, we have no ground of knowledge; but he fell upon his knees in the midst of the bridge like a man praying. On the rest of the journey to the manse, history is silent; but when they came to the door, the poor caitiff, taking the lantern from the child, looked upon her with so lost a countenance that her little courage died within her, and she fled home screaming to her parents. Not a soul would venture out; all that night, the minister dwelt alone with his terrors in the manse; and when the day dawned, and men made bold to go about the streets, they found the devil had come indeed for Mr. Thomson.

This manse of Anstruther Easter has another and a more cheerful association. It was early in the morning, about a century before the days of Mr. Thomson, that his predecessor[21] was called out of bed to welcome a Grandee of Spain, the Duke of Medina Sidonia, just landed in the harbour underneath. But sure there was never seen a more decayed grandee; sure there was never a duke welcomed from a stranger place of exile. Half-way between Orkney and Shetland, there lies a certain isle; on the one hand the Atlantic, on the other the North Sea, bombard its pillared cliffs; sore-eyed, short-living, inbred fishers and their families herd in its few huts; in the graveyard pieces of wreckwood stand for monuments; there is nowhere a more inhospitable

spot. *Belle-Isle-en-Mer*—Fair-Isle-at-Sea—that is a name that has always
rung in my mind's ear like music; but the only 'Fair Isle' on which I
ever set my foot, was this unhomely, rugged turret-top of submarine
sierras. Here, when his ship was broken, my lord Duke joyfully got
ashore; here for long months he and certain of his men were harboured; and it was from this durance that he landed at last to be
welcomed (as well as such a papist deserved, no doubt) by the godly
incumbent of Anstruther Easter; and after the Fair Isle, what a fine city
must that have appeared! and after the island diet, what a hospitable
spot the minister's table! And yet he must have lived on friendly terms
with his outlandish hosts. For to this day there still survives a relic of
the long winter evenings when the sailors of the great Armada crouched
about the hearths of the Fair-Islanders, the planks of their own lost
galleon perhaps lighting up the scene, and the gale and the surf that
beat about the coast contributing their melancholy voices. All the folk
of the north isles are great artificers of knitting: the Fair-Islanders
alone dye their fabrics in the Spanish manner. To this day, gloves and
nightcaps, innocently decorated, may be seen for sale in the Shetland
warehouse at Edinburgh, or on the Fair Isle itself in the catechist's
house; and to this day, they tell the story of the Duke of Medina
Sidonia's adventure.

It would seem as if the Fair Isle had some attraction for 'persons of
quality.' When I landed there myself, an elderly gentleman, unshaved,
poorly attired, his shoulders wrapped in a plaid, was seen walking to and
fro, with a book in his hand, upon the beach. He paid no heed to our
arrival, which we thought a strange thing in itself; but when one of the
officers of the *Pharos*,[22] passing narrowly by him, observed his book to be
a Greek Testament, our wonder and interest took a higher flight. The
catechist was cross-examined; he said the gentleman had been put across
some time before in Mr. Bruce of Sumburgh's[23] schooner, the only link
between the Fair Isle and the rest of the world; and that he held services
and was doing 'good.' So much came glibly enough; but when pressed a
little farther, the catechist displayed embarrassment. A singular diffi-
dence appeared upon his face: 'They tell me,' said he, in low tones, 'that
he's a lord.' And a lord he was; a peer of the realm pacing that inhospitable beach with his Greek Testament, and his plaid about his shoulders,
set upon doing good, as he understood it, worthy man! And his grandson, a good-looking little boy, much better dressed than the lordly
evangelist, and speaking with a silken English accent very foreign to the
scene, accompanied me for a while in my exploration of the island. I
suppose this little fellow is now my lord, and wonder how much he
remembers of the Fair Isle. Perhaps not much; for he seemed to accept

very quietly his savage situation; and under such guidance, it is like that this was not his first nor yet his last adventure.

Kirriemuir, Angus

From letter to J M Barrie from Vailima, 13 July 1894

I wonder my mother could resist the temptation of your proposed visit to Kirriemuir, which it was like your kindness to propose. By the way, I was twice in Kirriemuir, I believe in the year '77, when I was going on a visit to Glenogil.[1] It was Kirriemuir, was it not? I have a distinct recollection of an inn at the end—I think the upper end—of an irregular open place or square, in which I always see your characters evolve. But, indeed, I did not pay much attention; being all bent upon my visit to a shooting-box, where I should fish a real trout-stream, and I believe preserved. I did, too, and it was a charming stream, clear as crystal, without a trace of peat—a strange thing in Scotland—and alive with trout; the name of it I cannot remember, it was something like the Queen's River, and in some hazy way connected with memories of Mary Queen of Scots.[2] It formed an epoch in my life, being the end of all my trout-fishing; I had always been accustomed to pause and very laboriously to kill every fish as I took it. But in the Queen's River I took so good a basket that I forgot these niceties; and when I sat down, in a hard rain shower, under a bank, to take my sandwiches and sherry, lo and behold, there was the basketful of trouts still kicking in their agony. I had a very unpleasant conversation with my conscience. All that afternoon I persevered in fishing, brought home my basket in triumph, and sometime that night, 'in the wee sma' hours ayont the twal,'[3] I finally forswore the gentle craft of fishing. I daresay your local knowledge may identify this historic river; I wish it could go farther and identify also that particular Free Kirk[4] in which I sat and groaned on Sunday. While my hand is in I must tell you a story. At that antique epoch you must not fall into the vulgar error that I was myself ancient. I was, on the contrary, very young, very green, and (what you will appreciate, Mr. Barrie) very shy. There came one day to lunch at the house two very formidable old ladies—or one very formidable, and the other what you please—answering to the honoured and historic name of the Miss Carnegie Arbuthnotts of Balnamoon. At table I was exceedingly funny, and entertained the company with tales of geese and bubbly-jocks [turkey-cocks]. I was great in the expression of my terror

for these bipeds, and suddenly this horrid, severe, and eminently ma-
tronly old lady put up a pair of gold eyeglasses, looked at me awhile in
silence, and pronounced in a clangorous voice her verdict, 'You give
me very much the effect of a coward, Mr. Stevenson!' I had very nearly
left two vices behind me at Glenogil: fishing and jesting at table. And
of one thing you may be very sure, my lips were no more opened at
that meal.

Pitlochry

From letter to Sidney Colvin, from Kinnaird Cottage, Pitlochry, June 1881

My health improves. We have a lovely spot here: a little green glen
with a burn, a wonderful burn, gold and green and snow-white, singing
loud and low in different steps of its career, now pouring over miniature crags, now fretting itself to death in a maze of rocky stairs and
pots; never was so sweet a little river. Behind, great purple moorlands
reaching to Ben Vrackie. Hunger lives here, alone with larks and sheep.
Sweet spot, sweet spot.[1]

Blair Atholl

ATHOLE BROSE[1]

Willie an' I cam doun by Blair
   And in by Tullibardine,
The kye were at the waterside,
   An' bee-skeps in the garden.
I saw the reek of a private still –
   Says I, 'Gud Lord, I thank ye!'
As Willie and I cam in by Blair
   And out by Killiekrankie.

Ye hinny bees, ye smuggler lads,
   Thou, Muse, the bard's protector,
I never kent what kye were for
   Till I had drunk the nectar!

And shall I never drink it mair?
Gud troth, I beg your pardon!
The neist time I come doun by Blair
And in by Tullibardine.

Braemar

From letter to Mrs Frances Sitwell, from The Cottage, Castleton of Braemar, August 1881

Well I have been pretty mean, but I have not yet got over my cold so completely as to have recovered much energy. It is really extraordinary that I should have recovered as well as I have, in this blighting weather; the wind pipes, the rain comes in squalls, great black clouds are continually overhead; and it is as cold as March. The country is delightful, more cannot be said; it is very beautiful, a perfect joy when we get a blink of sun to see it in. The Queen knows a thing or two, I perceive; she has picked out the finest habitable spot in Britain. I wish however she had picked some other.[1]

Anstruther and Wick

'The Education of an Engineer'

Anstruther is a place sacred to the Muse; she inspired (really to a considerable extent) Tennant's vernacular poem *Anster Fair*;[1] and I have there waited upon her myself with much devotion.[2] This was when I came as a young man to glean engineering experience from the building of the breakwater. What I gleaned, I am sure I do not know; but indeed I had already my own private determination to be an author; I loved the art of words and the appearances of life; and *travellers*, and *headers*, and *rubble*, and *polished ashlar*, and *pierres perdues*, and even the thrilling question of the *string-course*, interested me only (if they interested me at all) as properties for some possible romance or as words to add to my vocabulary. To grow a little catholic is the compensation of years; youth is one-eyed; and in those days, though I haunted the breakwater by day, and even loved the place for the sake of the sunshine, the thrilling seaside air, the wash of waves on the sea-face,

72

the green glimmer of the divers' helmets far below, and the musical chinking of the masons, my one genuine preoccupation lay elsewhere, and my only industry was in the hours when I was not on duty. I lodged with a certain Bailie Brown, a carpenter by trade; and there, as soon as dinner was despatched, in a chamber scented with dry rose-leaves, drew in my chair to the table and proceeded to pour forth literature, at such a speed, and with such intimations of early death and immortality, as I now look back upon with wonder. Then it was that I wrote *Voces Fidelium*, a series of dramatic monologues in verse;[3] then that I indited the bulk of a covenanting novel—like so many others, never finished.[4] Late I sat into the night, toiling (as I thought) under the very dart of death, toiling to leave a memory behind me. I feel moved to thrust aside the curtain of the years, to hail that poor feverish idiot, to bid him go to bed and clap *Voces Fidelium* on the fire before he goes; so clear does he appear before me, sitting there between his candles in the rose-scented room and the late night; so ridiculous a picture (to my elderly wisdom) does the fool present! But he was driven to his bed at last without miraculous intervention; and the manner of his driving sets the last touch upon this eminently youthful business. The weather was then so warm that I must keep the windows open; the night without was populous with moths. As the late darkness deepened, my literary tapers beaconed forth more brightly; thicker and thicker came the dusty night-fliers, to gyrate for one brilliant instant round the flame and fall in agonies upon my paper. Flesh and blood could not endure the spectacle; to capture immortality was doubtless a noble enterprise, but not to capture it at such a cost of suffering; and out would go the candles, and off would I go to bed in the darkness, raging to think that the blow might fall on the morrow, and there was *Voces Fidelium* still incomplete. Well, the moths are all gone, and *Voces Fidelium* along with them; only the fool is still on hand and practises new follies.

Only one thing in connection with the harbour tempted me, and that was the diving, an experience I burned to taste of. But this was not to be, at least in Anstruther; and the subject involves a change of scene to the sub-arctic town of Wick.[5] You can never have dwelt in a country more unsightly than that part of Caithness, the land faintly swelling, faintly falling, not a tree, not a hedgerow, the fields divided by single slate stones set upon their edge, the wind always singing in your ears and (down the long road that led nowhere) thrumming in the telegraph wires. Only as you approached the coast was there anything to stir the heart. The plateau broke down to the North Sea in formidable cliffs, the tall out-stacks rose like pillars ringed about with surf, the coves were over-brimmed with clamorous froth, the sea-birds screamed, the wind sang in the thyme on the cliff's edge; here and there, small ancient castles toppled on the brim; here and there, it was possible to dip into a dell of shelter, where you might lie and tell yourself you were a little warm, and hear (near at hand) the whin-pods bursting in the afternoon sun, and (farther off) the rumour of the turbulent sea. As for Wick itself, it is one of the meanest of man's towns, and situate certainly on the baldest of God's bays. It lives for herring, and a strange sight it is to see (of an afternoon) the heights of Pulteney blackened by seaward-looking fishers, as when a city crowds to a review—or, as when bees have swarmed, the ground is horrible with lumps and clusters; and a strange sight, and a beautiful, to see the fleet put silently out against a rising moon, the sea-line rough as a wood with sails, and ever and again and one after another, a boat flitting swiftly by the silver disk. This mass of fishers, this great fleet of boats, is out of all proportion to the town itself; and the oars are manned and the nets hauled by immigrants from the Long Island (as we call the outer Hebrides), who come for that season only, and depart again, if 'the take' be poor, leaving debts behind them. In a bad year, the end of the herring fishery is therefore an exciting time; fights are common, riots often possible; an apple knocked from a child's hand was once the signal for something like a war; and even when I was there, a gunboat lay in the bay to assist the authorities. To contrary interests, it should be observed, the curse of Babel is here added: the Lews men are Gaelic speakers, those of Caithness have adopted English; an odd circumstance, if you reflect that both must be largely Norsemen by descent. I remember seeing one of the strongest instances of this division: a thing like a Punch-and-Judy box erected on the flat grave-stones of the churchyard; from the hutch or proscenium—I know not what to call it—an eldritch-looking preacher laying down the law in Gaelic about some one of the name of *Powl*, whom I at last divined to be the apostle to the Gentiles; a large congregation of the Lews men very devoutly listening; and on the outskirts of the crowd, some of the town's children (to whom the whole affair was Greek and Hebrew) profanely playing tigg. The same descent, the same country, the same narrow sect of the same religion, and all these bonds made very largely nugatory by an accidental difference of dialect!

Into the bay of Wick stretched the dark length of the unfinished breakwater, in its cage of open staging; the travellers (like frames of churches) over-plumbing all; and away at the extreme end, the divers toiling unseen on the foundation. On a platform of loose planks, the assistants turned their air-mills; a stone might be swinging between wind and water; underneath the swell ran gaily; and from time to time, a mailed dragon with a window-glass snout came dripping up the ladder. Youth is a blessed season after all; my stay at Wick was in the year of *Voces Fidelium* and the rose-leaf room at Bailie Brown's; and already I did not care two straws for literary glory. Posthumous ambition perhaps requires an atmosphere of roses; and the more rugged excitant of Wick east winds had made another boy of me. To go down in the diving-dress, that was my absorbing fancy; and with the countenance of a certain handsome scamp of a diver, Bob Bain by name, I gratified the whim.

It was grey, harsh, easterly weather, the swell ran pretty high, and out in the open there were 'skipper's daughters', when I found myself at last on the diver's platform, twenty pounds of lead upon each foot and my whole person swollen with ply and ply of woollen underclothing. One moment, the salt wind was whistling round my night-capped head; the next, I was crushed almost double under the weight of the helmet. As that intolerable burthen was laid upon me, I could have found it in my heart (only for shame's sake) to cry off from the whole enterprise. But it was too late. The attendants began to turn the hurdy-gurdy, and the air to whistle through the tube; some one screwed in the barred window of the vizor; and I was cut off in a moment from my fellow-men; standing there in their midst, but quite divorced from intercourse: a creature deaf and dumb, pathetically looking forth upon them from a climate of his own. Except that I could move and feel, I was like a man fallen in a catalepsy. But time was scarce given me to realise my isolation; the weights were hung upon my back and breast, the signal rope was thrust into my unresisting hand; and setting a twenty-pound foot upon the ladder, I began ponderously to descend.

Some twenty rounds below the platform, twilight fell. Looking up, I saw a low green heaven mottled with vanishing bells of white; looking around, except for the weedy spokes and shafts of the ladder, nothing but a green gloaming, somewhat opaque but very restful and delicious. Thirty rounds lower, I stepped off on the *pierres perdues* of the foundation; a dumb helmeted figure took me by the hand, and made a gesture (as I read it) of encouragement; and looking in at the creature's window, I beheld the face of Bain. There we were, hand to hand and (when it pleased us) eye to eye; and either might have burst himself with shouting, and not a whisper come to his companion's hearing. Each, in his own little world of air, stood incommunicably separate.

Bob had told me ere this a little tale, a five minutes' drama at the bottom of the sea, which at that moment possibly shot across my mind. He was down with another, settling a stone of the sea-wall. They had it well adjusted, Bob gave the signal, the scissors were slipped, the stone set home; and it was time to turn to something else. But still his companion remained bowed over the block like a mourner on a tomb, or only raised himself to make absurd contortions and mysterious signs unknown to the vocabulary of the diver. There, then, these two stood for a while, like the dead and the living; till there flashed a fortunate thought into Bob's mind, and he stooped, peered through the window of that other world, and beheld the face of its inhabitant wet with streaming tears. Ah! the man was in pain! And Bob, glancing downward, saw what was the trouble: the block had been lowered on the foot of that unfortunate—he was caught alive at the bottom of the sea under fifteen tons of rock.

That two men should handle a stone so heavy, even swinging in the scissors, may appear strange to the inexpert. These must bear in mind the great density of the water of the sea, and the surprising results of transplantation to that medium. To understand a little what these are, and how a man's weight, so far from being an encumbrance, is the very ground of his agility, was the chief lesson of my submarine experience. The knowledge came upon me by degrees. As I began to go forward with the hand of my estranged companion, a world of tumbled stones was visible, pillared with the weedy uprights of the staging: overhead, a flat roof of green: a little in front, the sea-wall, like an unfinished rampart. And presently in our upward progress, Bob motioned me to leap upon a stone; I looked to see if he were possibly in earnest, and he only signed to me the more imperiously. Now the block stood six feet high; it would have been quite a leap to me unencumbered; with the breast and back weights, and the twenty pounds upon each foot, and the staggering load of the helmet, the thing was out of reason. I laughed aloud in my tomb; and to prove to Bob how far he was astray, I gave a little impulse from my toes. Up I soared like a bird, my companion soaring at my side. As high as to the stone, and then higher, I pursued my impotent and empty flight. Even when the strong arm of Bob had checked my shoulders, my heels continued their ascent; so that I blew out sideways like an autumn leaf, and must be hauled in, hand over hand, as sailors haul in the slack of a sail, and propped upon my feet again like an intoxicated sparrow. Yet a little higher on the foundation, and we began to be affected by the bottom of the swell, running there like a strong breeze of wind. Or so I must suppose; for, safe in my cushion of air, I was conscious of no impact; only swayed idly like a weed, and was now borne helplessly abroad, and now swiftly—and yet with dream-like gentleness—impelled against my guide. So does a child's balloon divagate upon the currents of the air, and touch, and slide off again from every obstacle. So must have ineffectually swung, so resented their inefficiency, those light clouds that followed the Star of Hades, and uttered exiguous voices in the land beyond Cocytus.

There was something strangely exasperating, as well as strangely wearying, in these uncommanded evolutions. It is bitter to return to infancy, to be supported, and directed, and perpetually set upon your feet, by the hand of someone else. The air besides, as it is supplied to you by the busy millers on the platform, closes the eustachian tubes and keeps the neophyte perpetually swallowing, till his throat is grown so dry that he can swallow no longer. And for all these reasons— although I had a fine, dizzy, muddle-headed joy in my surroundings, and longed, and tried, and always failed, to lay hands on the fish that darted here and there about me, swift as humming-birds—yet I fancy I was rather relieved than otherwise when Bain brought me back to the ladder and signed to me to mount. And there was one more experience before me even then. Of a sudden, my ascending head passed into the trough of a swell. Out of the green, I shot at once into a glory of rosy, almost of sanguine light—the multitudinous seas incarnadined, the heaven above a vault of crimson. And then the glory faded into the hard, ugly daylight of a Caithness autumn, with a low sky, a grey sea, and a whistling wind.

Bob Bain had five shillings for his trouble, and I had done what I desired. It was one of the best things I got from my education as an engineer: of which, however, as a way of life, I wish to speak with sympathy. It takes a man into the open air; it keeps him hanging about harbour-sides, which is the richest form of idling; it carries him to wild islands; it gives him a taste of the genial dangers of the sea; it supplies him with dexterities to exercise; it makes demands upon his ingenuity; it will go far to cure him of any taste (if ever he had one) for the miserable life of cities. And when it has done so, it carries him back and shuts him in an office! From the roaring skerry and the wet thwart of the tossing boat, he passes to the stool and desk; and with a memory full of ships, and seas, and perilous headlands, and the shining pharos, he must apply his long-sighted eyes to the petty niceties of drawing, or measure his inaccurate mind with several pages of consecutive figures. He is a wise youth, to be sure, who can balance one part of genuine life against two parts of drudgery between four walls, and for the sake of the one, manfully accept the other.

Wick was scarce an eligible place of stay. But how much better it was to hang in the cold wind upon the pier, to go down with Bob Bain among the roots of the staging, to be all day in a boat coiling a wet rope and shouting orders—not always very wise—than to be warm and dry, and dull, and dead-alive, in the most comfortable office. And Wick itself had in those days a note of originality. It may have still, but I misdoubt it much. The old minister of Keiss would not preach, in these degenerate times, for an hour and a half upon the clock. The gipsies must be gone from their caverns; where you might see, from the mouth, the women tending their fire, like Meg Merrilies,[6] and the men sleeping off their coarse potations; and where, in winter gales, the surf would beleaguer them closely, bursting in their very door. A traveller to-day upon the Thurso coach would scarce observe a little cloud of smoke among the moorlands, and be told, quite openly, it marked a private still. He would not indeed make that journey, for there is now no Thurso coach. And even if he could, one little thing that happened to me could never happen to him, or not with the same trenchancy of contrast.

We had been upon the road all evening; the coach-top was crowded with Lews fishers going home, scarce anything but Gaelic had sounded in my ears; and our way had lain throughout over a moorish country very northern to behold. Latish at night, though it was still broad day in our sub-arctic latitude, we came down upon the shores of the roaring Pentland Firth, that grave of mariners; on one hand, the cliffs of Dunnet Head ran seaward; in front was the little bare, white town of Castleton, its streets full of blowing sand; nothing beyond, but the North Islands, the great deep, and the perennial ice-fields of the Pole. And here, in the last imaginable place, there sprang up young outlandish voices and a chatter of some foreign speech; and I saw, pursuing the coach with its load of Hebridean fishers—as they had pursued *vetturini* up the passes of the Apennines or perhaps along the grotto under Virgil's tomb—two little dark-eyed, white-toothed Italian vagabonds, of twelve to fourteen years of age, one with a hurdy-gurdy, the other with a cage of white mice. The coach passed on, and their small Italian chatter died in the distance; and I was left to marvel how they had wandered into that country, and how they fared in it, and what they thought of it, and when (if ever) they should see again the silver wind-breaks run among the olives, and the stone-pine stand guard upon Etruscan sepulchres.

Upon any American, the strangeness of this incident is somewhat lost. For as far back as he goes in his own land, he will find some alien camping there; the Cornish miner, the French or Mexican half-blood, the negro in the south, these are deep in the woods and far among the mountains. But in an old, cold, and rugged country such as mine, the days of immigration are long at an end; and away up there, which was at that time far beyond the northernmost extreme of railways, hard upon the shore of that ill-omened strait of whirlpools, in a land of moors where no stranger came, unless it should be a sportsman to shoot grouse or an antiquary to decipher runes, the presence of these small pedestrians struck the mind as though a bird of paradise had risen from the heather or an albatross come fishing in the bay of Wick. They were as strange to their surroundings as my lordly evangelist or the old Spanish grandee on the Fair Isle.[7]

Orkney—Kirkwall

Extracts from letters to his mother from the lighthouse steamer, 18-22 June 1869

The first sight one gets of Kirkwall is rather striking—a cluster of grey roofs with the red Cathedral[1] and a knot of umber ruin at the top, and the sea at its foot, running into a long and shallow creek which is severed from the open ocean by a ridge or bar of sand with some walls atop.

The whole aspect of the town is distinctly English. The houses, white with harl, present crowstepped gables and picturesque chimneys to the street; while on one hand, through an arched gateway, one catches a cool glimpse of a paven entrance court. Some of these arches are green with burdock and grass, and even with fern; and, to render the likeness to a village of the Riviera a thought more striking, on one occasion at least, there was a secondary arch within the first uselessly spanning the stone passage, a nest for weed and a roosting place for fowls. The slates are greyish white without the smallest tinge of colour; so it is a great relief to the general whiteness of wall and roof, to see green trees of decent size spreading in the court within. Above the doors there are inscriptions and emblems. On one, we saw a burning heart with some initials and the date 1743; on another 'Deo Soli Gloria'— 'To the one God Glory'; and on a third the emphatic and epigrammatic command 'Amet'—'Let him love', the allusion whereof it is hard to divine.

But the glory of Kirkwall, as of Salisbury, lies about its Cathedral. The High Street—which, I omitted to observe, is narrow and paven with the exception of a strip of causeway some two feet wide in the centre, so that there are four lines of kerb-stone in the width—opens out on your left into a sort of green. Just as you enter it, on the right, is the most noticeable courtyard and gate that we saw. Between two gables, rich in crowstep and weighted with squat stone chimneys, the arch stretched across supporting a somewhat heavy balcony, in the centre of which was the inscription 'Except the Lord' etc., and the date 1574; while an iron lamp, of a battered and rakish exterior was supported by an upright spike on the cornice. We went down into the broad cool court, lined on three sides with white houses and on the fourth with a high brown wall, out of whose shadow you could see the sunshine on the streets through the old archway. But what struck us most was an inner bartizan or terrace behind the cornice of the gate, attained by a flight of foot-broad stone steps, which it seemed must have been meant for defence in the time when the burgher who held it had to make good his house against the drunken servants of the earl or the pirate crews of Captain John Goffe[2] and his like.

The Cathedral, then, drawing back its skirts from the street, stands apart on a raised green, with its face towards the picturesque gables of the High Street and bordered on another side by a broad road that runs betwixt the graveyard and the twin ruins of the Bishop's and the Earl's Palaces. At the corner of this green between the High Street and this roadway, stands an old white house on a triple arcade closed with antique iron gratings and entered by an iron-studded door, which I believe I have identified with the Town House. The one remaining side of the High Street at this place is worthy of notice, because of two quaint old bow windows, projecting above the footway on massive corbelling; and between these houses and the church, within the two-foot wall that guards the precinct of the green, you see three broad stone steps, buried in dock and nettle, from the centre of which projects a forlorn spike of stone to show what was once the market cross. Going round the Town House again, turning up the road alongside of the burying ground, and passing an iron gate thereinto, somewhat in the fashion of the Town House rails and surmounted by a lamp similar to that above the old arch, you come to the twin palaces standing on either side of a pleasant looking lane. The Earl's Palace[3] stands among a thick grove of green plane trees, whence it shows its great corbelled bow windows, symptoms rather of manorial comfort than feudal warfare. The Bishop's adjoins to an old inhabited house which gives an air of homeliness to its quaint outline; for what with the umber-brown walls contrasting with scarlet quoins, and little pieces of statuary let into the solid masonry of the round tower, and the confused whirl of corbel and corner and stair and ragged gable which forms the projecting summit, one rarely sees so bizarre and uncouth a ruin.

And now, having disposed of the minor curiosities that cluster like chickens round a hen, about its lordly shadow, I may go on to the grand old Cathedral, which towers, with narrow gables and slope slate roof and wonder of red stonework and white, above the little green and the little grey town on the seaboard. You enter through the usual triple door of Gothic churches at the foot of the tall, narrow gables with moulding of alternate red and white and red columns crumbled down to the consistency of Madeira cake. Once in, you see the nave and the screen at the far end that shuts out the choir. It is as narrow and as tall as the outside has led you to expect. The roof, groined with red on dusky grey, is supported on tall black shafts, with no windows on the clerestory but a row of the dwarf Norman windows which prevail immediately above. In each aisle, there stands a row of dark monumental tablets. One in particular I noticed, showing the figure of a deformed woman with her back hair down weeping above a skull and cross bones, strangely mixed in with the following inscription: 'August 1756. Here was interred the corse of Margaret Young spouse of John Kiddoch, then one of the magistrates of Kirkwall and after Provost of the said Burgh. She lived regarded, and died regretted.' On a column not far distant was the tablet of another Kiddoch married to another Young; a system of intermarriage which seems in as great force now as ever, according to stories I was hearing today. For example, the two ministers of the Established Church have married sisters; and their brother-in-law has taken-to-wife a member of his mother's family which is in some way connected to them.

From the corner of the chancel just below the square tower you get the best look of the sombre church, with its black and scarlet stonework and its Catherine wheel at the chancel end; and hence you ascend to the belfry and the top of the church. And here I must fairly give up any hope, and my hope from the first has been feeble, to give you any idea of this delightful old church. From every corner of the tower, a corkscrew staircase ascends, giving admittance into passages along the blind clerestory of nave, choir and chancels: thence more stairs and narrower passages still—where one has to go on sidelong like a crab in a rock-cleft —leading along past the little windows of the nave, and between the double windows of the choir: thence more stairs to the dusty and lumbered lofts above the groined roof and to the belfry, criss-crossed by great unpainted wooden beams and hung with the big bells, on whose mellow sides the modern sacristan rings a stormy chime; and thence, by ladder to the outside of the tower. This is the climax: below you like a knife-edge the sharp ridge and swift slope of the two slate roofs each with its broad leaden gutters, the kirkyard with its stones, the little green, the ruins and the cluster of grey-slate roofs crouching at your feet. I wish I could let you feel, as I felt, these little stairs and passages—this network or web of dark and narrow alleys, with the very smallest windows sometimes, and sometimes with no windows at all. You expect to meet a 'priest in surplice white that defunctive music knows',[4] a sexton in hose and steeple hat, a tonsured monk, a mitred Bishop worn with conflict against Heathen Earls and savage boors, at every corner of the dusty maze; and when you come forth on the surface, the roof looks like that on which Dom Claude descends and breaks his fall, ere he plunges finally to the causeway below.[5] I know nothing so suggestive of legend, so full of superstition, so stimulating to a weird imagination, as the nooks and corners and bye-ways of such a church as St Magnus, in Kirkwall.

We then went down to the pier, where indeed we had a lamentable wakening and grievous revocation from Middle-Ages dreamland to everyday vulgarity and affectation. A London engineer has erected an iron jetty, like the ornamental bridge over the water in a cockney tea-garden—a gimcrack lane of carven lamp-posts—infinitely neat and infinitely shaky—a nursemaids' walk, that might have done at Greenwich, projecting into the easterly surge from Pomona the mainland of Orkney. Alas! alas!

Shetland—Whalsay—Unst—Lerwick

Extracts from letters to his mother from the lighthouse steamer, 18-22 June 1869

We are now fairly in Shetland—a fair, cold day with a low, leaden sky such as I am told they have here all the summer through: a bountiful provision of nature, by the way, as a very little sunshine would scorch their crops to nothing. It is higher, bleaker, and darker than Orkney; but, for the rest, the same—an archipelago of bare islets, with ruinous-looking cottages and brown ends of cliff cropping up here and there along the beach—and divided too by the same winding sounds with blind angles and tide races every mile or half-mile.

We have just passed a ruined castle on a hillock, built of mixed red and black like St Magnus and the Bishop's Palace and clasping in its walls a modern mansion house, resplendent with whitewash and called Burg Hall. The cottages about it seem mostly deserted; and this I am told is very much the way; for life is nearly impossible in Shetland

now-a-days. Before they lived on their knitting—took a pair of hose to
the store and brought back meal in exchange, or gave three eggs and
received a pirn of thread. In this way, however, they clad themselves
and got everything but the potatoes which they planted and the fish
they caught; and thus there was a man in Unst, whose yearly income
was fifteen shillings and whose yearly rent was ten, leaving a margin of
five solitary shillings—sixty copper pennies for himself and family.
Nowadays, this is impracticable; and the reason I understand is want of
wool to knit; but of this I am not sure.

This morning we landed on the Bound Skerry of Whalsey,[1] a shelf
of rock, the outmost of a group of islets to the east of Shetland. It is of
quartzose rock, of a salmon colour at a fracture, but growing black with
weather. Here the light was inspected, and the keepers took us down to
show us the rock torn up by the sea. One great big fellow ten feet long
and between two and three feet deep had been shifted about tremen-
dously, and had scored grooves, half an inch deep, wherever it went
with its knife-like edges. This is some fifty feet above the sea.

* * *

The coast beyond the embouchure of Blumel Sound, the western seaboard of Unst, is wild and rugged, dark cliffs riven with inky voes and
caverns, white with sea birds, marked here and there by natural arches,
and crowned with round hills of sere sun-burnt grass. In about half an
hour we sighted North Unst Lighthouse,[2] the most northern dwelling
house in Her Majesty's dominion. The mainland rises higher, with
great seams and landslips; and from the norwestern corner runs out a
string of shelving ledges, with a streak of green and purple seaweed and
a boil of white foam about their feet. The Lighthouse stands on the
highest—190 feet above the sea; and there is only an uninhabited reef
called the Out Stack[3] between it and the Faroe Islands.

* * *

We were pulled into the creek… between the Lighthouse and the other
rock, down the centre of which runs a line of reef… This is very
narrow, little broader than a knife edge; but its ridge has been cut into
stone steps and laid with iron grating and railed with an iron railing. It
was here that we landed, making a leap between the swells at a rusted
iron ladder laid slant-wise against the raking side [of] the ridge. Before
us a flight of stone steps led up the two hundred feet to the lighthouse
in its high yard-walls across whose foot the sea had cast a boulder

weighing twenty tons. On one side is a slippery face of clear sound rock; and on the other a chaos of pendulous boulder and rotten stone. On either side there was no vegetation save tufts of sea-pink in the crevices and a little white lichen on the lee faces. The lighthouse was in good order. We are now returning by Blumel Sound[4] to Sunday at Lerwick.

By the way, there is no part of Shetland three miles away from the sea: Mr Andrews and I tried it with the compass; so there is no mistake about it.

* * *

Lerwick lies in the hollow angle of a winding sound between the mainland of Shetland and the Island of Bressay. As we came up we saw many people on a gravel spit at the corner, drying fish on the baked white stones. The houses present their one gable to the water which laves their foundations and their other to the main street which runs parallel to the line of the shore. When we landed—about eight—this narrow way was swarming with people. It is paved from wall to wall with broad flat paving stones; and the resemblance to a Riviera village is further heightened by the narrow side-lanes, which climb the hillside on long flights of ruinous steps between high houses on either hand. At the north of the town stands Fort Charlotte,[5] founded, as I hear, by Cromwell. It overhangs the water with a circuit of heavy grass grown walls, backed by mounds supported by ruinous buttresses and pierced by some four arched gateways. The sea-pink blooms thickly among the lichened crevices of the old stonework. Inside there are two whitewashed buildings, a few sheds for the exercise of the naval reserve—four hundred of whom appear every winter on their return from the whale and seal fishing, and a great black looking tank, as old, I suppose, as the fort and lipping with repulsive looking water. The largest of these buildings is the jail and court-house—a long, low house with massive leaden gutters bearing the initials of George II[6] and the date seventeen hundred and eighty. The court is held in the upper part; and the lower windows each shaded by a wooden hutch have a melancholy interest in our eyes; for, not many days ago, a young man was sentenced to forty-five days imprisonment for shooting ducks at Unst, who hanged himself behind the midmost of these blank windows before the first night had come.

* * *

Four bells—midnight—has rung some time ago. Upstairs it is perfectly calm, the sky very dark with mottling of white and grey cirrus, and the yellow moon half out, half in the clouds above the houses of the town—the whole thing mirrored to perfection in the water of the Sound. Some fishermen are singing on the shore, probably in imitation of Italy; for they please themselves by calling Lerwick the northern Venice. This appearance is heightened by the excessive lightness.

Shetland—Lerwick—Pict's House—Sumburgh—Fair Isle

Extracts from letters to his mother from the lighthouse steamer, 18-22 June 1869

[More on Lerwick:] Between the house gables turned toward the Sound, there run down stairs and jetties every here and there, for more convenience of landing. One of these and that at which we have landed most frequently, was beside an old, square house with a belfry atop and a sort of terrace towards the street, with balustraded stair, used as the Town Hall. As with all the others, the green still water licks its very stones; but there is a projecting out house, butting forth among the wavelets, rendered noticeable by the wealth of some strange white blossom that hides its blue slate roof. The high street, too, as I forgot to notice, is not only irregular in direction, but also in width; sometimes a long house thrusts its gable far across and pens it in to a short ten feet; and sometimes the houses fall away in irregular open spaces, not unlike the little squares in the back slums of Venice.

* * *

The town of Lerwick stands on a low hill, circled in front by the sea, and behind by the loch of Klikomin[1] ('Klik'em in' is the way it's said), so that four roads alone join it to the island—one of them on an isthmus and the others on mere dykes. In this sheet of water, stands the Pict's House...

From a sandy point, on which the little ripple lays curves of strange looking emerald slime, there stretches out a causeway of rough stones, defended near the far end by two square piles of stones with a narrow pass between to act, I suppose, very much as the...[2] that covered the drawbridge of a feudal castle. The whole islet, thus joined to the mainland is buried in stones and stone ramparts, with many unroofed underground chambers; and the centre is occupied by a hollow round tower not unlike to a lime-kiln. In the thickness of its walls are passages along which I had to creep on all fours, stairs with steps three inches wide, round chambers buried in perfect darkness and small doorways, like coal hatches in a modern house, which seem to have led by covered ways to the outlying subterranean rooms. The people who built and occupied Maes-How[3] must have been two or three feet high at the outside; and there is I think something singularly disgusting in the whole idea. I fancied the place swarming with little dirty devils talking outlandish jargon and brandishing their flint-head axes; and, with the natural human hatred for swarms of minute life, I confess that I brought myself to share in the horror of these old 'Peghts' which is felt in Orkney and Shetland to this day.

In a note to the *Pirate*[4] you will find a good story illustrative of this. There came a travelling missionary to the island of North Ronaldsha, and, being wearied with journeying, he went straightway to the house of the teacher and there lay down to sleep. But, as ill luck would have it, he had been observed by the people, who instantly concluded from his small frame and dark visage that he was one of the old Picts, whether in the body or out of the body they could not tell; so they gathered about the house with evil intentions. The schoolmaster feared for his guest's bodily safety, and, bethinking him of my grandfather, who was then in the island, he sent a messenger for him and asked him to pacify the angry Norsemen. Unwilling to wake the fatigued man, he tried to convince them of their mistake by showing them the clumsy boots which he had left outside the door; but they would not be persuaded; and at last he was obliged to go in. Fortunately he recognized the man as having been a shopkeeper in Edinburgh before he became a missionary and set their suspicions at rest.

We then walked up the road a small way in a valley with a burn. The lowlands were cultivated after a skimble-skamble fashion: ruinous walls ran here and there sometimes wandering aimlessly into the middle of the fields and there ending with as little show of reason, sometimes gathering into gross heaps of loose stone more like an abortive cairn than an honest dry-stone dyke; for crop, it seemed that docken and the yellow wild mustard, which made bright patches every here and there, were much more plentiful than turnip or corn. Mixed up with this unwholesome looking wilderness were thatched cottages bearing every sign of desertion and decay except the curl of smoke from the place where the chimney should be and was not; and in some cases presenting bare gables and roofless walls to the bitter ocean breeze. The uplands were a sere yellow brown, with rich full-coloured streaks of peat, and grey stretches of outcropping rock. The whole place looks dreary and wretched; for here, nature, as Hawthorne would have said, has not sufficient power to take back to herself what the idleness and absence of man has let go. There is no ivy for the ruined cottage: no thorn or bramble for the waste way-side.

We returned again to the water-stair beside the town hall and waved a handkerchief for the gig, a romantic action which made me remember many old daydreams when it was my only wish to be a pirate or a smuggler.

* * *

This morning we have visited Sumburgh Head Lighthouse.[5] This, the southermost point of Shetland as Unst is the most northerly, is joined to the mainland by a very narrow isthmus of low sandhills and thin bent grass. There is shoal water on either hand or the sea would soon carry it away. Inshore of this isthmus, the land is high and bare, with the huge crags of Fitful Head running out a few miles off. Among these sandhills, on a grassy mound, stand some low and ruinous house-walls, all that remains of Jarlshof, so often mentioned in the *Pirate*;[6] and a little way above it, an elegant new house built by Mr Bruce of Sumburgh.[7]...

By the way is there not something grand in that name of Sumburgh— a low hollow boom, as it were of bursting surf.

We pulled in to a small slip on the beach with some grey houses at its head, one of which purported to sell 'Tea and Tobacco' with blotches where 'Spirits and Ale' had been painted out—a silent commentary on the habits of the people. We had then two miles to walk along the narrow headland, which rises in precipitous cliffs to the east and on the west stretches down to the sea in a gentle sweep of spring turf. Here and there, however, the voes run in on either hand with a rush of water and a screaming of gulls, and leave but a neck of land three hundred feet above the surf. For all that, the spray flies over it in clouds. Down in these voes, we saw the white gulls sitting on their eggs and the young ones beginning to walk about. We then visited the light and went on board again, passing easily through a jabble of short cresting waves which, in spring tides and heavy gales, is the fatal Sumburgh Roost.

* * *

87

The coast of the Fair Isle is the wildest and most unpitying that we have yet seen.[8] Continuous cliffs from one to four hundred feet high, torn by huge voes and echoing caverns, line the bare downs with scarcely a cove of sand or a practicable cleft in the belt of iron precipice. At intervals it runs out into strange peninsulas, square bluff headlands, and plumb faces of stone, tinged with the faint green of some sort of lichen.

* * *

The land... slopes almost continuously from the low shore on one side to the cliff top at the other; but in two places, the ground suddenly leaves your feet and you see a large rocky tank, some seventy feet deep, with a great arched doorway onto the ocean, right through the hill-side: the noise of a stone dropped in, reverberates with a hollow boom and splash up the rough sides on either hand. Close by there was a fine, graceful curve of beach, surrounded by red cliffs, and strangely marked by a great red stack or isolated pillar, standing among the heaped brown sea-weed on the sweep of the bay.

On our return we entered a house. They are here in three rooms. The first one is a byre; the second, the kitchen; the third, what they call 'the room'. This last was locked, so we did not see it; but the kitchen was open to curious eyes, with no more inhabitants than a large yellow cat and a small grey kitten. You entered by the door from the byre—none of the doors are above four feet high—and then saw opposite to you the door into 'the room', with the fire immediately in front of it on some large flat stones and with a stone standing upright behind it. The smoke escapes through three holes in the thatch and hangs in blue clouds among the rafters. All the furniture was on one side, and consisted principally of wooden armchairs and Fair Isle arm-chairs— that is with a frame of wood and a back of plaited straw. For such a cottage and croft, they only pay £4 or £3.10 a year; and the rent of the whole island, exclusive of fishing, is no more than £150.

* * *

We then went on to the church, a cottage set with plain unvarnished benches and a ditto pulpit—neat and tidy, however, and seated for two hundred and fifty. Outside was a small graveyard, with headstones consisting of rough slates about a foot high thrust into the ground. On two alone are there any letters; and these two are made of wood and cut by a man in the island. They were two of the oldest men that had ever died in the place, and yet the ages were but 61 and 64 respectively. Intermarriage and bad houses makes them a weak lot; and almost none of the women, as I hear, have good eyes. One of these inscriptions I had the curiosity to copy, by reason of the error it contains. 'In Memor*ium* of T. Wilson. Born January 5th 1801. Died January 13th 1865. Aged 64 years and 8 days. Time flies.' My father took out his knife to alter the mistake; but Mr MacFarlane stopped him, as the people would have looked on it as insulting the dead. Apropos of tombstones, the same gentleman told us that there [were] some lettered stones on the hill top, but what the inscriptions meant he was unable to tell us.

From the church we proceeded to the store, where tea, teapots, linen and blankets are sold to the inhabitants; and where the inhabitants expose, on the other hand, their quaint-patterned parti-coloured knitted socks, cowls, gloves and mittens.

During our absence, his Lordship had been taking Mr Curry about among the sick folk; and he said that of all the miserable people he had ever seen, they were the worst. Two twin old women of six and eighty years, literal skeletons, lived in misery and sickness in a wretched den waited on by the daughter of one, now well up in years herself. One of these had burnt her foot the day before, and the cloth she had wrapped about it was no finer than ordinary sacking. Their only hope was in death.

Such more or less seems the condition of the people. Beyond reach of all communication, receiving such stray letters as may come not once in six long months, with diseased bodies, and wretched homes, they drag out their lives in the wildest and most barren island of the north. Their crops, raised after hard labour from a cold and stony soil, can only support them for three months out of the twelve. Indeed their only life is from the sea. It is the sea that brings the fish to their nets: it is the sea that strews their shore with the spoils of wrecked vessels (thus we saw in the minister's house, a huge German musical box saved from the wreck of the *Lessing*).[9]

From Wick to Golspie

From Sketch, 'Night outside the Wick Mail'

First stage:[1] Lybster. A Roman Catholic priest travelling within, knowing that I was delicate, made me take his seat inside for the next stage. I dozed. When I woke, the moon was shining brightly. We were off the moors and up among the high grounds near the Ord of Caithness. I remember seeing a curious thing: the moon shone on the ocean, and on a river swollen to a great pool and between stretched a great black mass of rock; I wondered dimly how the river got out and then to doze again. When next I wake, we have passed the low Church of Berriedale, standing sentinel on the heathery plateau northward of the valley, and are descending the steep road past the Manse: I think it was about one: the moon was frosty but gloriously clear. In another minute—

Second stage: Berriedale. And of all lovely places, one of the loveliest. Two rivers run from the inner hills, at the bottom of two deep, Killiekrankie-like gorges, to meet in a narrow bare valley close to the grey North Ocean. The high Peninsula between and the banks, on either hand until they meet, are thickly wooded—birch and fir. On one side is the bleak plateau with the lonesome little church, on the other the bleaker, wilder mountain of the Ord. When I and the priest had lit our pipes, we crossed the streams, now speckled with the moonlight that filtered through the trees, and walked to the top of the Ord. There the coach overtook us and away we went for a stage, over great, bleak mountains, with here and there a hanging wood of silver birches and here and there a long look of the moonlit sea, the white ribbon of the road marked far in front by the newly erected telegraph posts. We were all broad awake with our walk, and made very merry outside, proffering 'fills' of tobacco and pinches of snuff and dipping surreptitiously into aristocratic flasks and plebeian pint bottles.

Third stage: Helmsdale. Round a great promontory with the gleaming sea far away in front, and rattling through some sleeping streets that shone strangely white in the moonlight, and then we pull up beside the Helmsdale posting-house, with a great mountain valley behind.

* * *

Fourth stage: name unknown. O sweet little spot, how often I have longed to be back to you! A lone farm-house on the sea-shore, shut in on three sides by the same, low, wooded hills. Men were waiting for us by the roadside, with the horses—sleepy, yawning men. What a peaceful place it was! Everything *steeped* in the moonlight, and the gentle plash of the waves coming to us from the beach. On again. Through Brora, where we stopped at the Post-Office and exchanged letter-bags through a practicable window-pane, as they say in stage directions. Then on again. Near Golspie now, and breakfast, and the roaring railway. Passed Dunrobin, the dew-steeped, tree-dotted park, the princely cluster of its towers, rising from bosky plantations and standing out against the moon-shimmering sea—all this sylvan and idyllic beauty so sweet and new to me! Then the Golspie Inn, and breakfast and another pipe, as the morning dawned, standing in the verandah. And then round to the station to fall asleep in the train.

Skye, Mull, Rhum, Eigg

Sing me a song of a lad that is gone,[1]
  Say, could that lad be I?
Merry of soul he sailed on a day
  Over the sea to Skye.

Mull was astern, Rhum on the port,
  Eigg on the starboard bow;
Glory of youth glowed in his soul:
  Where is that glory now?

Sing me a song of a lad that is gone,
  Say, could that lad be I?
Merry of soul he sailed on a day
  Over the sea to Skye.

Give me again all that was there,
  Give me the sun that shone!
Give me the eyes, give me the soul,
  Give me the lad that's gone!

Sing me a song of a lad that is gone,
  Say, could that lad be I?
Merry of soul he sailed on a day
  Over the sea to Skye.

Billow and breeze, islands and seas,
  Mountains of rain and sun,
All that was good, all that was fair,
  All that was me is gone.

Oban

Extract from letter to his mother from Earraid, 4th August 1870

At Oban, that night, it was delicious. Mr Stephenson's[1] yacht lay in the bay, and a splendid band on board played delightfully. The waters of the bay were as smooth as a millpond; and, in the dusk, the black shadows of the hills stretched across to our very feet and the lights were reflected in long lines. At intervals, blue lights were burned on the water; and rockets were sent up. Sometimes great stars of clear fire fell from them, until the bay received and quenched them. I hired a boat and sculled round the yacht in the dark. When I came in, a very pleasant Englishman on the steps fell into talk with me, till it was time to go to bed.

Next morning I slept on or I should have gone to Glencoe. As it was, it was blazing hot; so I hired a boat, pulled all forenoon along the coast and had a delicious bathe on a beautiful white beach.

Earraid

'Memoirs of An Islet'

Those who try to be artists use, time after time, the matter of their recollections, setting and resetting little coloured memories of men and scenes, rigging up (it may be) some especial friend in the attire of a buccaneer, and decreeing armies to manoeuvre, or murder to be done, on the playground of their youth. But the memories are a fairy gift which cannot be worn out in using. After a dozen services in various tales, the little sunbright pictures of the past still shine in the mind's eye with not a lineament defaced, not a tint impaired. *Glück und Unglück wird Gesang,*[1] if Goethe pleases; yet only by endless avatars, the original re-embodying after each. So that a writer, in time, begins to wonder at the perdurable life of these impressions; begins, perhaps, to fancy that he wrongs them when he weaves them in with fiction; and looking back on them with ever-growing kindness, puts them at last, substantive jewels, in a setting of their own.

One or two of these pleasant spectres I think I have laid. I used one but the other day: a little eyot of dense, freshwater sand, where I once waded deep in butterburrs, delighting to hear the song of the river on both sides, and to tell myself that I was indeed and at last upon an island. Two of my puppets lay there a summer's day, hearkening to the shearers at work in riverside fields and to the drums of the grey old garrison upon the neighbouring hill. And this was, I think, done rightly: the place was rightly peopled—and now belongs not to me but to my puppets—for a time at least. In time, perhaps, the puppets will grow faint; the original memory swim up instant as ever; and I shall once more lie in bed, and see the little sandy isle in Allan Water as it is in nature, and the child (that once was me) wading there in butterburrs; and wonder at the instancy and virgin freshness of that memory; and be pricked again, in season and out of season, by the desire to weave it into art.

There is another isle in my collection, the memory of which besieges me. I put a whole family there, in one of my tales;[2] and later on, threw upon its shores, and condemned to several days of rain and shellfish on its tumbled boulders, the hero of another.[3] The ink is not yet faded; the sound of the sentences is still in my mind's ear; and I am under a spell to write of that island again.

I

The little isle of Earraid[4] lies close in to the south-west corner of the Ross of Mull: the sound of Iona on one side, across which you may see the isle and church of Columba; the open sea to the other, where you shall be able to mark, on a clear, surfy day, the breakers running white on many sunken rocks. I first saw it, or first remembered seeing it, framed in the round bull's-eye of a cabin port, the sea lying smooth along its shores like the waters of a lake, the colourless, clear light of the early morning making plain its heathery and rocky hummocks. There stood upon it, in these days, a single rude house of uncemented stones, approached by a pier of wreckwood. It must have been very early, for it was then summer, and in summer, in that latitude, day scarcely withdraws; but even at that hour the house was making a sweet smoke of peats which came to me over the bay, and the bare-legged daughters of the cotter were wading by the pier. The same day we visited the shores of the isle in the ship's boats; rowed deep into Fiddler's Hole, sounding as we went; and having taken stock of all possible accommodation, pitched on the northern inlet as the scene of operations. For it was no accident that had brought the lighthouse steamer to anchor in the Bay of Earraid. Fifteen miles away to seaward, a certain black rock stood environed by the Atlantic rollers, the outpost of the Torran reefs.

Here was a tower to be built, and a star lighted, for the conduct of seamen. But as the rock was small, and hard of access, and far from land, the work would be one of years; and my father was now looking for a shore station, where the stones might be quarried and dressed, the men live, and the tender, with some degree of safety, lie at anchor.

I saw Earraid next from the stern thwart of an Iona lugger, Sam Bough[5] and I sitting there cheek by jowl, with our feet upon our baggage, in a beautiful, clear, northern summer eve. And behold! there was now a pier of stone, there were rows of sheds, railways, travelling-cranes, a street of cottages, an iron house for the resident engineer, wooden bothies for the men, a stage where the courses of the tower were put together experimentally, and behind the settlement a great gash in the hillside where granite was quarried. In the bay, the steamer lay at her moorings. All day long there hung about the place the music of chinking tools; and even in the dead of night, the watchman carried his lantern to and fro in the dark settlement, and could light the pipe of any midnight muser. It was, above all, strange to see Earraid on the Sunday, when the sound of the tools ceased and there fell a crystal quiet. All about the green compound men would be sauntering in their Sunday's best, walking with those lax joints of the reposing toiler, thoughtfully smoking, talking small, as if in honour of the stillness, or hearkening to the wailing of the gulls. And it was strange to see our Sabbath services, held, as they were, in one of the bothies, with Mr. Brebner reading at a table, and the congregation perched about in the double tier of sleeping bunks; and to hear the singing of the psalms, 'the chapters,' the inevitable Spurgeon's sermon, and the old, eloquent lighthouse prayer.

In fine weather, when by the spy-glass on the hill the sea was observed to run low upon the reef, there would be a sound of preparation in the very early morning; and before the sun had risen from behind Ben More, the tender would steam out of the bay. Over fifteen sea-miles of the great blue Atlantic rollers she ploughed her way, trailing at her tail a brace of wallowing stone-lighters. The open ocean widened upon either board, and the hills of the mainland began to go down on the horizon, before she came to her unhomely destination, and lay-to at last where the rock clapped its black head above the swell, with the tall iron barrack on its spider legs, and the truncated tower, and the cranes waving their arms, and the smoke of the engine-fire rising in the mid-sea. An ugly reef is this of the Dhu Heartach; no pleasant assemblage of shelves, and pools, and creeks, about which a child might play for a whole summer without weariness, like the Bell Rock[6] or the Skerryvore,[7] but one oval nodule of black-trap, sparsely bedabbled with an inconspicuous fucus, and alive in every crevice with a dingy insect between a slater and a bug. No other life was there but that of sea-birds, and of the sea itself, that here ran like a mill-race, and growled about the outer reef for ever, and ever and again, in the calmest weather, roared and spouted on the rock itself. Times were different upon Dhu Heartach when it blew, and the night fell dark, and the neighbour lights of Skerryvore and Rhu-val were quenched in fog, and the men sat prisoned high up in their iron drum, that then resounded with the lashing of the sprays. Fear sat with them in their sea-beleaguered dwelling; and the colour changed in anxious faces when some greater billow struck the barrack, and its pillars quivered and sprang under the blow. It was then that the foreman builder, Mr. Goodwillie, whom I see before me still in his rock-habit of undecipherable rags, would get his fiddle down and strike up human minstrelsy amid the music of the storm. But it was in sunshine only that I saw Dhu Heartach; and it was in sunshine, or the yet lovelier summer afterglow, that the steamer would return to Earraid, ploughing an enchanted sea; the obedient lighters, relieved of their deck cargo, riding in her wake more quietly; and the steersman upon each, as she rose on the long swell, standing tall and dark against the shining west.

II

But it was in Earraid itself that I delighted chiefly. The lighthouse settlement scarce encroached beyond its fences; over the top of the first brae the ground was all virgin, the world all shut out, the face of things unchanged by any of man's doings. Here was no living presence, save for the limpets on the rocks, for some old, grey, rain-beaten ram that I might rouse out of a ferny den betwixt two boulders, or for the haunting and the piping of the gulls. It was older than man; it was found so by incoming Celts, and seafaring Norsemen, and Columba's priests. The earthy savour of the bog plants, the rude disorder of the boulders, the inimitable seaside brightness of the air, the brine and the iodine, the lap of the billows among the weedy reefs, the sudden springing up of a great run of dashing surf along the sea-front of the isle, all that I saw and felt my predecessors must have seen and felt with scarce a difference. I steeped myself in open air and in past ages.

> 'Delightful would it be to me to be in *Uchd Ailiun*
>   On the pinnacle of a rock,
>   That I might often see
>   The face of the ocean;
>   That I might hear the song of the wonderful birds,

> Source of happiness;
> That I might hear the thunder of the crowding waves
>   Upon the rocks:
> At times at work without compulsion—
>   This would be delightful;
> At times plucking dulse from the rocks;
>   At times at fishing.'

So, about the next island of Iona, sang Columba himself twelve hundred years before. And so might I have sung of Earraid.

And all the while I was aware that this life of sea-bathing and sun-burning was for me but a holiday. In that year cannon were roaring for days together on French battlefields;[8] and I would sit in my isle (I call it mine, after the use of lovers) and think upon the war, and the loudness of these far-away battles, and the pain of the men's wounds, and the weariness of their marching. And I would think too of that other war which is as old as mankind, and is indeed the life of man: the unsparing war, the grinding slavery of competition; the toil of seventy years, dear-bought bread, precarious honour, the perils and pitfalls, and the poor rewards. It was a long look forward; the future summoned me as with trumpet calls, it warned me back as with a voice of weeping and beseeching; and I thrilled and trembled on the brink of life, like a childish bather on the beach.

There was another young man on Earraid in these days, and we were much together, bathing, clambering on the boulders, trying to sail a boat and spinning round instead in the oily whirlpools of the roost. But the most part of the time we spoke of the great uncharted desert of our futures; wondering together what should there befall us; hearing with surprise the sound of our own voices in the empty vestibule of youth. As far, and as hard, as it seemed then to look forward to the grave, so far it seems now to look backward upon these emotions; so hard to recall justly that loath submission, as of the sacrificial bull, with which we stooped our necks under the yoke of destiny. I met my old companion but the other day; I cannot tell of course what he was thinking; but, upon my part, I was wondering to see us both so much at home, and so composed and sedentary in the world; and how much we had gained, and how much we had lost, to attain to that composure; and which had been upon the whole our best estate: when we sat there prating sensibly like men of some experience, or when we shared our timorous and hopeful counsels in a western islet.

The Highlands

In the highlands, in the country places,[1]
Where the old plain men have rosy faces,
And the young fair maidens
Quiet eyes;
Where essential silence cheers and blesses,
And for ever in the hill-recesses
Her more lovely music
Broods and dies.

O to mount again where erst I haunted;
Where the old red hills are bird-enchanted,
And the low green meadows
Bright with sward;
And when even dies, the million-tinted,
And the night has come, and planets glinted,
Lo, the valley hollow
Lamp-bestarred!

O to dream, O to awake and wander
There, and with delight to take and render,
Through the trance of silence,
Quiet breath;
Lo! for there, among the flowers and grasses,
Only the mightier movement sounds and passes;
Only winds and rivers,
Life and death.

Appin—Mamore—Heugh of Corrynakiegh

From *Kidnapped*, Chapter 21: The Flight in the Heather:
the Heugh of Corrynakiegh

Early as day comes in the beginning of July, it was still dark when we
reached our destination, a cleft in the head of a great mountain, with a
water running through the midst, and upon the one hand a shallow

cave in a rock. Birches grew there in a thin, pretty wood, which a little further on was changed into a wood of pines. The burn was full of trout; the wood of cushat-doves; on the open side of the mountain beyond, whaups would be always whistling, and cuckoos were plentiful. From the mouth of the cleft we looked down upon a part of Mamore, and on the sea-loch that divides that country from Appin; and this from so great a height, as made it my continual wonder and pleasure to sit and behold them.

The name of the cleft was the Heugh of Corrynakiegh;[1] and although from its height and being so near upon the sea, it was often beset with clouds, yet it was on the whole a pleasant place, and the five days we lived in it went happily.

Cluny's Cage, Ben Alder

From Chapter 23 of *Kidnapped*: Cluny's Cage

We came at last to the foot of an exceeding steep wood, which scrambled up a craggy hillside, and was crowned by a naked precipice.

'It's here,' said one of the guides, and we struck up hill.

The trees clung upon the slope, like sailors on the shrouds of a ship; and their trunks were like the rounds of a ladder, by which we mounted.

Quite at the top, and just before the rocky face of the cliff sprang above the foliage, we found that strange house which was known in the country as 'Cluny's Cage.'[1] The trunks of several trees had been wattled across, the intervals strengthened with stakes, and the ground behind this barricade levelled up with earth to make the floor. A tree, which grew out from the hillside, was the living centre-beam of the roof. The walls were of wattle and covered with moss. The whole house had something of an egg shape; and it half hung, half stood in that steep, hillside thicket, like a wasp's nest in a green hawthorn.

Within, it was large enough to shelter five or six persons with some comfort. A projection of the cliff had been cunningly employed to be the fireplace; and the smoke rising against the face of the rock, and being not dissimilar in colour, readily escaped notice from below.

This was but one of Cluny's hiding-places; he had caves, besides, and underground chambers in several parts of his country; and following the reports of his scouts, he moved from one to another as the soldiers drew near or moved away. By this manner of living, and thanks to the affection of his clan, he had not only stayed all this time in safety, while so many others had fled or been taken and slain; but stayed four or five years longer, and only went to France at last by the express command of his master. There he soon died; and it is strange to reflect that he may have regretted his Cage upon Ben Alder.

Bridge of Allan

Extract from letter to Robert Stevenson, RLS's cousin, from Edinburgh, 17 November 1868

Lying here in my bed, I have been brooding over past walks. Especially our walk *up* the Allan—you remember it? And how after having passed all the wooded banks, we came out past a cavern[1] on a bit of river-meadow 'edged with Poplar pale',[2] surrounded on three sides by the retiring and then re-advancing wooded banks, and on the fourth by the brawling river and the high ground on the farther side. We passed through the meadow and came to a road betwixt two walls and two woods that sloped up the hillside... But where I chiefly long to be is at the immediate exit from the wood, where the river splashes through some rapids dewing with spray the over-hanging trees, and you see it bearing away its *taches* of foam, in a slow brown stream between 'the nodding horror of *two* shady brows'.[3]

Extract from letter to Mrs Frances Sitwell from probably Heriot Row, 31 January 1875

My dearest Mother,[1] I have been busy and knocked about and found no time to write. How the weather changes. On Friday, I went to Bridge of Allan.[2] A beautiful clear sunny winter's day, all the Highland hills standing about the horizon in their white robes. It was not cold. I went up my favourite walk by the riverside among the pines and ash trees. There is a little cavern here, by the side of a wide meadow, which has been a part of me any time these last twelve years—or more. On Friday it was wonderful. A large broken branch hung down over the mouth of it, and it was all cased in perfect ice. Every dock-leaf and long grass, too, was bearded with a shining icicle. And all the icicles kept dropping and dropping, and had made another little forest of clear ice among the grasses and fallen branches and dockens below them. I picked up one of these branches and threw it on the ground; and all the crystal broke with a little tinkle; and behold! a damp stick. Yesterday, a thick fog, rain and then snow, and then rain; and all along the roads the snow lay melting, and the pools froze and thawed alternately. And now today, a big blustering west wind and splendid sunshine, darkened ever and again by clouds and angry squalls of rain.

Strathyre—Allan Water—Stirling Castle, Brig

From Chapter 26 of *Kidnapped*: End of the Flight: we pass the Forth

'It's a chief principle in military affairs', said he [Alan Breck Stewart], 'to go where ye are least expected. Forth is our trouble; ye ken the saying, "Forth bridles the wild Hielandman." Well, if we seek to creep round about the head of that river and come down by Kippen or Balfron, it's just precisely there that they'll be looking to lay hands on us. But if we stave on straight to the auld Brig of Stirling, I'll lay my sword they let us pass unchallenged.'

The first night, accordingly, we pushed to the house of a Maclaren in Strathire, a friend of Duncan's, where we slept the twenty-first of the month, and whence we set forth again about the fall of night to make another easy stage. The twenty-second we lay in a heather bush on the hillside in Uam Var, within view of a herd of deer, the happiest ten hours of sleep in a fine, breathing sunshine and on bone-dry ground, that I have ever tasted. That night we struck Allan Water, and followed it down; and coming to the edge of the hills saw the whole Carse of Stirling underfoot, as flat as a pancake, with the town and castle on a hill in the midst of it, and the moon shining on the Links of Forth.[1]

'Now,' said Alan, 'I kenna if ye care, but ye're in your own land again. We passed the Hieland Line in the first hour; and now if we could but pass yon crooked water, we might cast our bonnets in the air.'

In Allan Water, near by where it falls into the Forth, we found a little sandy islet, overgrown with burdock, butterbur and the like low plants, that would just cover us if we lay flat. Here it was we made our camp, within plain view of Stirling Castle, whence we could hear the drums beat as some part of the garrison paraded. Shearers worked all day in a field on one side of the river, and we could hear the stones going on the hooks and the voices and even the words of the men talking. It behoved to lie close and keep silent. But the sand of the little isle was sun-warm, the green plants gave us shelter for our heads, we had food and drink in plenty; and to crown all, we were within sight of safety.

As soon as the shearers quit their work and the dusk began to fall, we waded ashore and struck for the Bridge of Stirling, keeping to the fields and under the field fences.

The bridge is close under the castle hill, an old, high, narrow bridge with pinnacles along the parapet; and you may conceive with how much interest I looked upon it, not only as a place famous in history, but as the very doors of salvation to Alan and myself. The moon was not yet up when we came there; a few lights shone along the front of the fortress, and lower down a few lighted windows in the town; but it was all mighty still, and there seemed to be no guard upon the passage.

The South-West

'A Winter's Walk in Carrick and Galloway' (a fragment)

At the famous bridge of Doon, Kyle, the central district of the shire of Ayr, marches with Carrick, the most southerly. On the Carrick side of the river rises a hill of somewhat gentle conformation, cleft with shallow dells, and sown here and there with farms and tufts of wood. Inland, it loses itself, joining, I suppose, the great herd of similar hills that occupies the centre of the Lowlands. Towards the sea, it swells out the coast-line into a protuberance, like a bay window in a plan, and is fortified against the surf behind bold crags. This hill is known as the Brown Hill of Carrick, or, more shortly, Brown Carrick.

It had snowed overnight. The fields were all sheeted up; they were tucked in among the snow, and their shape was modelled through the pliant counterpane, like children tucked in by a fond mother. The wind had made ripples and folds upon the surface, like what the sea, in quiet weather, leaves upon the sand. There was a frosty stifle in the air. An effusion of coppery light on the summit of Brown Carrick showed where the sun was trying to look through; but along the horizon clouds of cold fog had settled down, so that there was no distinction of sky and sea. Over the white shoulders of the headlands, or in the opening of bays, there was nothing but a great vacancy and blackness; and the road as it drew near the edge of the cliff seemed to skirt the shores of creation and void space. The snow crunched underfoot, and at farms all the dogs broke out barking as they smelt a passer-by upon the road. I met a fine old fellow, who might have sat as the father in 'The Cottar's Saturday Night,'[1] and who swore most heathenishly at a cow he was driving. And a little after I scraped acquaintance with a poor body tramping out to gather cockles. His face was wrinkled by exposure; it was broken up into flakes and channels, like mud beginning to dry, and weathered in two colours, an incongruous pink and grey. He had a faint air of being surprised—which, God knows, he might well be—that life had gone so ill with him. The shape of his trousers was in itself a jest, so strangely were they bagged and ravelled about his knees; and his coat was all bedaubed with clay as though he had lain in a rain-dub during the New Year's festivity. I will own I was not sorry to think he had had a merry New Year, and been young again for an evening; but I was sorry to see the mark still there. One could not expect such an old gentleman to be much of a dandy, or a great student of respectability in dress; but there might have been a wife at home, who had brushed out similar stains after fifty New Years, now become old, or a round-armed daughter, who would wish to have him neat, were it only out of self-respect and for the ploughman sweetheart when he looks round at night. Plainly, there was nothing of this in his life, and years and loneliness hung heavily on his old arms. He was seventy-six, he told me; and nobody would give a day's work to a man that age: they would think he couldn't do it. 'And, 'deed,' he went on, with a sad little chuckle, ' 'deed, I doubt if I could.' He said goodbye to me at a footpath, and crippled wearily off to his work. It will make your heart ache if you think of his old fingers groping in the snow.

He told me I was to turn down beside the school-house for Dunure. And so, when I found a lone house among the snow, and heard a babble of childish voices from within, I struck off into a steep road leading downwards to the sea. Dunure lies close under the steep hill: a haven among the rocks, a breakwater in consummate disrepair, much apparatus for drying nets, and a score or so of fishers' houses. Hard by, a few shards of ruined castle[2] overhang the sea, a few vaults, and one tall gable honeycombed with windows. The snow lay on the beach to the tidemark. It was daubed on to the sills of the ruin: it roosted in the crannies of the rock like white sea-birds; even on outlying reefs there would be a little cock of snow, like a toy lighthouse. Everything was grey and white in a cold and dolorous sort of shepherd's plaid. In the profound silence, broken only by the noise of oars at sea, a horn was sounded twice; and I saw the postman, girt with two bags, pause a

moment at the end of the clachan for letters. It is, perhaps, characteristic of Dunure that none were brought him.

The people at the public-house did not seem well pleased to see
me, and though I would fain have stayed by the kitchen fire, sent me
'ben the hoose' into the guest-room. This guest-room at Dunure was
painted in quite aesthetic fashion. There are rooms in the same taste
not a hundred miles from London, where persons of an extreme sensi-
bility meet together without embarrassment. It was all in a fine dull
bottle-green and black; a grave harmonious piece of colouring, with
nothing, so far as coarser folk can judge, to hurt the better feelings of
the most exquisite purist. A cherry-red half window-blind kept up an
imaginary warmth in the cold room, and threw quite a glow on the
floor. Twelve cockle-shells and a halfpenny china figure were ranged
solemnly along the mantel-shelf. Even the spittoon was an original
note, and instead of sawdust contained sea-shells. And as for the
hearthrug, it would merit an article to itself, and a coloured diagram to
help the text. It was patchwork, but the patchwork of the poor; no
glowing shreds of old brocade and Chinese silk, shaken together in the
kaleidoscope of some tasteful housewife's fancy; but a work of art in its
own way, and plainly a labour of love. The patches came exclusively
from people's raiment. There was no colour more brilliant than a heather
mixture; 'My Johnny's grey breeks,'[3] well polished over the oar on the
boat's thwart, entered largely into its composition. And the spoils of an
old black cloth coat, that had been many a Sunday to church, added
something (save the mark!) of preciousness to the material.

While I was at luncheon four carters came in—long-limbed, muscular
Ayrshire Scots, with lean, intelligent faces. Four quarts of stout were
ordered; they kept filling the tumbler with the other hand as they
drank; and in less time than it takes me to write these words the four
quarts were finished—another round was proposed, discussed, and
negatived—and they were creaking out of the village with their carts.

The ruins drew you towards them. You never saw any place more
desolate from a distance, nor one that less belied its promise near at
hand. Some crows and gulls flew away croaking as I scrambled in. The
snow had drifted into the vaults. The clachan dabbled with snow, the
white hills, the black sky, the sea marked in the coves with faint circu-
lar wrinkles, the whole world, as it looked from a loop-hole in Dunure,
was cold, wretched, and out-at-elbows. If you had been a wicked baron
and compelled to stay there all the afternoon, you would have had a
rare fit of remorse. How you would have heaped up the fire and gnawed
your fingers! I think it would have come to homicide before the evening—
if it were only for the pleasure of seeing something red! And the

masters of Dunure, it is to be noticed, were remarkable of old for inhumanity. One of these vaults where the snow had drifted was that 'black voute' where 'Mr. Alane Stewart, Commendatour of Crossraguel,' endured his fiery trials. On the 1st and 7th of September 1570 (ill dates for Mr. Alan!), Gilbert, Earl of Cassilis,[4] his chaplain, his baker, his cook, his pantryman, and another servant, bound the Poor Commendator 'betwix an iron chimlay and a fire,' and there cruelly roasted him until he signed away his abbacy. It is one of the ugliest stories of an ugly period, but not, somehow, without such a flavour of the ridiculous as makes it hard to sympathise quite seriously with the victim. And it is consoling to remember that he got away at last, and kept his abbacy, and, over and above, had a pension from the Earl until he died.

Some way beyond Dunure a wide bay, of somewhat less unkindly aspect, opened out. Colzean plantations lay all along the steep shore, and there was a wooded hill towards the centre, where the trees made a sort of shadowy etching over the snow. The road went down and up, and past a blacksmith's cottage that made fine music in the valley. Three compatriots of Burns drove up to me in a cart. They were all drunk, and asked me jeeringly if this was the way to Dunure. I told them it was; and my answer was received with unfeigned merriment. One gentleman was so much tickled he nearly fell out of the cart; indeed, he was only saved by a companion, who either had not so fine a sense of humour or had drunken less.

'The toune of Mayboll,' says the inimitable Abercrummie,[5] 'stands upon an ascending ground from east to west, and lyes open to the south. It hath one principall street, with houses upon both sides, built of freestone; and it is beautifyed with the situation of two castles, one at each end of this street. That on the east belongs to the Erle of Cassilis. On the west end is a castle, which belonged sometime to the laird of Blairquan, which is now the tolbuith, and is adorned with a pyremide [conical roof], and a row of ballesters round it raised from the top of the staircase, into which they have mounted a fyne clock. There be four lanes which pass from the principall street; one is called the Black Vennel, which is steep, declining to the south-west, and leads to a lower street, which is far larger than the high chiefe street, and it runs from the Kirkland to the Well Trees, in which there have been many pretty buildings, belonging to the severall gentry of the countrey, who were wont to resort thither in winter, and divert themselves in converse together at their owne houses. It was once the principall street of the town; but many of these houses of the gentry having been decayed and ruined, it has lost much of its ancient beautie. Just opposite to this vennel, there is another that leads north-west, from the chiefe street to the green, which is a pleasant plott of ground, enclosed round with an earthen wall, wherein they were wont to play football, but now at the Gowff and byasse-bowls. The houses of this towne, on both sides of the street, have their several gardens belonging to them; and in the lower street there be some pretty orchards, that yield store of good fruit.' As Patterson says, this description is near enough even today, and is mighty nicely written to boot. I am bound to add, of my own experience, that Maybole is tumbledown and dreary. Prosperous enough in reality, it has an air of decay; and though the population has increased, a roofless house every here and there seems to protest the contrary. The women are more than well-favoured, and the men fine tall fellows; but they look slipshod and dissipated. As they slouched at street corners, or stood about gossiping in the snow, it seemed they would have been more at home in the slums of a large city than here in a country place betwixt a village and a town. I heard a great deal about drinking, and a great deal about religious revivals: two things in which the Scottish character is emphatic and most unlovely. In particular, I heard of clergymen who were employing their time in explaining to a delighted audience the physics of the Second Coming. It is not very likely any of us will be asked to help. If we were, it is likely we should receive instructions for the occasion, and that on more reliable authority. And so I can only figure to myself a congregation truly curious in such flights of theological fancy, as one of veteran and accomplished saints, who have fought the good fight to an end and outlived all worldly passion, and are to be regarded rather as a part of the Church Triumphant than the poor, imperfect company on earth. And yet I saw some young fellows about the smoking-room who seemed, in the eyes of one who cannot count himself strait-laced, in need of some more practical sort of teaching. They seemed only eager to get drunk, and to do so speedily. It was not much more than a week after the New Year; and to hear them return on their past bouts with a gusto unspeakable was not altogether pleasing. Here is one snatch of talk, for the accuracy of which I can vouch—

'Ye had a spree here last Tuesday?'

'We had that!'

'I wasna able to be oot o' my bed. Man, I was awful bad on Wednesday.'

'Ay, ye were gey bad.'

And you should have seen the bright eyes, and heard the sensual accents! They recalled their doings with devout gusto and a sort of rational pride. Schoolboys, after their first drunkenness, are not more boastful; a cock does not plume himself with a more unmingled satisfaction as he paces forth among his harem; and yet these were grown men, and by no means short of wit. It was hard to suppose they were very eager about the Second Coming: it seemed as if some elementary notions of temperance for the men and seemliness for the women would have gone nearer the mark. And yet, as it seemed to me typical of much that is evil in Scotland, Maybole is also typical of much that is best. Some of the factories, which have taken the place of weaving in the town's economy, were originally founded and are still possessed by self-made men of the sterling, stout old breed—fellows who made some little bit of an invention, borrowed some little pocketful of capital, and then, step by step, in courage, thrift and industry, fought their way upwards to an assured position.

Abercrummie has told you enough of the Tolbooth; but, as a bit of spelling, this inscription on the Tolbooth bell seems too delicious to withhold: 'This bell is founded at Maiboll Bi Danel Geli, a Frenchman, the 6th November, 1696, Bi appointment of the heritors of the parish of Maiyboll.' The Castle deserves more notice. It is a large and shapely tower, plain from the ground upwards, but with a zone of ornamentation running about the top. In a general way this adornment is perched on the very summit of the chimney-stacks; but there is one corner more elaborate than the rest. A very heavy string-course runs round the upper story, and just above this, facing up the street, the tower carries a small oriel window, fluted and corbelled and carved about with stone heads. It is so ornate it has somewhat the air of a shrine. And it was, indeed, the casket of a very precious jewel, for in the room to which it gives light lay, for long years, the heroine of the sweet old ballad of 'Johnnie Faa'—she who, at the call of the gipsies' songs, 'came tripping down the stair, and all her maids before her.'[6] Some people say the ballad has no basis in fact, and have written, I believe, unanswerable papers to the proof. But in the face of all that, the very look of that high oriel window convinces the imagination, and we enter into all the sorrows of the imprisoned dame. We conceive the burthen of the long, lack-lustre days, when she leaned her sick head against the mullions, and saw the burghers loafing in Maybole High Street, and the children at play, and ruffling gallants riding by from hunt or foray. We conceive the passion of odd moments, when the wind threw up to her some snatch of song, and her heart grew hot within her, and her eyes overflowed at the memory of the past. And even if the tale be not true of this or that lady, or this or that old tower, it is true in the essence of all men and women: for all of us, some time or other, hear the gipsies singing; over all of us is the glamour cast. Some resist and sit resolutely by the fire. Most go and are brought back again, like Lady Cassilis. A few, of the tribe of Waring, go and are seen no more; only now and again, at springtime, when the gipsies' song is afloat in the amethyst evening, we can catch their voices in the glee.

By night it was cleared, and Maybole more visible than during the day. Clouds coursed over the sky in great masses; the full moon battled the other way, and lit up the snow with gleams of flying silver; the town came down the hill in a cascade of brown gables, bestridden by smooth white roofs, and spangled here and there with lighted windows. At either end the snow stood high up in the darkness, on the peak of the Tolbooth and among the chimneys of the Castle. As the moon flashed a bull's-eye glitter across the town between the racing clouds, the white roofs leaped into relief over the gables and the chimney-stacks, and their shadows over the white roofs. In the town itself the lit face of the clock peered down the street; an hour was hammered out on Mr. Geli's bell, and from behind the red curtains of a public-house some one trolled out—a compatriot of Burns, again!—'The saut tear blin's my e'e.'

Next morning there was sun and a flapping wind. From the street corners of Maybole I could catch breezy glimpses of green fields. The road underfoot was wet and heavy—part ice, part snow, part water, and any one I met greeted me, by way of salutation, with 'A fine thowe' (thaw). My way lay among rather bleak hills, and past bleak ponds and dilapidated castles and monasteries, to the Highland-looking village of Kirkoswald. It has little claim to notice, save that Burns came there to study surveying in the summer of 1777, and there also, in the kirkyard, the original of Tam o' Shanter sleeps his last sleep.[7] It is worth notic-ing, however, that this was the first place I thought 'Highland-looking.' Over the hill from Kirkoswald a farm-road leads to the coast. As I came down above Turnberry, the sea view was indeed strangely different from the day before. The cold fogs were all blown away; and there was Ailsa Craig, like a refraction, magnified and deformed, of the Bass Rock; and there were the chiselled mountain-tops of Arran, veined and tipped with snow; and behind, and fainter, the low, blue land of Cantyre. Cottony clouds stood, in a great castle, over the top of Arran, and blew out in long streamers to the south. The sea was bitten all over with white; little ships, tacking up and down the Firth, lay over at different angles in the wind. On Shanter they were ploughing lea; a cart foal, all in a field by himself, capered and whinnied as if the spring were in him.

The road from Turnberry to Girvan lies along the shore, among sandhills and by wildernesses of tumbled bent. Every here and there a few cottages stood together beside a bridge. They had one odd feature, not easy to describe in words: a triangular porch projected from above the door, supported at the apex by a single upright post; a secondary door was hinged to the post, and could be hasped on either cheek of the real entrance; so, whether the wind was north or south, the cotter could make himself a triangular bight of shelter where to set his chair and finish a pipe with comfort. There is one objection to this device: for, as the post stands in the middle of the fairway, any one precipitately issuing from the cottage must run his chance of a broken head. So far as I am aware, it is peculiar to the little corner of country about Girvan. And that corner is noticeable for more reasons: it is certainly one of the most characteristic districts in Scotland. It has this movable porch by way of architecture; it has, as we shall see, a sort of remnant of provincial costume, and it has the handsomest population in the Lowlands...

Dumfries and Vicinity

Extracts from a letter to Mrs Frances Sitwell from the Borders, 15-22 September 1873

Saturday

And today it came—warmth, sunlight, and a strong, hearty living wind among the trees. I found myself a new being. My father and I went off a long walk, through a country most beautifully wooded and various, under a range of hills. You should have seen one place where the road suddenly fell away in front of us down a long, steep hill between a double row of trees, with one small fair-haired child framed in shadow in the foreground; and when we got to the foot there was the little kirk and kirkyard of Irongray, among broken fields and woods by the side of the bright, rapid river. In the kirkyard, there was a wonderful congregation of tombstones, upright and recumbent on four legs (after our Scotch fashion), and of flat-armed fir trees. One gravestone was erected by Scott (at a cost, I learn, of £70) to the poor woman who served him as heroine in the *Heart of Midlothian*,[1] and the inscription in its stiff, Jedediah Cleishbotham fashion is not without something touching. We went up the stream a little farther to where two Covenanters lie buried in an oakwood;[2] the tombstone (as the custom is) containing the details of their grim little tragedy in funnily bad rhyme, one verse of which sticks in my memory:—

> 'We died, their furious rage to stay,
> Near to the kirk of Iron-Gray.'

We then fetched a long compass round about, through Holywood Kirk and Lincluden ruins to Dumfries.

Sunday
Another beautiful day. My father and I walked into Dumfries to church. When the service was done I noted the two halberts laid against the pillar of the churchyard gate; and as I had not seen the little weekly pomp of civic dignitaries in our Scotch country towns for some years, I made my father wait. You should have seen the Provost and three baillies going stately away down the sunlit street, and the two town-servants strutting in front of them, in red coats and cocked hats, and with the halberts most conspicuously shouldered. We saw Burns's house—a place that made me deeply sad, and spent the afternoon down the banks of the Nith.[3] I had not spent a day by a river since we lunched in the meadows near Sudbury. The air was as pure, and clear, and sparkling as spring water; beautiful, graceful outlines of hill and wood shut us in on every side; and the swift, brown river fled smoothly away from before our eyes, rippled over with oily eddies and dimples. White gulls had come up from the sea to fish, and hovered and flew hither and thither among the loops of the stream. By good fortune, too, it was a dead calm between my father and me.

The Borders

Extract from *Weir of Hermiston. An Unfinished Romance*: Introductory

In the wild end of a moorland parish, far out of the sight of any house, there stands a cairn among the heather, and a little by east of it, in the going down of the braeside, a monument with some verses half de-faced. It was here that Claverhouse[1] shot with his own hand the Praying Weaver of Balweary,[2] and the chisel of Old Mortality[3] has clinked on that lonely gravestone. Public and domestic history have thus marked with a bloody finger this hollow among the hills; and since the Cameronian[4] gave his life there, two hundred years ago, in a glorious folly, and without comprehension or regret, the silence of the moss has been broken once again by the report of firearms and the cry of the dying.

The Pentlands

Extract from *The Pentland Rising*

The sun, going down behind the Pentlands,[1] cast golden lights and blue shadows on their snow-clad summits, slanted obliquely into the rich plain before them, bathing with rosy splendour the leafless, snow-sprinkled trees, and fading gradually into shadow in the distance. To the south, too, they beheld a deep-shaded amphitheatre of heather and bracken; the course of the Esk, near Penicuik, winding about at the foot of its gorge; the broad, brown expanse of Maw moss; and, fading into blue indistinctness in the south, the wild heath-clad Peeblesshire hills. In sooth, that scene was fair, and many a yearning glance was cast over that peaceful evening scene from the spot where the rebels awaited their defeat; and when the fight was over, many a noble fellow lifted his head from the blood-stained heather to strive with darkening eyeballs to behold that landscape, over which, as o'er his life and his cause, the shadows of night and of gloom were falling and thickening.

Glencorse

Extract from 'The Body Snatcher'

At the same time there came the news of a burial in the rustic graveyard of Glencorse.[1] Time has little changed the place in question. It stood then, as now, upon a cross-road, out of call of human habitations, and buried fathom deep in the foliage of six cedar trees. The cries of the sheep upon the neighbouring hills, the streamlets upon either hand, one loudly singing among pebbles, the other dripping furtively from pond to pond, the stir of the wind in mountainous old flowering chestnuts, and once in seven days the voice of the bell and the old tunes of the precentor, were the only sounds that disturbed the silence around the rural church.

The Pentlands—Fisher's Tryst—
Glencorse

Extracts from letter to S R Crockett from Vailima, 17 May 1893

I shall never take that walk by the Fisher's Tryst and Glencorse; I shall never see Auld Reekie; I shall never set my foot again upon the heather. Here I am until I die, and here will I be buried. The word is out and the doom written. Or, if I do come, it will be a voyage to a further goal, and in fact a suicide; which, however, if I could get my family all fixed up in the money way, I might perhaps perform, or attempt. But there is a plaguey risk of breaking down by the way; and I believe I shall stay here until the end comes like a good boy, and a prolific milk cow, as I am. If I did it, I should put upon my trunks: 'Passenger to—Hades.'

* * *

Do you know where the road crosses the burn under Glencorse Church? Go there, and say a prayer for me: *Moriturus salutat.*[1] See that it's a sunny day; I would like it to be a Sunday, but that's not possible in the premises; and stand on the right-hand bank just where the road goes down into the water, and shut your eyes, and if I don't appear to you! well, it can't be helped, and will be extremely funny.

The Pentlands

To S. R. Crockett
(On receiving a Dedication)

Blows the wind today, and the sun and the rain are flying,
    Blows the wind on the moors today and now,
Where about the graves of the martyrs the whaups are crying,
    My heart remembers how!

Grey recumbent tombs of the dead in desert places,
    Standing-stones on the vacant wine-red moor,

111

Hills of sheep, and the howes of the silent vanished races,
  And winds, austere and pure:

Be it granted me to behold you again in dying,
  Hills of home! and to hear again the call;
Hear about the graves of the martyrs the pee-wees crying,
  And hear no more at all.[1]

View from the Pentlands

The tropics vanish, and meseems that I,
From Halkerside, from topmost Allermuir,
Or steep Caerketton, dreaming gaze again.
Far set in fields and woods, the town I see
Spring gallant from the shallows of her smoke,
Cragged, spired, and turreted, her virgin fort
Beflagged. About, on seaward-drooping hills,
New folds of city glitter. Last, the Forth
Wheels ample waters set with sacred isles,
And populous Fife smokes with a score of towns.

There, on the sunny frontage of a hill,
Hard by the house of kings, repose the dead,
My dead, the ready and the strong of word.
Their works, the salt-encrusted, still survive;[1]
The sea bombards their founded towers; the night
Thrills pierced with their strong lamps. The artificers,
One after one, here in this grated cell,[2]
Where the rain erases and the rust consumes,
Fell upon lasting silence. Continents
And continental oceans intervene;
A sea uncharted, on a lampless isle,
Environs and confines their wandering child
In vain. The voice of generations dead
Summons me, sitting distant, to arise,
My numerous footsteps nimbly to retrace,
And, all mutation over, stretch me down
In that devoted city of the dead.

Edinburgh—Lothian Road—Leith Walk

Extract from letter to Charles Baxter from Chalet am Stein, Davos, Switzerland, 5 December 1881

Pray write me something cheery. A little Edinburgh gossip, in Heaven's name. Ah! what would I not give to steal this evening with you through the big, echoing, college archway, and away south under the street lamps, and away to dear Brash's, now defunct! But the old time is dead also, never, never to revive. It was a sad time too, but so gay and so hopeful, and we had such sport with all our low spirits and all our distresses, that it looks like a kind of lamp-lit fairyland behind me. O for ten Edinburgh minutes—sixpence between us, and the ever-glorious Lothian Road, or dear mysterious Leith Walk![1] But here, a sheer hulk, lies poor Tom Bowling; here in this strange place, whose very strangeness would have been heaven to him then; and aspires, yes, C. B., with tears, after the past. See what comes of being left alone. Do you remember Brash? the sheet of glass that we followed along George Street? Granton? the night at Bonny mainhead? the compass near the sign of the *Twinkling Eye*? the night I lay on the pavement in misery?

Edinburgh—Drummond Street and Rutherford's

Extract from letter to Charles Baxter from the yacht *Casco*, 6 September 1888

My Dear Charles,—Last night as I lay under my blanket in the cockpit,[1] courting sleep, I had a comic seizure. There was nothing visible but the southern stars, and the steersman there out by the binnacle lamp; we were all looking forward to a most deplorable landfall on the morrow, praying God we should fetch a tuft of palms which are to indicate the Dangerous Archipelago; the night was as warm as milk; and all of a sudden I had a vision of—Drummond Street. It came on me like a flash of lightning; I simply returned thither, and into the past. And when I remembered all that I hoped and feared as I pickled about Rutherford's[2] in the rain and the east wind; how I feared I should make a mere shipwreck, and yet timidly hoped not; how I feared I should never have a friend far less a wife, and yet passionately hoped I might; how I hoped (if I did not take to drink) I should possibly write one little book, etc., etc. And then now—what a change! I feel somehow as if I should like the incident set upon a brass plate at the corner of that dreary thoroughfare, for all students to read, poor devils, when their hearts are down.[3]

Edinburgh—Lothian Road— Fergusson's Grave in the Canongate

Extracts from letter to Charles Baxter from Vailima, 18 May 1894

I wish to assure you of the greatness of the pleasure that this Edinburgh Edition[1] gives me. I suppose it was your idea to give it that name. No other would have affected me in the same manner. Do you remember, how many years ago, I would be afraid to hazard a guess, one night when I was very drunk indeed and communicated to you certain 'intimations of early death' and aspirations after fame? I was particularly maudlin; and my remorse the next morning on a review of my folly has written the matter very deeply in my mind; from yours it may easily have fled. If anyone at that moment could have shown me the Edinburgh Edition, I suppose I should have died. It is with gratitude and wonder that I consider 'the way in which I have been led'. Could a more preposterous idea have occurred to us in those days when we used to search our pockets for coppers, too often in vain, and combine forces to produce the threepence necessary for two glasses of beer, or wander down the Lothian Road without any, than that I should be well and strong at the age of forty-three in the island of Upolu, and that you should be at home bringing out the Edinburgh Edition? If it had been possible, I should have almost preferred the Lothian Road Edition, say, with a picture of the old Dutch smuggler on the covers.

I have now something heavy on my mind. I had always a great sense of kinship with poor Robert Fergusson[2]—so clever a boy, so wild, of such a mixed strain, so unfortunate, born in the same town with me, and, as I always felt rather by express intimation than from evidence, so like myself. Now the injustice with which the one Robert is rewarded and the other left out in the cold sits heavy on me, and I wish you could think of some way in which I could do honour to my unfortunate namesake. Do you think it would look like affectation to dedicate the whole edition to his memory? I think it would. The sentiment which would dictate it to me is too abstruse; and besides I think my wife is the proper person to receive the dedication of my life's work. At the same time—it is very odd—it really looks like transmigration of souls—I feel that I must do something for Fergusson; Burns has been before me with 'The Gravestone'. It occurs to me you might take a walk down the Canongate and see in what condition the stone is.[3] If it be at all uncared for, we might repair it and perhaps add a few words of inscription.

* * *

Suppose we do what I have proposed about Fergusson's monument. I wonder if an inscription like this would look arrogant.

> This stone originally erected by Robert Burns, has been
> repaired at the charges of Robert Louis Stevenson, and is
> by him re-dedicated to the Memory of Robert Fergusson
> as the gift of one Edinburgh lad to another.

In spacing this inscription I would detach the names of Fergusson and Burns; but leave mine in the text; or would that look like sham modesty and is it better to bring out the three Roberts?

Edinburgh—Precipitous City

To My Wife

I saw rain falling and the rainbow drawn
On Lammermuir. Hearkening I heard again
In my precipitous city beaten bells
Winnow the keen sea wind. And here afar
Intent on my own race and place I wrote.

Take thou the writing: thine it is. For who
Burnished the sword, blew on the drowsy coal,

Held still the target higher, chary of praise
And prodigal of censure—who but thou?[1]
So now, in the end, if this the least be good,
If any deed be done, if any fire
Burn in the imperfect page, the praise be thine.

Edinburgh or 'Auld Reekie'

Extract from 'The Scot Abroad'

Of all mysteries of the human heart, this is perhaps the most inscrutable. There is no special loveliness in that grey country, with its rainy, sea-beat archipelago; its fields of dark mountains; its unsightly places, black with coal; its treeless, sour, unfriendly-looking cornlands; its quaint, grey, castled city, where the bells clash of a Sunday, and the wind squalls, and the salt showers fly and beat. I do not even know if I desire to live there; but let me hear, in some far land, a kindred voice sing out, 'O why left I my hame?' and it seems at once as if no beauty under the kind heavens, and no society of the wise and good, can repay me for my absence from my country. And though I think I would rather die elsewhere, yet in my heart of hearts I long to be buried among good Scots clods.[1] I will say it fairly, it grows on me with every year: there are no stars so lovely as Edinburgh street-lamps. When I forget thee, Auld Reekie, may my right hand forget its cunning!

Select Bibliography

Collected Editions of the Works of Robert Louis Stevenson

It was the Edinburgh limited edition of 1,035 copies, all numbered, 28 vols, 1894-98, edited by Sidney Colvin, that made Stevenson a prestigious author. Other editions were, for example, named Pentland, Skerryvore, South Seas, Swanston and Vailima. The most popular edition of *The Works of Robert Louis Stevenson* was the unlimited Tusitala edition (35 volumes) edited by Lloyd Osbourne and Fanny van de Grift Stevenson and published in London by Heinemann, 1923-24. Although editorially dated, the volumes of this almost pocket-size edition remain very readable and some of them are indicated in the Notes. To his Samoan friends Stevenson was Tusitala, 'Teller of Tales'.

Available in one volume: *The Scottish Novels, Kidnapped, Catriona, The Master of Ballantrae and Weir of Hermiston,* Edinburgh, 1995, and reprints. With Introductions by Jenni Calder and Roderick Watson. (Canongate Classics 58.)

The New Lighthouse on the Dhu Heartach Rock, Argyllshire, edited with an introduction by Roger G Swearingen, St Helena, California, 1995. This previously unpublished essay was written in 1872; the manuscript (in the Huntington Library) has corrections by Stevenson's father.

The standard edition of *The Letters of Robert Louis Stevenson* is that edited by Bradford A Booth and Ernest Mehew, 8 vols, New Haven & London, 1994-95. There is also *The Selected Letters of Robert Louis Stevenson,* edited by Ernest Mehew, New Haven & London, 1997.

For Stevenson's poems see: *Collected Poems,* edited with an Introduction and Notes, by Janet Adam Smith, second edition, London, 1970; and *Selected Poems,* edited by Angus Calder, London, 1998. (Penguin Classics series.)

Further Reading

The first full biography was Graham Balfour's, *The Life of Robert Louis Stevenson,* London, 1901.
Other more recent biographies include:

117

Bell, Ian. *Dreams of Exile: Robert Louis Stevenson, a biography*, Edinburgh, 1992.

Calder, Jenni. *RLS: A Life Study*, London, 1980.

Callow, Philip. *Louis: A Life of Robert Louis Stevenson*, London, 2001.

Furnas, J C. *Voyage to Windward: the Life of Robert Louis Stevenson*, London, 1952.

McLynn, Frank. *Robert Louis Stevenson. A Biography*, London, 1993.

Angus, David. 'Robert Louis Stevenson at Bridge of Allan', *Forth Naturalist and Historian*, no 6, 1981.

Bathurst, Bella. *The Lighthouse Stevensons*, London, Edinburgh, 1999.

Buell, L M. 'Eilean Earraid: The Beloved Isle of Robert Louis Stevenson', *Scribner's Magazine*, no 71, February 1922.

Buchan, John. 'The Country of Kidnapped', *The Academy*, May 1898.

Calder, Jenni (edited). *The Robert Louis Stevenson Companion*, Edinburgh, 1980. With Introduction by Jenni Calder and writings by Sidney Colvin, Edmund Gosse, Will Low, J M Barrie, W E Henley, Henry James and J C Furnas.

Campbell, Thorbjörn. *Standing Witnesses. A Guide to the Scottish Covenanters and their Memorials with a Historical Introduction*, Edinburgh, 1996.

Daiches, David. *Robert Louis Stevenson and His World*, London, 1973.

——*Edinburgh*, London, 1978.

Findlay, J Patrick. *In the Footsteps of R.L.S.*, Edinburgh [1911].

Gelder, Kenneth. 'Introduction' and 'Explanatory Notes', *Robert Louis Stevenson. The Scottish Stories and Essays*, Edinburgh, 1989.

Glen, Duncan. *Makars' Walk. Walks in the Old Town of Edinburgh. With an Anthology of Poetry*, Edinburgh, 1990.

——*Historic Fife Murders at Falkland, St Andrews and Magus Muir*, Kirkcaldy, 2002.

——*Robert Louis Stevenson and the Covenanters on the Bass Rock and 'The Tale of Tod Lapraik'*, Kirkcaldy, 2002.

Haswell-Smith, Hamish. *The Scottish Islands*, Edinburgh, 1996.

Hendry, Alan. 'Stevenson's six weeks in grim, grey Wick', *John O'Groat Journal*, 3 November 2000.

Hill, Robin. *Pure Air and Good Milk—Robert Louis Stevenson at Swanston*, Edinburgh, 1995.

Hubbard, Tom. *Seeking Mr Hyde. Studies in Robert Louis Stevenson, Symbolism, Myth and the Pre-Modern*, Frankfurt am Main, 1995.

——'Edimbourg-la-Morte: the Fantastic in Charles Dickens and Robert Louis Stevenson', *Etudes Ecossaises*, no 7, 2001.

— —'North and South in the Writings of Robert Louis Stevenson', *The AnaChronist*, Budapest, 1997.

Knight, Alanna. *The Robert Louis Stevenson Treasury*, London, 1985.

Leslie, Jean and Paxton, Roland. *Bright Lights. The Stevenson Engineers 1752-1971*, Edinburgh, 1999.

MacCulloch, John A. *Stevenson and the Bridge of Allan*, Glasgow, 1927.

McLaren, Moray. *Stevenson and Edinburgh*, London, 1950.

McLynn, Frank. *Charles Edward Stuart: a tragedy in many acts*, London, 1988.

Masson, Flora. *Victorians All*, Edinburgh, 1931.

Masson, Rosaline (editor). *I Can Remember Robert Louis Stevenson*, Edinburgh, 1922.

Muir, Augustus. 'Stevenson's Scotland', *Scotland's Magazine*, November, 1950.

Nimmo, Ian and Seaton, Jim. 'The *Kidnapped* Walk', *Weekly Scotsman*, 5 January–2 February, 1961.

Rankin, Nick. *Dead Man's Chest: Travels after RLS*, London, 1987, reprinted 2001.

Stevenson, Robert. *The Bell Rock Lighthouse. Passages selected from 'An account of the Bell Rock Lighthouse' (published in 1824)*, edited by A F Collins, Cambridge, 1935.

Stott, Louis. *Robert Louis Stevenson and the Highlands and Islands of Scotland*, Milton-of-Aberfoyle, 1992.

Sutherland, John. *The Life of Walter Scott. A Critical Biography*, Oxford, 1995.

Swearingen, Roger G. *The Prose Writings of Robert Louis Stevenson*, London, 1980.

——*Robert Louis Stevenson's Edinburgh*, Edinburgh, 2001.

Thom, Valerie M. *Fair Isle. An Island Saga*, Edinburgh, 1989.

Tranter, Nigel. 'The Stevenson Coast', *The Scots Magazine*, March 1968 [on East Lothian in Stevenson's writings].

In addition, there is a new 56-minute film directed by Judith Dwan Hallet, *The Strange Case of Dr Jekyll and Mr Hyde*, produced by the Cronkite Ward Company for the Learning Channel's Great Books Series (USA), and released in 2002. The film situates the novella firmly in Edinburgh, with dramatised sequences shot in the Old Town, and there are interviews with Jenni Calder, Owen Dudley Edwards, Tom Hubbard, Ian Rankin, Roger Swearingen and other commentators on RLS.

Notes

See frontispiece map for significant places named by Stevenson.

Edinburgh Duality

Quoted by Graham Balfour, Stevenson's first biographer and cousin, in his *The Life of Robert Louis Stevenson*, Vol 1, pp 50-51, London, 1901. These 'Early Memories' date from October-November 1894.

1 Alison Cunningham, who became Louis's nurse when he was eighteen months old, see note to Limekilns, Fife, below.

Edinburgh: Picturesque Notes

Edinburgh: Picturesque Notes was first published in *The Portfolio* magazine, June to December 1878, and issued in book form in 1879 with three additional chapters: 'The Parliament Close', 'The Villa Quarters' and 'To the Pentland Hills'. Tusitala vol 26.

Chapter I: Introductory

1 The 'great bridge' is the North Bridge which joins the Old Town to the New. Encouraged by Provost George Drummond, precise proposals to bridge the valley to the north and so extend the city out of the overcrowded Old Town were made in 1752. Drainage of the North Loch (now Princes Street Gardens) began in 1759 and in July 1763 tenders were invited for a bridge across it which was first opened to pedestrians early in 1769. The way was open to create the Georgian New Town that Stevenson grew up in. Waverley Station was built in 1848 as the North British Railway's Edinburgh terminus. The great bridge that Stevenson knew was redesigned and rebuilt in the 1890s and opened in 1897. Today we can see the trains going out of Waverley station from Waverley Bridge, which joins Princes Street to Market Street and Cockburn Street, but the first Waverley Bridge was not completed until 1873 when RLS went south to France.

2 Holyrood Abbey, with its small Abbey Church, became a major ecclesiastical establishment that was important to King James II who was born, married to Mary of Gueldres, and buried there. James IV extended the parts of the abbey used as a royal residence but it was James V who built 'his fayre Pallais with three toweres'

and both Charles I and II enlarged and modernised the Palace of Holyroodhouse. Stevenson would be surprised to see how much this area around the ruined Abbey, and well-maintained Palace (which is the official residence of the Queen in Scotland) has been restored, and also to see the Scottish Parliament building standing close to the Palace.

3   David Rizzio, Mary Queen of Scots' secretary, was murdered in Holyrood in March 1566 by those, including Lord Darnley, Mary's husband, who were jealous of his influence at Court.

4   Prince Charles Edward Stuart rode into Holyrood on 17 September 1745, making the Palace his headquarters. The Prince and his army left Edinburgh on 1 November after a remarkably peaceful occupation of the city.

5   Greenside is at the foot of Calton Hill facing Leith Street, Leith Walk and Picardy Place. This open space was given in 1456 by James II to the burgesses for recreational use. Sir David Lyndsay's *Ane Satyre of the Thrie Estaitis* was performed at this Playfield on Sunday 12th August 1554 before Marie de Lorraine, Queen-Regent.

6   John Knox returned to Edinburgh in 1558 to lead the extreme Reformers and the overthrow of the Catholic Church in Scotland. Knox gave his biased view of his outspoken 'interviews' with Queen Mary in his *The History of the Reformation of Religion within the Realme of Scotland.*

7   King James VI, son of Mary, Queen of Scots, and Lord Darnley, was King of Scots from 1567, and from 1603 also King of England where he is known as James I.

8   George Heriot, who was popularly referred to as 'Jinglin Geordie', was appointed goldsmith to the King whom he followed to London in 1603. As Stevenson said, Heriot's shop in Edinburgh was close to St Giles Cathedral but perhaps not in a very small premises— see note on the 'krames' below. Just before his death in 1624 Heriot assigned his fortune to the Town Council for the education of fatherless boys and he also made provision for the endowment of 'Heriot's Hospital'. Work began on the building (now George Heriot's School) in 1628 on land to the west of Greyfriars Kirkyard but was not completed until 1659 when thirty fatherless boys were admitted.

9   The fanatical Covenanting heroes of the seventeenth century interested Stevenson from his boyhood through to his death. His first book, *The Pentland Rising*, is dated 28 November 1866 and marked

the bicentenary of the insurrection by Covenanters from the south-west that ended in defeat on the Pentland Hills at Rullion Green. One hundred copies of the young Stevenson's *The Pentland Rising* were printed anonymously (as a sixteen-page pamphlet), at Stevenson's father's expense. Perhaps Thomas Stevenson had second thoughts, as he bought in as many copies as he could find. At this time Stevenson had also started a novel on the 1666 Pentland insurrection but he was encouraged by his father away from Scott-like romances set in Covenanting times to write this factual account of the events that culminated at Rullion Green. For Stevenson's continuing interest in the Covenanters see his essay 'The Coast of Fife' reprinted here.

10 John Graham of Claverhouse, first Viscount Dundee, was known as 'Bloody Clavers' to the Covenanters whom he suppressed and as 'Bonny Dundee' to others who admired his 'dash'. He fought for the Stuart cause against William of Orange and in 1689 led a Jacobite army against a much larger Orange one at the Battle of Killiecrankie where he was killed by a stray bullet.

11 Thomas Aikenhead, an Edinburgh student who was hanged in 1696 for heresy, having proclaimed himself an atheist.

12 David Hume died in 1776, and Robert Burns arrived in Edinburgh on Tuesday 28 November 1786, coming through the West Port, at the west end of the Grassmarket, to ride up the West Bow to the Lawnmarket and lodgings in Baxter's Close near today's Writers' Museum where he is remembered alongside Stevenson and Sir Walter Scott.

Chapter II: Old Town—The Lands

13 Sir William Chambers, Lord Provost, was involved in the movement to improve the city. Old squares were cleared to make possible the seventy-foot wide Chambers Street which linked the South Bridge to George IV Bridge. The South Bridge, which spanned the valley of the Cowgate south of the North Bridge, was completed in 1789. George IV Bridge, which runs parallel to South Bridge and crosses the Cowgate and Merchant Street, was opened in 1834.

Chapter III: The Parliament Close

14 The 'krames' were open stalls, many of which sold toys; the 'luckenbooths' were larger locked shops and round the corner in what was Parliament Close (which, in the words of Sir Walter

Scott in *Redgauntlet*, 'new-fangled affectation has termed a square'), were other small shops, some of which were the premises of watchmakers and jewellers—George Heriot, goldsmith to King James VI, had premises there.

15 In the fifteenth century the Old Tolbooth at the north-west corner of St Giles was the centre of the town, being where the Town Council sat, the law courts and sometimes even Parliament met. Also, tolls were collected there and there was accommodation for a prison which became this building's sole use. It is as a prison that Scott's *The Heart of Midlothian* made it notorious.

16 The six-ton lead equestrian statue, which shows King Charles II mounted on horseback and dressed as a Roman general, was first erected in 1685, just before the King's death. It gets a mention in Scott's *The Heart of Midlothian* in the context of a phantom member of the City Guard that 'creeps, I have been informed, round the statue'.

17 Stevenson's 'hall with a carved roof' is the historic Parliament Hall (or House), which dates from 1639; the hammer-beam roof is splendid. When the independent Scottish Parliament ceased to exist in 1707 Parliament House became the centre of the Scottish legal establishment. The lawyers still pace its floor as they discuss cases. Stevenson qualified as an advocate in July 1875 but the artists' colony at Fontainebleau interested him more than treading these historic boards. Following a holiday with his parents in Germany, he did spend some autumn mornings in Parliament House in wig and gown but soon saw that as a waste of time that could be better spent on literary matters.

Chapter IV: Legends

18 In 1814 Sir Walter Scott gathered some background information that he was to use in *The Pirate*, 1822, when he accompanied RLS's grandfather, Robert Stevenson, and the Northern Lighthouse Commissioners on one of their official voyages to inspect lighthouses. When Scott left on this exciting voyage in July 1814 *Waverley* was being promoted by Archibald Constable, its publisher, but had yet to become a bestseller. Scott was the most distinguished guest on board but there were three sheriffs of the northern territories. One was Scott's friend William Erskine, Sheriff of Orkney and Zetland. Scott was famous as the author of *The Lady of the Lake* and on the voyage he made notes for *The Lord of the Isles*, but the idea that became *The Pirate* was not thought of

until Constable suggested it to Scott in 1820. Scott wrote the novel in the summer and autumn of 1821 but, recognising that he was 'making my bricks with a very limited amount of straw', consulted William Erskine at Abbotsford in September 1821. Unlike Scott, Erskine, who had been on the voyage of 1814, knew Orkney and Shetland and so could provide the novelist with the history and Norse lore which Scott introduced into *The Pirate*.

19 William Burke and William Hare together committed many murders in Edinburgh to make money by supplying corpses for dissection by the distinguished anatomist Dr Knox. Burke was hanged after Hare turned King's evidence.

20 It was, in part, Deacon William Brodie's career that gave RLS the idea for Jekyll and Hyde. By day a respectable cabinet-maker, Deacon of Wrights, and member of the Town Council, he was by night a reckless burglar. He was hanged on 1 October 1788 on a gallows he had designed for the Edinburgh civic authorities.

21 Major Thomas Weir, who lived, with his sister, a respectable and seemingly God-fearing life in his house in the Head of the Bow, became ill and confessed to acts of incest, bestiality and sorcery. He was strangled and burnt at the stake near today's Picardy Place on 12 April 1670. His sister was hanged in the Grassmarket. For a century their empty house in the West Bow was a place to avoid, not least by the young James Boswell who went to school in the West Bow. W E Henley, whom RLS first met in Edinburgh in 1875, suggested that the name Weir, as used in *Weir of Hermiston*, was specially significant to Stevenson because of the life of Major Weir.

Chapter V: Greyfriars

22 Old Milne. The Mylnes were a dynasty of master masons who enjoyed Royal patronage; Mylnes Court off the Lawnmarket on the Royal Mile takes its name from them. The Mylne memorial in Greyfriars Kirkyard remains impressive.

23 Sir George Mackenzie of Rosenhaugh (1636-91) founded the Advocates' Library which evolved to become the National Library of Scotland. His *Discourse upon the Laws and Customs of Scotland in Matters Criminal*, 1674, remained a standard work for over one hundred years. His *Aretina*, a romance, wore less well. To fanatical Covenanters, whom, as King's Advocate in Scotland, he suppressed, he was 'Bloody McKenzie' or 'the bluidy Advocate'.

24 The Battle of Bothwell Bridge, 1679, saw the royal army led by the

Duke of Monmouth, Charles II's favourite illegitimate son, rout the Covenanters who had experienced victory at Drumclog when John Graham of Claverhouse ('Bloody Clavers') had attacked an armed gathering (Conventicle). Amongst the Covenanters who fought at both Drumclog and Bothwell were John Balfour and David Hackston, both of whom had been involved in the murder of Archbishop James Sharpe at Magus Muir. See notes to Stevenson's essay 'The Coast of Fife' printed here.

25 Many Covenanters were executed in the Grassmarket.

26 Patrick Walker was a favourite Covenanting writer of RLS's nurse, Alison Cunningham, and his influence can be seen in the young Stevenson's *The Pentland Rising*, 1866. Walker's writings, *Biographia Presbyteriana*, c.1732, were edited by J Stevenson, 1827. RLS also drew on the writings of: James Kirkton, *The Secret and True History of the Church of Scotland from the Restoration to the Year 1678. To which is added an account of the Murder of Archbishop Sharp by James Russell, an actor therein*, edited from the MSS by Charles Kirkpatrick Sharpe, 1817; and Robert Wodrow, *The History of the Sufferings of the Church of Scotland from the Reformation to the Revolution*, edited by Robert Burns, 4 vols, 1828-30.

Chapter VI: New Town—Town and Country

27 The poem by Robert Fergusson (1750-74) is 'On Seeing a Butterfly in the Street' which was included by Alexander Manson Kinghorn and Alexander Law in their selection *Poems by Allan Ramsay and Robert Fergusson*, 1974. See also the extract from Stevenson's letter to Charles Baxter, 18 May 1894, in which he wrote, 'I had always a great sense of kinship with poor Robert Fergusson…'.

28 Anst'er is the local usage for Anstruther, Fife, and the May is the Isle of May, which lies off Anstruther; see RLS's 'The Coast of Fife' reprinted here. Since 1815 the May has been owned by the Northern Lighthouse Commissioners who paid the Duchess of Portland £60,000 for it. During 1815-16 the historic beacon tower was replaced by a Robert Stevenson lighthouse which was modernised in 1886 and 1924.

29 RLS's mother was born in Colinton where her father was minister; see RLS's 'The Manse' reprinted here.

CHAPTER VII: THE VILLA QUARTERS

30 See John Ruskin's *Edinburgh Lectures* which includes these words on being in Edinburgh, 'There is hardly a day passes but you may

see some rent or flaw in bad buildings... You may see one when-ever you choose, in one of your most costly and most ugly buildings, the great church with the dome, at the end of George Street. I think I never saw a building with a principal entrance so utterly ghastly and oppressive; and it is as weak as it is ghastly.'

Chapter VIII: The Calton Hill

31 The six-ton foundation stone for the unfinished National Monu-ment on Calton Hill to those who died in the Napoleonic wars was laid by George IV in 1822 during his visit that Sir Walter Scott theatrically staged. The idea of Edinburgh as the Athens of the North is seen not only on Calton Hill but down in Waterloo Place, built in 1815, which leads into Regent Road. The terraces on Calton Hill, including Royal Terrace where RLS's cousin Charles Stevenson lived, although envisaged earlier were not built until the middle of the century. William Playfair, who designed these terraces, the Observatory and the National Monument on Calton Hill, and many other important buildings, is obviously of major importance in the development of the 'Athens of the North' but that truly formidable man, RLS's grandfather, Robert Stevenson, not only built light-houses, and enabled his sons and grandsons to do likewise, but also helped to change the face of the east end of Edinburgh. He blasted out the shelf on which Regent Road lies as it goes round Calton Hill and carried it over ravines and built massive supporting walls.

When Robert Stevenson created Regent Road he had to take it through Old Calton Cemetery and he moved the graves of his family to the New Calton Burying Ground where he also is buried. The old cemetery remains divided, with a smaller part behind Waterloo Place. In the larger part of the cemetery there is a new-looking memorial stone to Thomas Smith (1752-1815) and his third wife Jean Stevenson (1751-1820); she was born Jean (or Jane) Lillie and her first husband was Alan Stevenson who died in 1774— these are the great-grandparents of RLS. Also, since Robert Stevenson (RLS's grandfather) married Thomas Smith's eldest daughter, Thomas Smith is both father-in-law and stepfather of RLS's grandfather.

32 The New-Athens-style monuments to Dugald Stewart and to Robert Burns were built in the early 1830s. Dugald Stewart (1753-1828), an eloquent and influential lecturer, was Professor of Moral Philosophy in Edinburgh.

33 The Ballad of Sir Patrick Spens. The Queen they sought was

Margaret, the Maid of Norway. She was the granddaughter of King Alexander III, who was killed in a fall from his horse near Kinghorn in Fife. Margaret was a girl of three, daughter of Alexander's late daughter, Margaret, who had married Eric II of Norway. The little Queen died in 1290 not having seen Scotland.

34 Mucklebackit in Walter Scott's *The Antiquary*, 1816.

Chapter X: To the Pentland Hills

35 Flodden, the battle of 9 September 1513 when King James IV, Scotland's Renaissance Prince, was slain, as were nine earls, thirteen barons, an archbishop, and many thousands more, named and unnamed, of the English and Scottish armies.

36 From Burns's 'Tam o' Shanter'.

37 In 1867 Thomas Stevenson, RLS's father, leased Swanston Cottage, at Swanston village, on the slopes of the Pentland Hills, some five miles from the family house in Heriot Row.

38 Sam Bough, landscape painter and 'thorough Bohemian', who became a member of the Royal Scottish Academy. In 1870 he toured the Western Isles with Stevenson and others soon after Louis left the islet of Earraid. RLS's essay 'The Late Sam Bough, RSA' was printed in *The Academy*, 30 November 1878.

Edinburgh—The Water of Leith

Unpublished fragment written in late 1890 or early 1891, possibly later. The manuscript, of slightly more than a page with many revisions and deletions, is held at Yale (Beinecke 6506).

1 Rising in the Pentland Hills, the Water of Leith passes through Colinton, where Louis's grandfather was the minister (see essay 'The Manse' reprinted here) and in Edinburgh passes through Gorgie, Murrayfield, Dean Village and under Thomas Telford's spectacular Dean Bridge (1831) to pass near Henderson Row (with Edinburgh Academy which Louis attended) before curving round to Canonmills and through Leith to enter the Forth at Leith Docks.

Edinburgh—Colinton
'The Manse'

'The Manse' was first published in *Scribner's Magazine*, May 1887, and in that same year was printed in *Memories and Portraits*, 1887. Tusitala vol 29.

1   RLS's maternal grandfather, Rev Dr Lewis Balfour, was the minister at Colinton. RLS's mother, Margaret Isabella Balfour, was born at Colinton Manse.

2   From the Metrical Psalm 121 which begins, 'I to the hills will lift mine eyes'.

3   Alexander Adam, Rector of the High School, Edinburgh, was a distinguished classical scholar who introduced Greek into the school curriculum in 1772. In 1780 Edinburgh University conferred on him the degree of LL.D and so he was generally known as Dr Adam. He taught both Lord Cockburn and Sir Walter Scott; the former saying that Dr Adam was 'born to teach Latin, some Greek, and all virtue', and Scott writing, 'It was from this respectable man that I first learned the value of the knowledge I had hitherto considered only as a burdensome task.' William Nicol, Robert Burns's friend and drinking and travelling companion, who taught Latin at the High School, thought less well of Dr Adam, conducting a vindictive campaign against the Rector.

4   'Smith opens out his cauld harangues' is a line from Burns's 'The Holy Fair' with the following line reading, 'On *practice* and on *morals*'. In his biography of RLS, Graham Balfour writes that when he was about the age of twenty the Rev Lewis Balfour went to his first parish in Ayrshire and there met and married a daughter of Dr George Smith (died 1823), minister of Galston, the moralistic Smith of Burns's 'Holy Fair' (lines 122-35) who was RLS's maternal great-grandfather.

5   In his *Records of a Family of Engineers*, Stevenson wrote of Thomas Smith, stepfather and father-in-law (see note on Calton Hill above) of RLS's paternal grandfather, Robert Stevenson, founding a 'solid business in lamps and oils'. Also, having designed a system of oil lights to replace the primitive coal fires formerly used, Thomas Smith became Engineer to the Board of Commissioners of Northern Lighthouses. Robert Stevenson followed John Smith as engineer to the Board; in other words this is the start of the dynasty of lighthouse designers and of the prosperity which allowed Thomas Stevenson to support his son Louis financially.

The reference to a possible family link to a French barber to Cardinal David Beaton who, in 1546, was murdered in his castle at St Andrews, and to other improbable family associations can also be found in *Records of a Family of Engineers*. Since Baillie Nicol Jarvie is a merchant in Scott's fictional *Rob Roy*, Stevenson has added another reality to these biographical imaginings. As Tom Hubbard notes, Stevenson wrote as 'an unreal realist'

The details on the career of Robert Stevenson (1772-1850), RLS's engineer grandfather, are accurate as he made his name by building the Bell Rock lighthouse which stands on a sharp sandstone reef twenty-seven miles east of Dundee and eleven miles south of Arbroath. Also, in 1814 Sir Walter Scott did gather some background information for *The Pirate*, 1822, when he accompanied Robert Stevenson and the Northern Lighthouse Commissioners on one of their official voyages to inspect lighthouses, see note to *Edinburgh: Picturesque Notes* above.

Midlothian

'The Antiquities of Midlothian'. A translation of this piece first appeared in Michel Le Bris, *A travers l'Ecosse*, 1992. The original English of RLS's essay is published for the first time in the present work. Michel Le Bris worked from a manuscript in the Beinecke Library, Yale, where it is MS5970.

1   The eleven-year-old Louis made an excursion to Craigmillar Castle and Corstorphine Church in March 1861 and dictated his work to his mother in that same year. The great central tower of Craigmillar, south-east of Edinburgh off the A68, was built by the Prestons in the fourteenth century and enclosed in the early years of the next century by an embattled curtain wall. Within that defensive wall are stately apartments that date from the sixteenth and seventeenth centuries. A meeting of Queen Mary's nobles within these walls in 1567 involved plotting the death of her husband Darnley.

2   The Battle of Carberry Hill, which is about eight miles from Edinburgh, took place on 15 June and saw the Queen's army, led by Bothwell whom she had married at Holyrood on 15 May, defeated by lords who were jealous of Bothwell's rise to power. By evening Mary had accepted a safe conduct for Bothwell and entrusted herself to the lords. This was the prelude to Mary's imprisonment in Lochleven Castle where on 24 July 1567 she signed her abdication in favour of her son. She did not see Bothwell again.

North Berwick

Extract from 'The Lantern-Bearers'.

'The Lantern-Bearers' was first published in *Scribner's Magazine*, February 1888, and it was reprinted in *Across the Plains*, 1892. Tusitala vol 30. In November 1887, from Saranac Lake, RLS wrote to E L Burlingame, editor of *Scribner's Magazine*, 'I was glad you liked the "Lantern Bearers"; I did too... ingeniously put together.'

1 North Berwick is where RLS spent holidays in the early 1860s. His cousin Charles Stevenson gave an excellent account of his and Louis's boyhood days at North Berwick, 'On many days a joyous lot of boys would proceed along the Longskelly Beach to the Eel Burn referred to by Louis in *Catriona* as a "cressy burn" about a mile west of the end of North Berwick Links in the days of our boyhood.' Charles Stevenson also wrote that 'Fidra, the Lamb, Craigleith and the Bass were all left behind after the ice-age had passed by, going from west to east... Louis described Fidra [in *Catriona*, see extracts printed here] as "a strange grey islet of two humps, made the more conspicuous by a piece of ruin and I mind that (as we drew close to it) the sea peeped through like a man's eye." The eye is a hole through the main hump of the island about 29 feet in height. In Louis's day (and mine of course) the Eye used to be a marked and lovely feature of Fidra on the road leading out of Dirleton towards North Berwick and with the sea behind it, it looked like a great waterfall but grown trees have now [c.1940] shut off this unique angle. There was of course no lighthouse in those days.' The engineer for the Bass lighthouse of 1902 was David A Stevenson.

2 Once the Latin name given to the solan goose, or gannet, was *Pelecanus Bassanus* indicating that it belonged to the pelican family; today it is named *Sula Bassana*.

3 Tantallon Castle, east of North Berwick off the A198, was a stronghold of the Red Douglases. Bell-the-Cat was the nickname of Archibald, fifth Earl of Angus. His third son was Gavin Douglas (c.1475-1522), poet and translator of Virgil's *Aeneid*.

4 Berwick Law, or hill, faces the very similar Largo Law across the Forth.

Gillane Sands—Tantallon

From Chapter 13 of *Catriona:* Gillane Sands.

Catriona. A Sequel to Kidnapped was first published in 1893. Stevenson's novel *Kidnapped* had been published in 1886 but it was not until February 1892, at Vailima, Samoa, that he continued the story of David Balfour, his most-admired hero. Like *Kidnapped* it is dedicated to Charles Baxter, a very good and supportive friend from his student days who had remained in Edinburgh as a lawyer and who as such handled the exiled Stevenson's business affairs, and more besides. For notes on North Berwick see above extract from 'The Lantern Bearers'.

1 See Charles Stevenson, RLS's cousin, quoted in the note to North Berwick above.

The Bass Rock

From Chapter 14 of *Catriona:* The Bass.

1 The Bass Rock rises abruptly to a height of 420 feet above the sea; it is a distinct landmark from the Fife coast but it belongs to East Lothian, being about two miles from the shore and three miles east of the ancient royal burgh of North Berwick.

2 The 'auld saints' were the Covenanters who were imprisoned on the Bass in the seventeenth century and feature in RLS's 'The Tale of Tod Lapraik' in which he wrote, 'In thir days, dwalled upon the Bass a man of God, Peden the Prophet was his name'. Memorably, Stevenson has Black Andie say of Peden that 'The voice of him was like a solan's and dinnle'd in folk's lugs, and the words of him like coals of fire.' Alexander Peden, minister of New Luce, Galloway, was one of those who on being 'outed' from his ministry continued his preaching in the fields. Although he was not at Rullion Green, Peden was arrested for having been involved in the Rising of 1666. See also my *Robert Louis Stevenson and the Covenanters on the Bass Rock*, Kirkcaldy, 2002.

Edinburgh/Granton—Cramond

Letter to Mrs Frances Sitwell from 17 Heriot Row, Edinburgh, 12 September 1873.

1 It was in 1873 after Louis, aged twenty-two-years, had told his father that he was an agnostic if not an atheist, that the tension between him and his father was at its worst. To avoid too many

confrontations, Louis was given a study of his own on the top floor of Heriot Row and in July, to further ease that tension, he went on a holiday to stay with his Balfour cousin Maud (Mrs Churchill Babington) at Cockfield Rectory, Suffolk. It was during his 1873 visit to Cockfield Rectory that Louis met Mrs Frances Sitwell who was twelve years older than the gauche but interestingly complex youth. Mrs Sitwell not only gave the young and impressionable Louis sympathy and moral support but introductions which helped his literary career. His poem in *Underwoods*, 'To F. J. S' is easily seen to be to Mrs Sitwell, but it is only more recently that it has been known that 'Claire', of the early poems, was a poetic name for Mrs Sitwell.

1873 also saw the beginning of RLS's friendship with Sidney Colvin who, in 1903, married Mrs Sitwell. Colvin encouraged the young Louis and introduced him to literary circles in London. Colvin edited the Edinburgh edition of Stevenson's *Works*, 28 vols, 1894-98 and RLS chose him to prepare for publication, 'a selection of his letters and a sketch of his life'—see Introduction by Sir Sidney Colvin to the Tusitala edition (vols 31-35) of the *Letters*.

Edinburgh/Granton—South Queensferry

Letter to Mrs Frances Sitwell from Heriot Row, Edinburgh, 24 September 1873.

1   South Queensferry takes its name from the second wife of Malcolm III, the saintly Queen Margaret, who, in the eleventh century established a free ferry to provide transport across the Forth for pilgrims travelling to St Andrews.

South Queensferry and Hawes Inn

From Chapter 6 of *Kidnapped:* I Go to the Queen's Ferry.
Kidnapped was first published in 1886.

1   At South Queensferry, the Hawes Inn remains in business, over-looked by the Forth Rail Bridge, which was opened for use on 4 March 1890, and the nearby Road Bridge which was opened by the Queen on 4 September 1964. South Queensferry once had a busy fishing harbour which was rebuilt by Robert Stevenson and John Rennie between 1809 and 1818.

Limekilns, Fife

From Chapter 26 of *Kidnapped:* End of the Flight: We Pass the Forth.

1   Stevensonians may go to Limekilns to find the Ship Inn where Balfour and Alan Breck supposedly stopped, but they could also visit nearby Torryburn as it was there that Alison Cunningham, Louis's nurse, was born. Louis was eighteen months old when 'Cummy', as the child was to call her, arrived in the Stevensons' home. When Stevenson published his *A Child's Garden of Verses* in 1885 he dedicated the book 'To Alison Cunningham from her boy'. Alison Cunningham told her charge the stories of the Old Testament and of Scottish Covenanting history. For an imaginative child some of these may have been rather too vivid. In an autobiographical piece Stevenson wrote,

> I had an extreme terror of Hell, implanted in me, I suppose, by my good nurse, which used to haunt me terribly on stormy nights, when the wind had broken loose and was going about the town like a bedlamite. I remember that the noises on such occasions always grouped themselves for me into the sound of a horseman, or rather a succession of horsemen, riding furiously past the bottom of the street and away up the hill into town: I think even now that I hear the terrible *howl* of his passage, and the clinking that I used to attribute to his bit and stirrups.

These memories were used by Stevenson in the early poem 'Stormy Nights', but that is a prosy work when set against the direct scariness expressed in 'Windy Nights', which was printed as the ninth poem of *A Child's Garden of Verses*.

From Inverkeithing to Anstruther

'The Coast of Fife'. 'Contributions to the History of Fife: Random Memories' which included 'The Coast of Fife', was first published in *Scribner's Magazine*, October 1888. It was first collected in *Across the Plains*, 1892. Tusitala vol 30.

It was in July 1868 that Louis went to Anstruther to see the harbour works. In a letter from Anstruther to his father that July he wrote, 'My lodgings are very nice, and I don't think there are any children. There is a box of mignonette in the window and a factory of dried rose-leaves, which make the atmosphere a trifle heavy, but very pleasant.'

1   In addition to its association with the King (Alexander III) drinking

the blood-red wine as reported in the ballad of Sir Patrick Spens, Dunfermline is the burial place of King Robert I, the Bruce, and the poet Robert Henryson added another kind of lustre to the burgh, as did Andrew Carnegie who was born there.

2   The 'bonny face' that was spoiled was that of the Earl of Moray. On a green point east of St David's Bay, below Donibristle Castle, James Stewart, the bonnie Earl of Moray of ballad fame, was killed in February 1592 by the Earl of Huntly and his soldiers. St David's Bay, like its neighbour Dalgety Bay, is now part of a large housing development.

3   John Paul Jones (1747-92) was born at Kirkbean, Kirkcudbright, but became famous as an American naval commander during the War of Independence. Rev Mr Shirra was a minister of the Secession church in Kirkcaldy when Jones was involved in a raid on Scotland in September 1778. As reported by J W Taylor, who was the minister of the Free Church, Flisk and Creich, the brave Mr Shirra 'knelt on the wet sands, and prayed fervently to the Lord that He would interpose on behalf of the defenceless towns, and send Paul Jones and his privateers by the way by which they had come. The prayer was visibly and speedily answered. The wind veered round, and blew freshly from the west. The hostile ships hovered about for a time, uncertainly, and then, turning their prows, bore down the Forth, and outwards to the ocean.' See J W Taylor, *Some Historical Notices, Chiefly Ecclesiastical, Connected with Kirkcaldy and Abbotshall*, Kirkcaldy, 1869. Incidentally, the Edinburgh distributor of this booklet was Andrew Elliot who published RLS's *The Pentland Rising*. See also Sir Robert Sibbald's *The History Ancient and Modern of the Sheriffdoms of Fife and Kinross*, new edition, 1803, which may also have influenced Stevenson. Herman Melville recounts the Shirra-Jones episode in his novel *Israel Potter* (1855). Melville's paternal ancestors came from Fife.

4   Alexander III who fell to his death on a dark night in March 1286 as he rode along the cliff between Burntisland and Kinghorn; a memorial marks the spot. The death of Alexander left Scotland without a clear successor to the throne and this led to what RLS terms the 'English wars', otherwise the Wars of Independence.

5   The Wemyss caves are especially important for the prehistoric drawings that decorate their walls.

6   Stevenson wrote that *The Master of Ballantrae* had been conceived on the moors between Pitlochry and Strathairdle and in 'Highland rain, in the blend of the smell of heather and bog-plants, and with

Notes

a mind full of the Athole correspondence and the Memoirs of the Chevalier de Johnstone.' For Chevalier de Johnstone see James de Johnstone, *Memoirs of the Chevalier de Johnstone*, translated by Charles Winchester, 1870-71.

7   Dr John Balfour was in the medical service of the East India Company, and the Mutiny referred to by RLS is that in Delhi in May 1857.

8   Alexander Selkirk (1676-1721), the model for Daniel Defoe's *Robinson Crusoe*, was born in Lower Largo. His cottage has gone but its replacement carries a statue of Selkirk dressed as 'Robinson Crusoe', and the Crusoe Hotel stands beside Lower Largo harbour.

9   Archbishop James Sharp was murdered by Covenanters on 3 May 1679 by the roadside near Magus Muir between Ceres and St Andrews. See notes on John Balfour and David Hackston below and also my *Historic Fife Murders at Falkland, St Andrews and Magus Muir*, Kirkcaldy, 2002.

10 Cardinal David Beaton was murdered in his castle in St Andrews on 29 May 1546. John Knox gave a detailed description of the murder in his *History of the Reformation* which included these seemingly heartless words, 'And so was he brought to the east blockhouse head, and shown dead over the wall to the faithless multitude, which would not believe before it saw. How miserably lay David Beaton, careful Cardinal... These things we write merrily.'

11 Andrew Lang came to St Andrews in 1860 as a student and he retained a genuine liking for the small grey town on the Forth, writing in his poem 'Almae matres', 'St Andrews by the northern sea, / A haunted town it is to me!' He published his *St Andrews in 1893*. Stevenson's poem 'To Andrew Lang', printed in *Underwoods*, 1887, begins, 'Dear Andrew, with the brindled hair'.

12 RLS's grandfather, Robert Stevenson, died four months before his grandson was born. See RLS's uncompleted *Records of a Family of Engineers* and Robert Stevenson's own *An Account of the Bell Rock Lighthouse*, 1824. See also Bella Bathurst, *The Lighthouse Stevensons*, 1999, and Jean Leslie and Roland Paxton, *Bright Lights. The Stevenson Engineers 1752-1971*, 1999. Mrs Jean Leslie (born in 1916) is the granddaughter of Charles Stevenson (1885-1950) and daughter of Frances Margaret Stevenson (later Douglas) (1892-1974).

13 Thomas Rowlandson's *The English Dance of Death* appeared in two volumes, 1815-16.

14 See James Kirkton, *The Secret and True History of the Church of*

Scotland from the Restoration to the Year 1678. To which is added an account of the Murder of Archbishop Sharp by James Russell, an actor therein, edited from the MSS by Charles Kirkpatrick Sharpe, 1817. John Balfour of Kinloch led the murderers of Archbishop Sharp at Magus Muir. He escaped west and, as a Covenanting officer at the Battle of Bothwell Bridge, as at Drumclog, showed that he was a natural fighter, being one of the last to leave the scene of the battle. After his heroic exploits at Bothwell a wounded Balfour disappeared into the shadows of legend as a crazed figure on wild moors and soaring rock faces; almost a King Lear of the Fife lairds. Sir Walter Scott invented a history for Balfour in *Old Mortality* where he appears under the name of Burley:

> Burley, only altered from what he had been formerly by the addition of a grisly beard, stood in the midst of the cave with his clasped Bible in one hand and his drawn sword in the other. His figure, dimly ruddied in the red light of the red charcoal, seems that of a fiend in the lurid atmosphere of Pandemonium.

15 The relevant passage from James Russell's account, as printed in James Kirkton's *History*, of the murder of Archbishop Sharp that haunted Stevenson's imagination is where he describes an event at the scene of the murder. With the Archbishop dead,

> James Russell desired his servants to take up their priest now. All this time Andrew Guillan pleaded for his life. John Balfour threatening him to be quiet, he came to Rathillet, who was standing at a distance with his cloak about his mouth all the time on horseback, and desired him to come and cause save his life, who answered, as he meddled not with them nor desired them to take his life, so he durst not plead for him nor forbid them. Then they all mounted, and going west gathered up some pistols which they had thrown away after fired.

Having fought and led his troop of horse with great courage at Bothwell Bridge, David Hackston of Rathillet, in Fife, escaped to join Richard Cameron. Hackston was taken prisoner in July 1680 at a battle fought at Airds Moss, near Muirkirk in Ayrshire. An exceptionally brave man amongst many brave Covenanting martyrs, he was taken to Edinburgh for trial and sentencing. He was drawn backwards on a hurdle to the place of execution at the Cross of Edinburgh where he bravely died a cruel and slow death. In his essay 'My First Book [ie first novel]: *Treasure Island*', published in

1894, RLS wrote of his 'mania' to write novels, 'as soon I was able to write, I became a good friend to the papermakers. Reams upon reams must have gone into the making of "Rathillet", the "Pentland Rising" [a novel and not the 'slim green pamphlet']...'. Stevenson was not yet fifteen when he worked on 'Rathillet' and his almost lifelong interest in the Covenanters can be seen in the posthumously published *Weir of Hermiston* and in another unfinished novel, *Heathercat*, which he spasmodically worked on from July 1893 through to the summer of 1894.

16 Robert Wodrow, *The History of the Sufferings of the Church of Scotland from the Reformation to the Revolution*, edited by Robert Burns, 4 vols, 1828-30.

17 See Lt Col Alexander Fergusson, *Chronicles of the Cumming Club, and Memories of Old Academy Days*, 1887. Stevenson wrote several poems relating to Edinburgh Academy: 'Their Laureate to an Academy Class Dinner Club' (the class of D'Arcy Wentworth Thompson), that met for a dinner in 1883, and 'Poem for a Class Re-union' (of 1875).

18 Henry Charles Fleeming Jenkin (1833-85), Professor of Engineering at Edinburgh, taught RLS who wrote *Memoir of Fleeming Jenkin*, 1887, Tusitala vol 19. RLS was to write to Mrs Fleeming Jenkin, 'I never knew a better man.' Louis's engineering education at Edinburgh University was more about truancy than attendance. We learn from the 'Memoir' that, after much pleading by Louis, Professor Jenkin gave his student a certificate that he could show to his father to the effect that he had satisfactorily completed the classwork in engineering. His first response had been, 'It is quite useless for you to come to me, Mr Stevenson. There may be doubtful cases, there is no doubt about yours. You have simply not attended my class.'

19 *The Abode of Snow: Observations on a Journey from Chinese Tibet to the Indian Caucasus, through the Upper Valleys of the Himalaya*, 1875. Lt Col Alexander Fergusson, note above, wrote that the president of the Philosophical Society was 'poor "Skinny Wilson"— that is to say, Andrew Wilson, whose *Abode of Snow* is not likely to be forgotten'.

20 Stevenson took the story of the Rev Edward Thomson from Kirkton's *History of the Church*, where it is an illustration of the fate of those who betrayed the Covenanting cause. It has been seen as an influence on 'Thrawn Janet' and 'The Tale of Tod Lapraik'.

21 Mr Thomson's predecessor as minister in Anstruther was Rev James Melville (1556-1614) nephew of Andrew Melville who famously informed King James VI that he was 'bot God's sillie [weak] vassal'. In his *Diaries*, the Rev Melville told the story of how the Spanish general and his captains and soldiers sought shelter in Anstruther following the battle with the English and having run onto the rocks off Fair Isle. Melville gave the names of the Spanish commanders as, 'Jan Gomes de Medina, Generall of twentie houlkes, Capitan Patricio, Capitan de Legoretto, Capitan de Luffera, Capitan Mauritio and Seingour Serrano'. See Rev James Melville, *The Autobiography and Diary*, edited by Robert Pitcairn, 1827. Stevenson's interest in the Spanish Armada may have been fuelled by Sibbald's *The History Ancient and Modern of Fife and Kinross*. Stevenson also showed interest in the Armada in 'The Merry Men', which he began in the Summer of 1881.

22 In June 1869 RLS sailed in the lighthouse steamer *Pharos* on a voyage to inspect lighthouses in Orkney and Shetland including North Unst (Muckle Flugga) Lighthouse, which Louis described in a letter to his mother as 'the most northerly dwelling house in Her Majesty's domain.' He also visited Fair Isle. See extracts from letters printed here.

23 John Bruce (1798-1885), of Sumburgh and of Fair Isle, see also note to 'Shetland—Lerwick—Pict's House—Sumburgh—Fair Isle'.

Kirriemuir, Angus

From letter to J M Barrie from Vailima, 13 July 1894.

1 According to his mother's diary RLS visited Glenogil, ten miles north-east of Kirriemuir, Barrie's birthplace, in 1877. He was visiting John Leveson Douglas Stewart (1842-87).

2 The 'Queen's River' is the Noran Water. Alex J Warden wrote in his *Angus, or Forfarshire*, 1883, of how a Scottish Queen, having washed her linen cap in it, said that the Noran Water was the clearest stream in Scotland.

3 'Some wee, short hour ayont the *twal*' (twelve midnight) is a line in the final stanza of Robert Burns's 'Death and Doctor Hornbook. A True Story'.

4 The Free Kirk was at Memus, five miles north-east of Kirriemuir.

Pitlochry

From letter to Sidney Colvin, from Kinnaird Cottage, Pitlochry, June 1881.

1   Stevenson was in Pitlochry from June to July 1881. The weather was bad and RLS had bouts of ill health but he wrote 'Thrawn Janet' and also 'The Merry Men' which in a cheerful letter to W E Henley (Pitlochry, July 1881) he described as 'a fantastic sonata about the sea and wrecks'. He also saw 'a little of Scott's *The Pirate* in it'.

Blair Atholl

'Athole Brose', a poem.

1   In Chapter 25 of *Kidnapped*: 'In Balquidder', Stevenson described the constituents of Atholl Brose, 'Duncan Dhu made haste to bring out the pair of pipes that was his principal possession, and to set before his guests a mutton-ham and a bottle of that drink which they call Athole brose, and which is made of old whiskey, strained honey, and sweet cream, slowly beaten together in the right order and proportion'. Duncan Dhu's wife was 'out of Atholl and had a name far and wide for her skill in that confection.'

Braemar

From letter to Mrs Frances Sitwell, from The Cottage, Castleton of Braemar, August 1881.

1   The Stevensons were at Braemar during August and September 1881. It was there that Stevenson began to write *Treasure Island*. The Cottage was known as 'the late Miss McGregor's cottage' but RLS wrote in a NB to a letter to Edmund Gosse, 10 August 1881, who was to edit the Pentland edition (20 vols 1906-7) of his *Works*, 'The reference to a deceased Highland lady (tending as it does to foster unavailing sorrow) may with advantage be omitted from the address, which would therefore run—The Cottage, Castleton of Braemar.'

Anstruther and Wick

'The Education of an Engineer'. 'The Education of an Engineer' was first published in *Scribner's Magazine* in November 1888 and first collected in *Across the Plains*, 1892. Tusitala vol 30. There are various titlings of this essay, linking it to 'Contribution to the History of Fife: Random Memories', which also included 'The Coast of Fife'.

1   The poet William Tennant was born in 1784 in a house on Anstruther High Street that now carries a plaque. As the plaque says, Tennant became Professor of Oriental Languages in St Mary's College, St Andrews. He is buried in Anstruther at St Adrian's Kirkyard on Burial Brae. Tennant is best known for the long poem *Anster Fair*, but his 'Papistry Storm'd' is another *tour de force*. See *The Comic Poems of William Tennant*, edited by Alexander Scott and Maurice Lindsay, 1989.

2   Stevenson was in Anstruther in July 1868, and later that same year in Wick—see extracts from letters reprinted here.

3   *Voces Fidelium* is mentioned by Graham Balfour, in his *Life*, 1901, (see vol 1, p.104,) and by J C Furnas in his *Voyage to Windward*, 1952, p.48.

4   Stevenson's early unfinished Covenanting novels included one on David Hackston.

5   Stevenson was in Wick from 27 August to 6 October 1868—see extracts from letters written from Wick printed here. He also wrote about Wick in his essay 'On the Enjoyment of Unpleasant Places', first published in *Portfolio Magazine*, November 1874. Tusitala vol 25.

6   Meg Merrilies, the gypsy in Walter Scott's *Guy Mannering*, 1815.

7   Another reference to the Spanish Armada shipwrecked off Fair Isle. For the Commander's arrival in Anstruther, see the essay 'The Coast of Fife' reprinted here.

Orkney—Kirkwall

Extracts from letters to his mother from the lighthouse steamer, 18-22 June 1869.

Selections from RLS's Letters, edited by Sidney Colvin, were printed in *Scribner's Magazine* during 1899. The first group of letters printed in the magazine was a selection from those he wrote to his parents in 1868 and 1869 from Anstruther, Wick and Orkney and Shetland. The long letters written by Louis to his mother, when he accompanied his father on board the 'Pharos', the official steamer of the Northern Lighthouse Commissioners, on a tour of inspection to Orkney and Shetland, are journals of that voyage. Louis inserted details of time and date and

where the steamer was when he wrote a particular section of the journal-
letters, eg: 'Between Cantick and Hoy'; 'Off Lerwick'; 'Between
Sumburgh and Fair Isle'; and 'Between Fair Isle and Ronaldsha'.

1   The massive early-Norman style Cathedral of St Magnus in Kirkwall
    was completed in the fifteenth century but has a history going back
    to 1137 and Rognvald III, nephew of Magnus. This impressive
    Gothic structure survived the Reformation but Cromwell's army
    used it as a prison and a stable. For many years only the choir
    remained in use as a parish church and the building deteriorated
    until a restoration of 1912-20.

2   Captain John Gow, captured in Orkney and executed for piracy in
    1725. Walter Scott used the story as the basis for *The Pirate*, where
    he also used the name Goffe.

3   The ruined Bishop's Palace has a hall-house that dates from the
    thirteenth century but was much altered in the sixteenth century
    and again by Patrick Stewart, Earl of Orkney. The roofless but
    otherwise very complete Earl's Palace, which was built by Earl
    Patrick Stewart in the early years of the seventeenth century, has
    been described as 'the most mature and accomplished piece of
    Renaissance architecture left in Scotland'. The notoriously tyran-
    nical Earl Patrick, son of an illegitimate son of James V, also built
    Scalloway Castle in Shetland about 1600. Earl Patrick was ex-
    ecuted in Edinburgh in 1615.

4   From Shakespeare, 'The Phoenix and the Turtle', lines 13-14.

5   Archdeacon Claude Frollo, who was pushed by the hunchback
    from one of the towers of Notre-Dame in Victor Hugo's novel.

Shetland—Whalsay—Unst—Lerwick

Extracts from letters to his mother from the lighthouse steamer, 18-22
June 1869, see note to 'Orkney—Kirkwall' above.

1   Whalsay is the 'bonny Isle' with green pastures and low hills offset
    by small lochs. From the small port of Symbister, in the south, a
    road passes Symbister House which became a school in 1940, to
    Sudheim and the now-ruined cottage where Hugh MacDiarmid
    (Christopher Murray Grieve) (1892-1978) lived from April 1933 to
    February 1942. To the delight of MacDiarmid, the Anglicising
    mapmakers gave Sudheim (south home) as Sodom.

    Even for a lighthouse engineer, Thomas Stevenson was more
    than usually interested in the generation and force of waves. Despite

his scientific approach, Thomas seemed to lapse, in his private notes, into the idea that there were forces at work beyond scientific explanation. Standing on the cliff at Whalsay he examined 'indications of a violent, destructive agency which seemed to have been lately at work upon the hard rock... Here then was a phenomenon so remarkable as almost to stagger belief—a mass of 5.5 tons not only moved at a spot which is 72 feet above high water spring tides, but actually quarried from its position *in situ*'. This is as dramatic as his young son's words on the 'great big fellow'.

2   A temporary light was built at North Unst (Muckle Flugga) by RLS's uncle David Stevenson in 1854 and a permanent lighthouse was completed in 1857 and modernised in 1927. David also built a light at Out Skerries [Whalsay Skerries], Shetland, 1852-54. Temporary lights were built at Whalsay, and also North Unst, because the Admiralty asked to have lights exhibited on the north-east coast of Shetland not later than 1st October 1854. The purpose of these lights was to indicate to the fleet bound for Russia during the Crimean War the northern and eastern coasts of the Shetland islands. Dubh Artach, or Dhu Heartach (1867-72) was David and Thomas Stevenson's finest lighthouse. Thomas was working on this light in the summer of 1870 when Louis visited the Isle of Earraid off Mull from where he visited Dhu Heartach lighthouse. See the essay 'Memoirs of an Islet' reprinted here. The Muckle Flugga light was automated in 1995 which meant that Wick of Skaw, a crofter's house, became Britain's most northerly dwelling.

3   Standing on the summit of Unst's Saxa Vord (284m), the bare rock of Out Stack can be seen 3km further north but it is the sea-battered cliffs and Muckle Flugga that visitors remember. In 1849 Lady Franklin landed on Out Stack to pray for her husband when he had not returned from his North West Passage expedition.

4   Today's maps spell RLS's Blumel Sound, between Unst and Yell, as Bluemull Sound which takes its name from the headland Blue Mull on which stands the Kirk of Lund or St Olaf's Chapel.

5   Fort Charlotte was named in honour of Queen Charlotte. Norsemen are likely to have been first in settling what is now Lerwick, but it was the Dutch who, in the early seventeenth century, established it as a seasonal centre for their fishing, and the Shetlanders welcomed them as customers for their goods in what was essentially a shanty town. Before the Dutch made Lerwick important, Scalloway was the capital of Shetland. Cromwellians expelled the Dutch and built the fort but the Dutch returned to fire the fort in

1673 and to resume fishing. The repaired fort was modernised and a barrack block added in 1781.

6   In fact George III.

Shetland—Lerwick—Pict's House—Sumburgh— Fair Isle

Extracts from letters to his mother from the lighthouse steamer, 18-22 June 1869, see note to 'Orkney—Kirkwall' above.

1   Loch Clickhimin, which has been surrounded by houses since Stevenson's day. In the loch, but connected to the shore by a causeway, is Clickhimin Broch which is a good example of a broch tower with other buildings dating to the Iron Age (first centuries BC-AD). It has been suggested that the Victorian woman who excavated the site may have tidied it up somewhat. Walter Scott can be said to have tidied up the varied ruins at Sumburgh Head by naming them, in *The Pirate*, the fictional Norse-sounding Jarlshof, see note below.

2   RLS left a blank at this point in the letter; perhaps he was thinking of 'barbican'.

3   Maes Howe (west of Kirkwall on the A965) the great chambered tomb of the Neolithic period, had only recently (1861) been uncovered when RLS was in Orkney. Described as 'the finest megalithic tomb in Britain, the masonry being unsurpassed in Western Europe', the craftsmanship of the men who built Maes Howe certainly matches that of the best masons employed in the nineteenth century by the Stevenson family. Today visitors can see an exhibition and video display on the ground floor of nearby Tormiston Mill. Near Maes Howe are the standing stones of Stenness and on the west coast at the Bay of Skaill (north-west of Kirkwall on the B9056) is the prehistoric village of Skara Brae, which became known when it was cleared by an exceptional storm in 1824. Today within Skara Brae and Skaill House Centre there is a tearoom, shop, exhibition area and audio/visual room.

4   As previous notes: in 1814 Sir Walter Scott gathered some slight background information that he later used for *The Pirate*, 1822, when he accompanied RLS's grandfather, Robert Stevenson, and the Lighthouse Commissioners on one of their official voyages to inspect lighthouses.

5   Sumburgh Head Lighthouse was built by Robert Stevenson in 1821; his structure was superseded by a second tower built in 1914.

6   Jarlshof, which is one of the most remarkable archeological sites in Britain, is now known not so much for the ruined walls of the seventeenth-century house built by Earl Patrick Stewart but as the site of Norse ruins of the 9th-14th centuries, important Bronze Age buildings and a broch from the Iron Age. The seventeenth-century 'Laird's House' on the crest of the sandy mound is, however, the original of Scott's 'Jarlshof', the home of the fictitious Mr Mertoun in *The Pirate*.

7   John Bruce (1798-1885), of Sumburgh, owned Fair Isle from 1866.

8   Fair Isle is also described by RLS in 'The Coast of Fife' (reprinted here). Since 1954 the National Trust for Scotland has owned Fair Isle, having bought it from George Waterston, the ornithologist who founded the Bird Observatory in 1948.

9   The *Lessing*, from Bremen, was wrecked on Fair Isle on 23 May 1868.

From Wick to Golspie

From sketch, 'Night outside the Wick Mail'. Written into letter to Robert Stevenson from Edinburgh, 17 November 1868.

All his life RLS looked up to his older cousin Robert (Bob) Alan Mowbray Stevenson (1847-1900), son of Alan Stevenson (1807-65). It was his cousin Bob who was blamed by Louis's father for introducing the younger youth into the low life of Edinburgh and undermining his Christian faith. There was an extreme example of what Louis described as 'the thunderbolt of paternal anger' when Bob, Louis, Charles Baxter and others formed a Society whose constitution opened with the words, 'Disregard everything our parents taught us.' That may have been not uncommon youthful rebellion, but Bob also introduced Louis not only to the fashionable European 'wide-awake' hat and velvet jacket but to the artists' colony at Barbizon, in the forest of Fontainebleau, where, in the summer of 1876, he met Fanny Osbourne. Throughout Stevenson's work filial relationships that involve tension occur. One is central to *The Master of Ballantrae* and they occur not only in *Weir of Hermiston* in which Archie Weir, son of Lord Hermiston, is in a stressful relationship with his father, but also in *The Wrecker*, 'The Story of a Lie', and 'The Misadventures of John Nicholson' with John Binding, in a Penguin edition of *Weir of Hermiston and other stories*, 1979, going so far as to suggest that Mr Nicholson is a 'portrait' of Thomas Stevenson.

1   In October 1868 Louis took the stagecoach from Wick to Golspie from where he continued south by train. He travelled to Wick with

his father but soon Thomas Stevenson left Louis on his own to attend to other work. Louis had already been that summer to Anstruther, where harbour improvements were ongoing, to add to his engineering knowledge. In Wick, he took lodgings with Mrs Sutherland, where his father had previously stayed, in what is now named Harbour Terrace and from where he had a splendid view of the then busy Pulteneytown Harbour, and in Louis's words, 'the baldest of God's bays'. In 1907 a plaque was placed above the door which says 'Robert Louis Stevenson lived here in Autumn 1868. Erected by the Literary Society, Wick, 1907'. During the six weeks he was in Wick Louis was befriended by Sheriff Hamilton Russell and his wife Mary, who were old friends of his father. The Russells lived at 9 Breadalbane Crescent and dinner there involved, as Louis wrote to his mother, 'spotless blacks, white tie, etcetera, and finished off below with a pair of navvies' boots. How true that the devil is betrayed by his feet! A message to Cummy at last. Why, O treacherous woman! Were my dress boots withheld.'

Wick was not a place that Thomas Stevenson liked to remember. As Iain Sutherland wrote in his *Wick Harbour and the Herring Fishing*, the breakwater scheme was 'a disaster from start to finish, representing the only failure that this company was ever to experience in all its undertakings. Two hundred feet of the works were demolished by a storm on December 21, 1868, it was replaced and another 400 feet was destroyed on February 10, 1870. Another section was destroyed in 1872 and by 1873 the [British Fisheries] Society had had enough and its engineers declared the construction to be a ruin and abandoned it.' In late May 1887, after his father's death on the 8th, Louis wrote, 'Many harbours were successfully carried out; one, the harbour at Wick, the chief disaster of my father's life, was a failure; the sea proved too strong for man's arts; and after expedients hitherto unthought of, and on a scale hyper-cyclopean, the work must be deserted, and now stands a ruin in that bleak, God-forsaken bay, ten miles from John O'Groats.' ('Thomas Stevenson: Civil Engineer', *The Contemporary Review*, no 51, June 1887, and reprinted in *Memories and Portraits*, 1887.)

During his six-week stay in Caithness Louis visited Thurso and it was on the coach trip to Thurso via Castleton that there occurred the dream-like incident, remembered in 'The Education of an Engineer', 1888, involving two Italians and from which came the 'blood and thunder tale', 'The Pavilion on the Links' of 1880. It could also be that Jim Hawkins' encounter with Ben Gunn, a ragged 'creature of the woods', came from RLS's memory of an incident that happened near Wick. Also, as Ian Bell noted, 'In the Wick area the name Gunn was common, and there was more than one local named Ben.' Others, including Tom Hubbard, have suggested that in writing *Treasure Island* Stevenson may also have remembered a cave, on a walk he favoured, by the Allan Water between Bridge of Allan and Dunblane, see note to 'Bridge of Allan' below. In 1868 Louis also visited Scrabster before leaving Wick in early October to take the journey by stagecoach to Golspie which he described so well in the 'sketch' printed here.

Skye, Mull, Rhum, Eigg

'Sing me a song of a lad that is gone'. This poem, or song, was published in *Songs of Travel*, in Vol 14 of the Edinburgh Edition of Stevenson's *Works*, December 1895, edited by Sidney Colvin, and as a separate volume published by Chatto & Windus in September 1896.

1   This poem is dated by Graham Balfour as having been written in 1887. Mrs Stevenson, in her Prefatory Note to *Underwoods*, explained, 'The writing of *Over the Sea to Skye* grew out of a visit from one of the last of the old school of Scots Gentlewomen, Miss Ferrier, a granddaughter of Professor Wilson (Christopher North). Her singing was a great delight to my husband, who would beg for song after song, especially the Jacobite airs, which had always to be repeated several times. The words to one of these seemed unworthy, so he made a new set of verses more in harmony with the plaintive tune.' According to the *Oxford Companion to Music*, 'One half of the tune is a sea-shanty heard in 1879 by Miss Annie MacLeod (later Lady Wilson) when going by boat from Toran to Loch Coruisk; the other half is by Miss MacLeod herself. The words, by Sir Harold Boulton, Bart, [*Speed bonnie boat, like a bird on the wing*] date from 1884. Later some other words were written to the tune by Robert Louis Stevenson, who apparently believed the tune to be a pure folk tune and in the public domain.'

Oban

Extract from letter to his mother from Earraid, 4th August 1870.

1   George Robert Stephenson (1819-1905) of Glen Caladh Castle, Kyles of Bute, nephew of the railway engineer who was himself an engineer and owner of locomotive works at Newcastle-upon-Tyne.

Earraid

'Memoirs of an Islet'. 'Memoirs of an Islet' was written about spring-summer 1887 and first published in *Memories and Portraits*, 1887. Tusitala, vol 29.

1 'Happiness and unhappiness become song'.

2 'The Merry Men'.

3 David Balfour in *Kidnapped*.

4 Stevenson spent three weeks on Earraid, off Mull, in August 1870 during the construction of Dhu Heartach lighthouse (now given as Dubh Artach) fifteen miles to the south-west. Earraid (or Erraid) lies at the southern edge of the Sound of Iona and, being tidal, is accessible across the sands for two hours at low tide. The island has its surrounding islets and rocks with fine names, Eilean Dubh, Eilean Ghòmain, Eilean nam Muc, Eilean Chalmain, Eilean na Seamair, etc. The Torran Rocks lie to the south, with the sea mostly hiding the shipwrecking teeth that the white spray can lead the eye to. Until 1967 Earraid was the shore station for not only Dubh Artach but also Skerryvore.

   Thomas Stevenson worked with his brother David on Dubh Artach and it is their finest achievement, being not only an elegant structure but standing on a very difficult deep-sea site. Louis saw the rock of Dubh Artach as 'the first outpost of a great black brotherhood'; and these 'fatal rocks' of the Torran reef were moved nearer to Earraid, to become the 'place' where David Balfour and Alan Breck were shipwrecked in *Kidnapped*. As David Balfour explained in the novel, 'the reef on which we had struck was close in under the south-west end of Mull, off a little isle they call Earraid, which lay low and black upon the larboard.' Earraid is also the setting for 'The Merry Men' which RLS began at Pitlochry in 1881. Incidentally, *The Cornhill Magazine*, no. 45, June 1882, paid RLS (via his account with Mitchell and Baxter) 18 guineas for 'The Merry Men'.

5 Sam Bough (1822-78), landscape painter and 'thorough Bohemian'; see note to *Edinburgh: Picturesque Notes* above.

6 Robert Stevenson made his name through building the Bell Rock lighthouse which was completed in 1811.

7 Skerryvore was built by RLS's uncle Alan Stevenson (1807-65). If the Bell Rock lighthouse was a major challenge to the indefatigable and mentally strong Robert Stevenson, then Skerryvore stretched

Alan Stevenson, his more imaginative son, to his physical and mental limits. Skerryvore, which is undoubtedly the finest monument to the Stevenson family, stands on rocks twelve miles west of Tiree on an exposed reef that is swept by the full might of Atlantic storms. It is accepted by those who know, that this was a more scientifically designed lighthouse than any of its predecessors with 'its sides curved in the form of a solid generated by the revolution of a rectangular hyperbole about its asymptote as a vertical axis' which had the lowest centre of gravity of various possibilities considered. To Alan Stevenson's fellow engineers Skerryvore was 'the finest combination of mass with elegance to be met with in architectural or engineering structures.' To his nephew Louis it was 'the noblest of all the extant deep-sea lights', and 'we are all very proud of the family achievements, and the name of my house here in Bournemouth is stolen from one of the sea-towers of the Hebrides which are our pyramids and monuments.' (Letter of June 1886 to a Miss Monroe in Chicago).

8   The Franco-Prussian War. In a letter to James Payn (11 August 1894) from Vailima, when the rebels of Atua were being bombarded by British ships, Stevenson wrote, 'I can well remember, when the Franco-Prussian war began, and I was in Eilean Earraid, far enough from the sound of the loudest cannonade, I could *hear* the shots fired, and I felt the pang in my breast of a man struck. It was sometimes so distressing, so instant, that I lay in the heather on the top of the island, with my face hid, kicking my heels for agony. And now, when I can hear the actual concussion of the air and hills, when I *know* personally the people who stand exposed to it, I am able to go on *tant bien que mal* with a letter to James Payn! The blessings of age, though mighty small, are tangible.'

The Highlands

'In the highlands, in the country places', poem. This much-admired poem was printed in *The Pall Mall Gazette*, 21 December, 1894, where it was accompanied by a facsimile of the original manuscript. Published in *Songs of Travel*, in Vol 14 of the Edinburgh Edition of Stevenson's *Works*, December 1895, edited by Sidney Colvin, and as a separate volume published by Chatto & Windus in September 1896.

1   Stevenson knew the 'country places' and ways of those who lived around his grandfather's manse at Colinton and at the week-end cottage at Swanston near the 'hill-recesses' of the Pentlands, but

the lyricism of these very literary lines seems to lie outside such places where the language of the people was Scots.

Appin—Mamore—Heugh of Corrynakiegh

From *Kidnapped*, Chapter 21: The Flight in the Heather: the Heugh of Corrynakiegh.

1   The Heugh of Corrynakiegh is named by RLS, as is the little clachan not far from Corrynakiegh, which 'has the name of Koalisnacoan' but not the 'sea-loch that divides that country from Appin'. It may be that the Heugh is a fictional name but there is a hamlet called Caolasnacon. We can take the sea-loch to be Loch Leven with Heugh of Corrynakiegh seemingly somewhere high on the north side of Aonach Eagach above Glen Coe. In Chapter 22 of *Kidnapped* we learn that 'More than eleven hours of incessant, hard travelling brought us to the end of a range of mountains. In front of us there lay a piece of low, broken desert land, which we must now cross.' This 'desert' is not given a geographical placing or naming but it is described in details that are an example of, as Tom Hubbard notes, Stevenson representing things through 'significant simplicity',

> The mist rose and died away, and showed us that country lying as waste as the sea; only the moorfowl and the peewees crying upon it, and far over to the east, a herd of deer, moving like dots. Much of it was red with heather; much of the rest broken up with bogs and hags and peaty pools; some had been burnt black in a heath fire; and in another place there was quite a forest of dead firs, standing like skeletons. A wearier looking desert man never saw; but at least it was clear of troops, which was our point. We went down accordingly into the waste, and began to make our toilsome and devious travel towards the eastern verge. There were the tops of mountains all round (you are to remember)...

Only later, as they come near it, is Ben Alder named by Alan Breck to the exhausted David Balfour.

Cluny's Cage, Ben Alder

From Chapter 23 of *Kidnapped*: Cluny's Cage.

1   From Chapter 22 of *Kidnapped*: 'The Flight in the Heather: The

Moor' we learn, 'Now Cluny Macpherson, the chief of the clan Vourich, had been one of the leaders of the great rebellion six years before; there was a price on his life; and I had supposed him long ago in France, with the rest of the heads of that desperate party. Even tired as I was, the surprise of what I heard half wakened me. "What?" I cried. "Is Cluny still here?" "Ay is he so!" said Alan. "Still in his own country and kept by his own clan. King George can do no more."'

Cluny's Cage was built on the face of a very rough and steep rocky spur on the south face of Ben Alder overlooking Loch Ericht. It comprised a rough shelter on two levels, made of large rocks laid at various angles. The lower 'room' was kitchen and larder and those sheltering there slept on the upper space. When Prince Charles Edward Stuart took shelter there Cluny's men excavated a subterranean 'room' in which he could spend the winter if he could not get away to France. A nearby spring provided water and there was plenty of whisky and no shortage of food as Cluny's country was rich in game, especially hares and moorfowl. Also, his herds and flocks had not been found by the enemy although his valuable collection of brood mares had been taken after Culloden. For further details of the Cage and how the Prince may have coped during his five months on the run see Frank McLynn, *Charles Edward Stuart: a tragedy in many acts*, London, 1988.

Bridge of Allan

Extract from letter to Robert Stevenson, RLS's cousin, from Edinburgh, 17 November 1868.

1   This cavern has been seen as having been in Stevenson's mind when he wrote in *Treasure Island* of Jim Hawkins' encounter with Ben Gunn, see also note to 'From Wick to Golspie' above. The cavern is reputed to have been the entrance to a copper mine.

2   From John Milton, 'Hymn on the Morning of Christ's Nativity'.

3   From Milton, *Comus*. RLS received a three-volume set of Milton's works from his mother on his eighteenth birthday. In his *Seeking Mr Hyde*, 1995, Tom Hubbard suggested that 'A real-life chemist of Bridge of Allan may have served as a model for both [Stevenson's] Hyde and Gourlay [of George Douglas Brown's *The House with the Green Shutters*]. See RLS, "Memoirs of Himself", ("Fairy, the hunchback druggist... was a terror to me by day and haunted my dreams at night; but my pity was stronger than my distaste"); and David Angus... cites the druggist's name as Gilbert Farie.'

Extract from letter to Mrs Frances Sitwell from probably Heriot Row, 31 January 1875.

1 The 'My dearest Mother' perhaps needs a comment if not a Freudianesque theory. A few weeks later, in another letter to Mrs Sitwell, RLS wrote,

> Dearest Mother, ... I do not know to whom it was that I wrote last spring, when I was at the bottom of sorrow at Mentone—but I think it was to Bob; if it was not to him it was to you—calling for a mother; I felt so lonely just then; I cannot tell you what sense of desertion and loss I had in my heart; and I wrote, I remember, to someone, crying out for the want of a mother—nay, when I fainted one afternoon at the Villa Marina, and the first sound I heard was Madame Garschine saying 'Berecchino' so softly, I was glad—O, so glad I—to take her by the hand as a mother, and make a mother of her at the time, so far as it would go. You do not know, perhaps—I do not think I knew myself, perhaps, until I thought it out to-day—how dear a hope, how sorry a want, this has been for me. For my mother is my father's wife; to have a French mother, there must be a French marriage; the children of lovers are orphans. I am very young at heart—or (God knows) very old—and what I want is a mother, and I have one now, have I not?

2 RLS went to Bridge of Allan with his parents on Friday 29 January 1875 and returned home alone on the Sunday when he may have written this letter.

Strathyre—Allan Water—Stirling Castle, Brig

From Chapter 26 of *Kidnapped*: End of the Flight: we pass the Forth.

1 Near Stirling and Cambuskenneth the Forth twists and turns so much that it almost seems to be turning back on itself.

The South-West

'A Winter's Walk in Carrick and Galloway'. This uncompleted essay was published posthumously in the *Illustrated London News*, Summer 1896. Tusitala, vol 30.

Stevenson set out on this walk in January 1876, and the essay was probably begun just after the walking tour but it remained unfinished and unpublished during his lifetime. See letter to Sidney Colvin, February 1876, in which he wrote, 'I'm as fit as a fiddle after my walk. I am four inches bigger about the waist than last July!... I went to Ayr, Maybole, Girvan, Ballantrae, Stranraer, Glenluce and Wigton. I shall make an article of it some day soon.'

1   Robert Burns's 'The Cottar's Saturday Night', the cottar being a farm tenant, a cottager like the poet's father.

2   The now-ruined Dunure Castle belonged to the Kennedys of Dunure, Earls of Cassillis (see note below on the fourth Earl) who also owned nearby Culzean Castle which was rebuilt for the ninth and tenth Earls of Cassillis by Robert Adam and is now (with its Country Park) in the care of the National Trust for Scotland. Dunure, a ruined 13th-century keep, stands on a rocky promontory near the old fishing village of Dunure and 5 miles north-west of Maybole; it has been excavated and consolidated so that the ruins could be opened to the public.

3   'Johnnie's Grey Breeks' is a traditional song in which the breeks are 'threadbare worn'.

4   In 1570 Gilbert Kennedy, fourth Earl of Cassillis, kidnapped Allan Stewart the Commendator of Crossraguel Abbey, south of Maybole (on the A77) and, in 'the black voute' of Dunure demanded that he sign various deeds conveying the lands of the Abbey to the Earl. When the Commendator refused the Earl 'roasted' him over a large fire in the vaults. Kennedy of Bargany, hearing of the kidnapping, came to Dunure which he captured. Stevenson knew James Paterson's *History of the County of Ayr, with a genealogical account of the Families of Ayrshire*, 2 vols, 1847 and 1852.

5   William Abercrombie was minister at Maybole from 1673 to 1690. Stevenson noted Hew Scott's *Fasti Ecclesiae Scoticanae, under 'Maybole' (Part III)*, but again Stevenson drew on Paterson's *History*.

6   The lady seduced by Jonnie Faa, the wandering gypsy, away from the Castle was popularly believed to be Lady Cassillis, wife of John, sixth Earl of Cassillis, and the man no true gypsy but Sir John Faa of Dunbar disguised as one.

7   Within Ayrshire it was accepted that the original for Burns's 'Tam o' Shanter' was Douglas Graham (1739-1811) who was tenant of the farm 'Shanter', in Carrick, near Turnberry, where as Stevenson passed they were 'ploughing lea'. Graham sailed a boat named 'Tam o' Shanter'. The original for Souter Johnny is accepted as being John Davidson, whose thatched cottage is in Kirkoswald

where both 'originals' are buried in the kirkyard. The tavern referred to by Tam's wife Kate at line 28 was that in Kirkoswald
kept by 'Kirkton Jean' or Jean Kennedy. We know that in the
summer of 1775, Burns was sent by his father from Mount Oliphant
to a 'noted school' in Kirkoswald, run by Hugh Rodger, to learn
'Mensuration, Surveying, Dialling, etc'. Souter Johnny's cottage in
Kirkoswald (on the A77 south-west of Maybole) is now owned by
the National Trust for Scotland and life-sized stone figures of
Johnny and cronies can be seen (April to September) in the garden
of the restored ale-house.

Dumfries and Vicinity

Extracts from a long letter to Mrs Frances Sitwell. Written during a
week-long journey through the Borders, 15-22 September 1873.

Following the first extract a quarrel with his father took place, see
note to 'Edinburgh/Granton—Cramond' above.

1   In the churchyard at Irongray, seven miles from Dumfries, there is
    a gravestone with an inscription written by Walter Scott in memory
    of Helen Walker (died 1791) who 'practised in real life the virtues
    with which fiction has invested the imaginary character of Jeanie
    Deans' in *The Heart of Midlothian.* Jedediah Cleishbotham is part
    of an elaborate and comic apparatus which Scott created for his
    'Tales of a Grandfather'; Jedediah is the (fictitious) ultra-pedantic
    transcriber and preserver of the work of his (fictitious) dead friend
    and fellow teacher, Peter Pattieson, which is based on stories re-
    putedly collected orally from the historical figure of Old Mortality,
    Robert Paterson. See also note on Robert Paterson,'The Borders'
    below. RLS mentions Irongray in the chapter on Greyfriars in
    Edinburgh: Picturesque Notes.

2   The two Covenanters are 'Edward Gordon and Alexander
    McCubine, martyrs, hanged 'without law by Lagg and Cap Bruce';
    and the date was March 3, 1685.

3   Robert Burns lived in Dumfries from November 1791 until his
    death there in July 1796.

The Borders

Extract from *Weir of Hermiston. An Unfinished Romance*: Introductory.

Weir of Hermiston was posthumously published; serialised in
Cosmopolis, January-April 1896, and published in book form by Cassell

in 1896. Stevenson began the novel in October 1892 and worked inter-
mittently on it through 1893 and also in 1894. On 30 November 1894,
less than a week before Stevenson died, Isobel Strong reported that
they were 'pegging away at Hermiston like one o'clock. I hardly drew
breath, but flew over the paper; Louis thinks it is good.' And Lloyd
Osbourne wrote of the day Stevenson died, 'he wrote hard all that
morning of the last day, his half-finished book, *Hermiston*, he judged
the best he had ever written.' Charles Baxter, who was on his way to
visit Stevenson when he learned of his death, brought the manuscript
back to Britain. Stevenson's friends, including Henry James, suggested
that it be published immediately, and Sidney Colvin prepared the type-
script for publication. Its last words, as published, are, 'It seemed
unprovoked, a wilful convulsion of brute nature....'

1   John Graham of Claverhouse, Viscount Dundee, otherwise both
    'Bloody Clavers' and 'Bonnie Dundee'. See note to *Edinburgh:
    Picturesque Notes*.

2   Balweary is also the fictional village of Stevenson's story 'Thrawn
    Janet' and of the fragment *Heathercat*. It has been proposed that
    Stevenson may have wished to suggest the ruined Balwearie Cas-
    tle, near Kirkcaldy in Fife, which is associated with Sir Michael
    Scott or Scot, who wrote scholarly works on astrology, medicine,
    and alchemy but was popularly regarded as a wizard. The myth of
    the man is more influential than any documented biography. Sir
    Walter Scott continued the tradition of the wizard in *The Lay of
    the Last Minstrel*; and in *Anster Fair* William Tennant wrote in
    good high spirits of Scott 'Who there, in Satan's arts alignly bold,
    / His books of dev'lish efficiency wrote.' Tom Hubbard has writ-
    ten poems and a play in which he explores the Faustian theme in
    literature and within these works can be discerned the shadowy
    figure of Michael Scott.

3   Old Mortality was the name given to Robert Paterson, a commit-
    ted Covenanting stonemason who travelled around Scotland renewing
    Covenanting inscriptions. Paterson, who died on 14 February 1801
    aged 88, is buried in Caerlaverock but there is a memorial stone to
    him at Balmaclellan where the second significant incident took
    place that led to the Pentland Rising. Walter Scott's novel *Old
    Mortality* of 1816 takes its title from this man; Scott had encoun-
    tered Paterson whilst he was working on a stone in Dunnottar
    Churchyard, in the Mearns. In his 1830 'Introduction' to *Old
    Mortality* Scott wrote that this meeting took place 'about thirty years
    since, or more'. See also note to 'Dumfries and Vicinity' above.

4   Cameronian: the name given to the followers of Richard Cameron
     who broke away from any idea of moderation. In 1680 he returned
     from Holland to preach in the fields and hills and on 20 June 1680
     publicly denounced the King's authority. He died at the 'battle' of
     Airds Moss on 20 July 1680, when a wounded David Hackston of
     Rathillet was captured and taken to Edinburgh to be executed.

The Pentlands

Extract from *The Pentland Rising: a Page of History, 1666*. *The Pentland
Rising*, a sixteen page pamphlet, was published anonymously in Edinburgh in 1866 by Andrew Elliot. The essay is dated 28 November 1866
and was written by the sixteen-year-old youth to mark the bicentenary
of the Pentland Rising. One hundred copies were printed anonymously
at Stevenson's father's expense. Tusitala vol 28.

1 See note to *Edinburgh: Picturesque Notes* above.

Glencorse

Extract from 'The Body Snatcher'. Stevenson began 'The Body Snatcher'
in June 1881 but put it aside as 'being horrid'; it was, however, completed by early August 1881. It appeared in the Christmas extra number
of the *Pall Mall Gazette*, No 13, December 1884, when 'Markheim'
was found to be too short for the space that had been allocated to it.
'The Body Snatcher' was not published in book form until the Edinburgh edition of Stevenson's *Works*, edited by Sidney Colvin, 28 vols,
1894-98. 'Markheim' was revised by RLS and published in his *The
Merry Men and Other Tales and Fables*, 1887.

1   In exile, Glencorse cemetery remained important to Stevenson.
     His grandfather, Lewis Balfour, was minister at nearby Colinton,
     and the Stevensons' cottage at Swanston was also close to Glencorse.
     The relevance of the graveyard to the story of 'The Body-Snatcher'
     may be related to Stevenson having remembered, as reported by
     Graham Balfour in his *Life*, 1901, that as a child he had imagined
     a dead man at Glencorse 'sitting up in his coffin and watching us
     with that strange fixed eye.'

The Pentlands—Fisher's Tryst—Glencorse

Extracts from letter to S R Crockett from Vailima, 17 May 1893.

1   *Moriturus salutat, He who is about to die salutes you.* Stevenson is

referring to the gladiators in the arena who saluted the Roman Emperor with the words, 'Hail Caesar: those who are about to die salute you.'

The Pentlands

Poem entitled in *Songs of Travel*, 'To S R Crockett. On Receiving a Dedication'.

1   'To S. R. Crockett', written in Samoa, is one of Stevenson's most anthologised poems. Crockett (1860-1914) was a minister of the Free Church and his first charge was in Penicuik, near the Pentlands. Crockett had dedicated his collection of sketches, *The Stickit Minister*, 1893, 'To Robert Louis Stevenson of Scotland and Samoa I dedicate these stories of that Grey Galloway land where About the Graves of the Martyrs The Whaups are crying—his heart remembers how.' Stevenson confessed in a letter to Sidney Colvin (23 August 1893) 'And then you could actually see Vailima, which I *would* like you to, for it's beautiful and my home and tomb that is to be; though it's a wrench not to be planted in Scotland—that I never can deny—if I could only be buried in the hills, under the heather and a table tombstone like the martyrs, where the whaups and plovers are crying! Did you see a man who wrote *The Stickit Minister,* and dedicated it to me, in words that brought the tears to my eyes every time I looked at them. "Where about the graves of the martyrs the whaups are crying. *His* heart remembers how." Ah, my God, it does!' The poem was printed as a prefatory poem, and reproduced in facsimile, in the eighth, limited edition of *The Stickit Minister*, 1894, and in subsequent editions. It was also published in the *Pall Mall Gazette*, 12 December 1894, under the title 'Home Thoughts from Samoa'. *Howes* in line 7 is often printed as *homes,* howes being valleys or glens.

View from the Pentlands

Untitled poem printed in *Songs of Travel*, 'The tropics vanish; and meseems that I'.

1   The lighthouses built by the Stevensons.

2   The 'grated cell' is in New Calton Cemetery where Robert Stevenson, born in 1772, was buried in July 1850. The Stevenson burial chamber is the only one in that bright and airy cemetery to

retain its original roof and that is due to the Stevensons having used the same method in its construction of 'dove-tailing' the stones into each other that Robert had employed in building the Bell Rock lighthouse. The upright memorial stone of Robert Stevenson and his wife Jane Smith faces the impressive iron gates of that well-preserved burial chamber. The bust of Robert is in the shadows of the 'cell' but the inscription which informs us that he 'designed and erected the Bell Rock Lighthouse' remains sharp and clear. Also buried in that grated burial house are Alan Stevenson, 'of the Skerryvore Lighthouse', his wife Margaret Scott Jones and their two children, Robert Alan Mowbray Stevenson (1847-1900) and Katharine de Mattos. Like her brother Bob, Katherine was one of RLS's favourite cousins and he dedicated *Dr Jekyll and Mr Hyde* to her. She caused a family scandal by marrying and divorcing Sydney de Mattos, a 'Cambridge Atheist'. The flat memorial stone on the floor of the burial ground commemorates not only Thomas (1818-87) and Margaret Isabel Balfour, 'wife and mother born at Colinton Manse February 11th 1828, died at Edinburgh May 14th 1897', but also RLS's death in Samoa. That grated, or gated, cell in New Calton Cemetery is now overlooked not only by the Burns Monument, the steeples of the Tron Kirk and St Giles, the dome of the University's Old College, Arthur's Seat and the Salisbury Crags, but also the new Scottish Parliament building. Below the cemetery also stands the Palace of Holyroodhouse which in RLS's poem is 'the house of kings'.

Edinburgh—Lothian Road—Leith Walk

Extract from letter to Charles Baxter from Chalet am Stein, Davos, Switzerland, 5 December 1881.

1   In Stevenson's time, Lothian Road was lined by public houses frequented by prostitutes, with the public house of the ill-tempered Peter Brash a favourite of Stevenson and Charles Baxter when they were students. Stevenson wrote a series of sonnets published under the general tile of 'Brasheanna' which he dedicated to Baxter. Stevenson wished to make a pamphlet of these and Baxter had the first two sonnets set in type and sent proofs to Stevenson who replied jokily from Nice on 12 January 1883. These proofs are very rare Stevensoniana but the poems are printed in *Collected Poems* edited by Janet Adam Smith.

Edinburgh—Drummond Street and Rutherford's

Extract from letter to Charles Baxter from the yacht *Casco*, 6 September 1888. Written at sea, near the Paumotus 'with a dreadful pen' and dated 7 a.m. 6 September 1888. The letter was mislaid and not posted until 19 June 1889 with Baxter noting receipt on 22 July 1889. The yacht had sailed from Hiva-oa in the Marquesas Islands on the morning of 4 September on a voyage through many coral atolls bound for Fakarava in the Paumotu Archipelago, also known as the Dangerous or Low Archipelago (now Tuamotu). See Stevenson's *In the South Seas* for his account of these alarming days.

1   Stevenson was taking risks by sleeping on deck 'upon the cockpit bench' with the steersman for company.

2   A public house in Drummond Street, near the University's Old College, and still in business.

3   A plaque quoting RLS's words has recently been placed at the corner of Drummond Street, 'presented on behalf of all Stevenson lovers' by an anonymous donor.

Edinburgh—Lothian Road—Fergusson's Grave in the Canongate

Extracts from letter to Charles Baxter from Vailima, 18 May 1894.

1   Edinburgh edition, edited by Sidney Colvin, London, 1894-98.

2   It was while Burns was in Edinburgh in 1786 that he arranged for a headstone to be put on Robert Fergusson's pauper's grave in Canongate Kirkyard. The invoice for the stone can be seen in the Writer's Museum, Edinburgh. Robert Fergusson, the successor to Allan Ramsay and the most important eighteenth-century predecessor to Robert Burns, was born in 1750 in one of the now-demolished alleys off the High Street and educated at St Andrews University. He died on 17 October 1774, aged twenty-four years and one month, in the Edinburgh Bedlam where he had been confined as a 'pauper lunatic'. The old Minute-book of the Charity workhouse reported Fergusson's death with these chilling words, 'Mr Ferguson, in the Cels.'

3   Charles Baxter replied to RLS on 11 July 1894 that he had been to Canongate Kirkyard and found that Fergusson's headstone was 'in perfect preservation and kept freshly painted'.

Edinburgh—Precipitous City

Poem 'To My Wife'.

1 'To my Wife' was printed posthumously in 1896 as the dedication to *Weir of Hermiston*. In a letter to Sidney Colvin, Fanny Stevenson explained, as quoted in F V Lucas's *The Colvins and their Friends*, 'In looking over further papers to give Mr Balfour to carry to you, I found the dedication to me as Louis first [wrote] it for *Hermiston*. Please put it in as he meant it to be. He pinned it to my bed curtains when I was asleep, with other explanatory verses.' There are three drafts of the poem in the Beinecke Collection at Yale and there is also an early version in a letter to Charles Baxter of 18 May 1894. At that time Stevenson was considering whether to use these verses, although designed for *Weir*, as a general dedication to the Edinburgh edition. The Vailima and Tusitala editions print an early version which has two lines more than that published in the novel and reprinted here.

Edinburgh or 'Auld Reekie'

Extract from 'The Scot Abroad'. 'The Scot Abroad' from *The Silverado Squatters*, was serialised in the *Century Illustrated Monthly Magazine*, November and December 1883. The American, Boston, and London editions were published simultaneously in 1883.

1 See also extract from letter to S R Crockett, May 1893, 'The Pentlands—Fisher's Tryst—Glencorse', above.

DUNCAN GLEN